UNEQUAL
AMERICANS

Contributions in Political Science
SERIES EDITOR: Bernard K. Johnpoll

UNEQUAL AMERICANS

Practices and Politics of Intergroup Relations

JOHN SLAWSON
in collaboration with Marc Vosk

CONTRIBUTIONS IN POLITICAL SCIENCE, NUMBER 24

GREENWOOD PRESS
WESTPORT, CONNECTICUT • LONDON, ENGLAND

Library of Congress Cataloging in Publication Data

Slawson, John, 1896-
    Unequal Americans.
    (Contributions in political science ; no. 24
    ISSN 0147-1066)
    Includes index.
    1. Minorities—United States. 2. United States—
Social conditions—1960-   3. Civil rights—United
States. 4. Social interaction—United States
I. Vosk, Marc, joint author.   II. Title.   III. Series.
E184.A1S63   301.45′1′0973   78-26318
ISBN 0-313-21118-3

Library of Congress Catalog Card Number: 78-26318
ISBN: 0-313-21118-3
ISSN: 0147-1066

First published in 1979

Greenwood Press, Inc.
51 Riverside Avenue, Westport, Connecticut 06880

Printed in the United States of America

10 9 8 7 6 5 4 3 2 1

To Ada Schupper Slawson,
an understanding and loving wife;
none better ever graced man's good fortune.

Contents

Acknowledgments

In any study conducted over a long period of time and covering diverse areas, such as this one represents, the assistance of colleagues and friends is not only helpful but essential. This I have had the good fortune of receiving.

Selma Hirsh, associate director of the American Jewish Committee (AJC), stands out in this role above all others. She initiated and produced the John Slawson Fund for Research, Training and Education, which made possible not only this study but also a number of useful projects both here and in Israel. I express my profound gratitude to her and to the generous AJC board members who made the contributions. I do the same to the late Irving M. Engel, former honorary president of AJC, who assumed the responsibility of chairman of the fund.

Bertram Gold, the executive vice-president of the agency, my successor, has been generous, gracious, and cooperative in every way.

My interviewees supplied the basic data of the study, and to them I convey my thanks for their time, their interest, and their effort.

Dr. Marc Vosk, a former colleague of many years' standing, worked diligently in a collaborative role during the last phases of the study. His role is indicated on the title page.

Martha S. Cherkis faithfully and diligently carried out the tasks of a research assistant. Her services were invaluable.

My gratitude is conveyed for the helpfulness given me by many AJC staff members, especially Morris Fine, Harry Fleischman, the late Judith Herman, Sonya Kaufer, Irma and Milton Krents, Irving Levine, Sam Rabinove, Rabbi A. James Rubin, and Dr. Neil Sandberg. I trust I will be forgiven if, inadvertently, I omitted names that should be on this list.

In addition, I wish to express my gratitude to Oscar Cohen, Professors Lucy S. Dawidowicz, Sigmund Diamond, Herbert H. Hyman, and Jack Rothman for their advice.

Outstanding, of course, in helpfulness and support in every way was my dear wife, Ada Schupper Slawson, to whom this book is happily dedicated.

Introduction

This book examines the principles underlying the treatment of problems in intergroup relations and analyzes the methods employed in ameliorating and preventing them from arising.

"Unequal Americans" rather than "Minority Groups" has been selected as the title because the former term does not emphasize the numbers involved and at the same time retains the connotation of "minority groups"—namely, those who are disadvantaged in pursuing equality of opportunity because of race, ethnicity, religion, or sex. In addition, the designation "unequal Americans" accommodates the group "women," which is not a "minority." Throughout the text, however, the term "minority group" is retained because of its more common usage.

This book is concerned primarily with clarifying the methodology in the field of intergroup relations. It seeks to ascertain the kind of social change and alterations in mental attitude that might contribute to (1) improved relationships among racial, ethnic, and religious groups in the United States, (2) the achievement of equality of oppportunity for all groups, and (3) the improvement of the social quality of life within these groups.

In addition, this work attempts to ascertain the relationships between the historic events of the past several decades and the group problems that were faced during these years, as well as to determine and, to the extent possible, evaluate the strategies employed to alleviate these problems.

The basic data in the study come from tape recordings of individual interviews with selected representatives of the intergroup relations field.[1] Most of the interviews were conducted in 1970. The questions were formulated in advance, but were not followed strictly, serving primarily as discussion guides for the interviewer. With very few exceptions, the interviewer is the author of this volume; at times, the interviewee himself posed certain queries.

The interviewees are classified as informants rather than as respondents.[2] Their knowledge is based on their actual work experience in the field as policy-makers, practitioners, or specialists. The discussions prompted by their responses to the queries are interpreted in light of the author's thirty-five years of experience in the field. These interviews generally lasted from one to one and one-half hours and were designed to draw out all possible substantive content from the specific topics. Thus, there was no intention of deriving statistical data from any of the responses or of achieving a stratified statistical sampling of responses with respect to any of the items selected for inquiry.

It is hoped that the intensive consultations on each of the items discussed with the interviewees will yield some insights into the best known methods of alleviating and preventing intergroup discord (racial, religious, ethnic, and sexual). The process employed by the author in the analysis of the tapes might best be designated as "distillation of ideas."

The procedures used in the study are described in Appendix A, which includes the names and positions of those interviewed. Informants were selected on the basis of their competence and status in the field in a particular area. In order to ensure a balanced analysis, members of the public and private sectors, the national and local community, and the sectarian and nonsectarian areas are represented. A total of forty-one public and private agencies are represented, and seventy-six individuals were interviewed. Most of these individuals reside in New York City and Washington, D.C.; several who live in neither city were interviewed while visiting New York.

In this study, the quantitative is subordinate to the qualitative dimension; hence, deletions from and amalgamations of material are frequent, and disparate items related either to the issues or the objectives of the study are often fused. The goals of the study are to determine the dynamics involved and to identify the processes which the intergroup relations personnel use as aids.

One slight advantage and a positive byproduct of the methodology employed in this work was that it allowed frequent updating; the situation at the time of the taping could be compared with the later situation. In addition to the use of the tape recordings, the published research in this area was liberally perused.

The study deals with the empirical, conceptual, and ideological aspects of intergroup relations. It is hoped that it will be helpful to the professional person in the field and of interest to the layman concerned with the problems of human relations, for without the latter's active participation, efforts to improve any facet of human relations will be well-nigh futile.

As much as practicable, the views of the informants are presented in their own language. Often the discussion with the informant stimulated new thinking on the part of the interviewer, and this new thinking is generally incorporated in the book. As noted earlier, the interviews constitute the basic data for the study, but other subject matter is included. For example, there is a lengthy discussion of the fact that currently, the economic situation appears to have overshadowed all other factors, thus relegating concern with human attitudes to a secondary role.

The concern here is largely with intergroup relations in the United States, even though international events inevitably influence domestic affairs. Even the Arab-Israeli struggle and the racial strife in South Africa have important repercussions for our domestic group relationships. Nevertheless, the focus here is on the domestic scene.

As is seen in the text, we have a long way to go before racism and bigotry are eradicated from our society, but great progress has been made in destroying overt discrimination. This progress is the unique achievement of a democracy: only in a democracy could the people themselves take hold and, through a variety of organizations and a diversity of approaches, achieve this encouraging outcome. However, overt discrimination can be brought under control far more readily than prejudice. And as long as prejudice persists, crisis situations are inevitable. Racial outbreaks continue to occur much too often. We should not forget that the greatest exhibition of man's inhumanity to man in all of human history, the Holocaust, took place only a little over three decades ago.

Notes

1. All quoted portions that are unattributed are drawn from the interviews.
2. The distinction between "informant" and "respondent" is presented in Appendix A.

UNEQUAL
AMERICANS

1

Overview

Intergroup relations generally pursues three aims—improved group relationships, intragroup advancement, and equality of opportunity for its members. Since there is a close correlation between the welfare of the group and that of society as a whole, the advancement of the latter also becomes a concern of intergroup relations. Hence, the particularistic concern for the one often acts as a stimulus to the universalist concern for the many.

Effective intergroup relations can be achieved by restructuring the relations among groups, i.e., through redistributing the power resources among the groups, not by being taught "to be nice to each other." This restructuring of power relationships among groups is essential to harmonious intergroup relationships.

The past quarter century has witnessed major developments in the intergroup relations field. There has been a shift from a sociopsychological orientation to a politicoeconomic approach in coping with intergroup problems, that is, from modification of individual attitudes to social change. While the root of prejudice, as has been so amply demonstrated by social science and supported by observation, lies within the prejudiced person, it has been concluded that it is more effective generally to deal with the external situation (environment) than with the person (personality), without, of course, neglecting the person.

This choice is based on the consideration of a number of factors. First, there is the prevailing view that in the long run the behavior induced by the changed situation—be it by virtue of law or administration—may eventually affect the attitude of the person. Second, for the victim of discrimination, the creation of equal opportunity for all regardless of race, religion, ethnicity, or sex removes frustration, and for the person inclined to discriminate, it enhances an atmosphere conducive to the acceptance, rather than rejection, of group differences.

The social change requisite for eliminating or reducing prejudicial inequities may be achieved by a process of negotiation leading to consensus. Quite frequently, the resolution is achieved by protest leading to conflict. Conflict as a process, not as a goal, should not be considered a necessarily negative manifestation; it often is essential to progress. It should be kept in mind, however, that the attitudinal factor cannot be totally neglected—for several reasons. The failure to modify attitude by either direct or indirect means will often result in the avoidance and evasion of externally imposed regulations (legal or administrative). In addition, prejudices may be submerged more deeply, only to surface on an opportune occasion. The relatively recent anti-Semitic expressions by former high government officials illustrate this phenomenon.

The intergroup relations field today is not as distinctive as it was in the past. Economics and political science have made deep inroads into it and have begun to compete for attention with civil rights and civil liberties. Moreover, since minorities are in the worst position in a "sick society," the intergroup relations field must concern itself with the society as a whole in addition to specific groups. As a result, intergroup relations is concerned not only with "fairness" in making employment, housing, and education accessible to all groups regardless of race, ethnicity, religion, or sex, but also with "fullness"—i.e., with the availability of those resources for all. Here we go beyond the former restriction to "equality" and extend our concern to "availability." Intergroup relations thus expands its horizon to what may be termed the macro level, i.e., the community or the nation, while still retaining its concern with the micro level, i.e., the individual group, a category to which intergroup relations tended to be largely confined in the past. Agencies such as the American Jewish Committee and the National Urban League further their individual group's advancement by also working for the removal of all racial, ethnic, religious, and sexual barriers to upward mobility.

Over and above the commitment to the sanctity of the person and the inviolability of human rights, intergroup relations rests on two underlying convictions. First, no distinctions can be made among racial or ethnic groups in terms of presumed *genetic* superiority or inferiority. It has been a persistent fallacy to confuse the relative *performance* or lack of performance of a given group at given times with its relative *genetic capacities*. Performance and capacity need not always be correlated, in groups or even in individuals. Historical evidence offers abundant proof of a particular racial, ethnic, or national group, overwhelmingly dominant in achievement at one time, which ceased to be so a few centuries later. Or, conversely, peoples who had been rated lowest in capacity in time became leaders on the world scene. A striking current example are the Jews, long considered a physically passive people, incapable of fighting, who suddenly emerged in Israel as among the world's bravest, most effective soldiers, able pilots, and brilliant military tacticians. In sum, to quote Amram Scheinfeld:

Not until human beings of all racial groups everywhere have had the same opportunities for education, training and advancement can we draw fair conclusions as to their relative genetic capacities. As matters stand, there is enough evidence to suggest that the genes for all types of achievement are spread among all racial groups, and that each group abounds in far more gifted individuals than have had a chance to assert themselves.[1]

Hence, social policy should aim at improving the environmental situation, which includes the elimination of discriminatory and exclusionary practices with respect to all groups, as well as making special training opportunities (compensatory) available to those handicapped by earlier environmental deprivation. Such a policy will tend eventually to reduce the gap even in the quality of *performance* among all groups (as groups) to the extent that the handicap exists. In this connection, the "self-fulfilling prophecy"[2] is much too frequently encountered in dealing with minority groups. By our own doing we create the undesirable conditions that we supposedly wish to avoid. For instance, it might be said that a member of a culturally deprived group will not be able to profit much from education; therefore, why waste training on this person. Such a conclusion assures that person's inability to function satisfactorily in the future.

The second pillar on which the practice of intergroup relations rests is the scientifically based conviction that group prejudice is a product of the bigot and not of the victim. To be sure, there is the occasional person who practices ethnic, religious, or racial discrimination, not because of deeply felt prejudice but as a matter of expediency; for example, he believes that his social circle and his colleagues expect it of him. Aside from this category, which is rapidly becoming extinct, the definitively group-prejudiced individual is generally the product of an early childhood learning experience at home, in the neighborhood, or in the schoolroom.

About a quarter of a century ago, it was demonstrated that prejudice which expresses itself in bigoted action may meet a personality need; i.e., it is an emotional problem of the personality. An example is "the authoritarian personality," characterized by a number of symptoms including an abnormal fluctuation between aggressive-assertive and dependent-submissive behavior, excessive fear, rigidity, and excessive deference to authority. Since such personalities are almost wholly outer-directed, they have little or no capacity to respond to the inner conscience. The latter characteristic is generally attributed to emotional deprivation in early childhood.[3]

Because of these personality problems as well as the difficulties encountered in coping with them, intergroup agencies have generally found it more rewarding to deal with institutional racism than with individual prejudices or individual discriminatory practices. It is in the factory, the school, the neighborhood, the housing development—yes, and even in the community —that the discrimination that results in deprivation for minorities breeds and is experienced. Dealing with the individual instance is gradually giving way to coping with the total pattern of which it is a part.

Important changes in social perceptions that have a bearing on intergroup relations both conceptually and pragmatically have taken place in recent years, especially since World War II. The most far-reaching change is the increased consciousness that the white peoples of the world constitute only about one-third of mankind and that with the accelerated increase of the nonwhite population this proportion continues to diminish. The Judeo-Christian civilization comprises only one-quarter of mankind. Today 36 million Americans are nonwhite, 25 million of whom are black. The nonwhites consist of more than a dozen different national and ethnic groups.

The United States is a composite of various religious, ethnic, and racial groups; it contains more than one hundred different ethnic groups[4] and approximately one hundred creeds,[5] and about seventy languages[6] are spoken. It is therefore easy to understand why we are experiencing difficulties in our intergroup relationships. It has been conjectured that two hundred years from now historians writing of our period may wonder how, given such a diverse aggregation, it was possible for us to live together as well as we have. Moreover, our society is getting increasingly pluralistic; the monolithic conception is receding at a rapid pace.

To some extent, as a result of the growing importance given to ethnicity in recent years, intergroup relations in the United States has tended to take on a multinational and international character. For example, blacks in the United States are concerned with blacks in South Africa. The Urban League characterizes the U.S. efforts "on the side of black Africans in their struggle to achieve majority rule" as "the year's [1977] most important occurrence in the area of foreign relations" (for black Americans).[7] American Jews are intensively concerned with Israel, with the plight of Russian Jewry, and with Jews elsewhere in the Diaspora as an expression of their age-old sense of responsibility for their brethren the world over. In the case of Israel, the religious and Biblical ties have existed since time immemorial. These factors have a domestic impact—for instance, on the relationship between Jews and Christians on the one hand and Jews and blacks in the United States on the other hand. Most other ethnic groups in our pluralistic nation exhibit similar relationships and concerns.

In line with this same stress on the values of ethnicity in a pluralistic America is the weight assigned today to inner-group strength—strength basic to good intergroup functioning. Corollary to this orientation is the emphasis on the full participation of the people *themselves* in coping with their group problems, with an added focus on self-help as a means of effecting social change.[8]

At the same time as America becomes increasingly depersonalized, "groupism" and ethnicity serve the added important function of reducing anomie—the feeling of social isolation. Hence, the internal life of groups such as Jews, blacks, Spanish-Americans, or Asian-Americans that has a bearing on human interrelationships becomes the natural concern of the intergroup relations agency. The nature of the person's identification with his own group is important, among other reasons, because it is basic to the quality of his relationship with other groups. This need for identification with a group is particularly acute today when, as Ross tells us, "the dominant impetus for change today is technological, is pressing toward increased industrialization and urbanization, with comparatively little consideration of the effects of such movement on social relations."[9]

Consequently, private agencies in the intergroup relations field are becoming increasingly occupied with developing a healthy group identity for each individual. They recognize that the self-acceptance that flows from the awareness of one's own group identity contributes to the inner strength requisite for an easy and understanding relationship with other groups. Through this self-acceptance, America's various religious, ethnic, racial, and sex groups have become more assertive with respect to their roles in American society. Their self-acceptance as groups has encouraged them to learn more about their ancestry and their traditional values, as well as their group contributions to America. A case in point is the reception given to Haley's *Roots*.[10]

In turn, this newly acquired self-image tends to sharpen group aspirations which are enhanced by a number of stimuli, including the mass media, (especially television). These stimuli bring vividly to the attention of the deprived the relative affluence of the more fortunate. Here we have the phenomenon of "relative deprivation."[11]

Intergroup relations actionists have come to realize that it is sometimes advisable that a measure of temporary "planned separateness" for the development of inner-group strength precede the attempt to achieve a cooperative relationship. A cooperative relationship can then more readily follow and lead to the desired collaboration. This preparatory period may be designated as the intensification of internal group cohesiveness.

Groups do well to attain near equality in strength or status before any efforts toward a joint venture are made. According to Allport, "Prejudice (unless deeply rooted in the character structure of the individual) may be reduced by equal status contact between majority and minority groups in the pursuit of common goals."[12]

Correlative with the various groups' need to achieve unified action in furthering common goals, *community organization* has become integral to intergroup relations. The job is not finished when the laws are changed in the desired direction or when new administrative procedures are launched. Motivation for a continuing process of change, primarily on a self-help and mutual-aid basis, becomes imperative for the successful implementation of legislation or an executive order.

The social sciences have had considerable impact on the field of inter-

group relations and continue to do so. In earlier years, when attitude modification occupied a prominent position in the treatment program, the sociopsychological sciences were substantially relied upon in the evolution of
methods for developing insight into negative attitudes toward religious,
ethnic, or racial groups. The group-dynamics procedure gave a strong impetus to the use of the face-to-face, intragroup (small) technique for the
penetration into one's own biases and misapprehensions. As we moved into
the "do it yourself" or self-examination approach, the scientific method of
getting at the facts objectively played a valuable role, whether in revealing
the presence of prejudicial content in religious teaching material for the
young or in uncovering bias in the selection process of candidates for the
"executive suite" in industry. This self-examination approach which has
been used by the religious and industrial organizations themselves in an objective, scientific manner has been known to produce fairly durable change.

The general view is that a healthy society will do everything possible to
make decision-making free and open, thus facilitating the collective "arriving at the common good."[13] The goal of the "common good" presupposes
the interrelatedness of various objectives and the means for attaining them.
Consequently, the systems approach in the field of intergroup relations is
beginning to attract the attention of policy-makers. This is overall planning
as opposed to planning on a piecemeal basis. Not only is it more effective,
but also it can often prevent consequences that are opposite to those intended, and that are sometimes even harmful.

The need for community planning can best be illustrated in the job and
housing fields. Simply constructing a low-cost housing facility in the inner
city—beneficial though this may be in the short run—might result in further
impoverishment of the area and a further lowering of its tax base, with the
consequences that flow from such a development. Regional planning involves taking into consideration more related relevant factors than called
for by planning for the inner city alone. One may decide to go ahead anyway, but one should be aware of the possible negative consequences.

With the entry of government into the intergroup relations field, com-
mencing with the enactment of civil rights legislation and the Supreme
Court decisions in the 1950s and continuing through the 1960s and early
1970s, the field expanded greatly. (In recent years, some contraction has
taken place largely because of budgetary stringency.) Government, both
national and local, transformed the objectives of intergroup relations into a
public responsibility by monitoring compliance with legislative acts and
judicial decisions. There can be little question that governmental involvement greatly expanded the services and accelerated the establishment of
"group equality of opportunity" as the standard orientation in our nation.

In fact, equality of opportunity can generally be achieved only as our
areas of concern enter the public domain. This holds for the job, the home,
the school, or the leisure-time activity. Redressing inequality is one of the

major responsibilities of the public institution. Christopher Jencks tells us that "equalizing opportunity is almost impossible without greatly reducing the absolute level of inequality, and the same is true of eliminating deprivation."[14]

Some believe that, today, the rewards of competitive success appear to be much too high in contrast to the cost of failure. Jencks concludes that "if all the non-genetic causes of inequality were eliminated, and if America still placed the same value it now places on various kinds of skill, the income gap between the top and the bottom fifths of all male workers would fall from around 7 to 1 to around 1.4 to 1."[15]

It is generally conceded that economic growth is essential to harmonious intergroup relations, since the competition for a limited number of occupational opportunities by members of the various racial, religio-ethnic, and sexual groups can and often does result in intergroup hostility. As already indicated, because the mass media and other communications underscore the contrast between the affluent and the deprived, this disparity tends to take on a more damaging aspect in the form of relative deprivation. Minority poverty has become a well-defined affliction, dreaded for its effect both on the poor and on society as a whole. Continuous want can undermine one's dignity, a basic ingredient of wholesome intergroup relations.

Many students of intergroup relations still disagree with the conclusion of the National Advisory Commission on Civil Disorders that "our Nation is moving toward two societies, one black, one white—separate and unequal."[16] Their position is that "we have had two societies from the beginning and that is how it will be for a long, long time." Without doubt, the persistence of such a condition will inevitably result in increased group hostility.

Poverty and ignorance are relative as well as absolute conditions. Personal and group anxiety is heightened by feelings of economic insecurity. Economic insecurity is a basic problem in any attempt to change the feelings of hostility between America's racial and religiocultural groups. The "side by side" inequality manifestations in contiguous neighborhoods and the vast gap between the top members of the minority groups and the deplorable condition of their masses in the ghettos is fertile soil for the breeding of discontent leading to intergroup hostility and violence.

Regrettably, one of the principal actors on the stage of "economic growth"—corporate America—has yet to assume a sufficiently responsible role. Many intergroup relations professionals believe that corporate America must become more responsive to community relations needs; it possesses vast resources, approximating those of government itself, and in some cases it is beginning to influence or control vital communal decisions—decisions as large as those made by government. Hence, society has a right not only to regulate certain corporate actions, but also to change their values.[17]

Yet, meeting only a portion of the need may not always be the best solu-

tion and may merely stimulate "rising expectations" that may remain unfulfilled. The conditions under which "rising expectations" develop were well
illustrated by de Tocqueville early in the nineteenth century. In analyzing
the impact of the French Revolution, he stated: "The evil which was suffered patiently as inevitable seemed unendurable as soon as the idea of es-
caping from it crossed men's minds."[18]

Generally, the black revolts in the United States have followed a period
of some improvement in their condition: "As is nearly always true in a revolutionary movement, it is not those on the bottom but those who have experienced significant gains and then been stalled, who revolt."[19] Prior to the
most recent riots in Detroit, for example, it was widely felt that "it can't
happen here" because "many progressive measures" had been introduced
there. However, revolutions occur as a consequence of frustrated hope;
those who harbor frustrated hopes are more likely to rebel than those with
no hope at all.[20]

One encouraging sign is that according to a recent analysis related to
Stouffer's classic study in 1955, tolerance in the United States has increased
greatly over the past two decades.[21]

Jews have long constituted a special minority. It is true that they have
their own burden of the poor, chiefly but not exclusively among the elderly.[22]
But through diligence, resourcefulness, and painful struggle, they have
achieved a prominent economic, cultural, and educational position; their
professional representation is equal to that of the topmost American religious, ethnic, or racial group. Nonetheless, the old stereotypes and negative
prejudgments persist, especially in the social club and to a considerable extent in the "executive suite"—selection and advancement in major American
business and industrial corporations.

The one hundred or more professional anti-Semitic organizations that
were still active in 1948 were practically defunct in 1970. All the same, anti-
Semitism remains deeply imbedded in Western culture and in Christian religious institutions and can be raised to fever pitch by conditions and incidents of unpredictable potency. It is the oldest form of prejudice, dating
back twenty centuries. A recent study showed that "at least one-fourth of
America's anti-Semites [those considered such by the investigators' criteria]
have a religious basis for their prejudice, while nearly another fifth have this
religious basis in considerable part."[23]

The late Bernhard Olson, a distinguished Christian religious researcher,
stated:

These teachings of contempt (as examined by Jules Isaac) thus gave rise to and justified the system of degradation under which Christians have forced Jews to live.
Banishments, killings, burnings, drownings, tortures, forced baptisms, segregation,
restrictions on their human and religious freedom, confiscations of their property,

curbs on their means of livelihood, burnings of their sacred book, mandatory attendance at church services to hear themselves denounced as a perverse and godless people—these and many other acts continuously flowed from such teachings.[24]

The wounds of human misery, frustration, status anxiety, economic want, and political upheavals have served as fertile breeding grounds for anti-Semitic outbreaks since time immemorial.

It is possibly because of their long experience with prejudice and discrimination that Jews have been intimately concerned with the problems of particularism and universalism. (Witness the Hillel dictum: "If I am not for myself, who will be; if I am only for myself, what am I, and if not now, when?") This concern is well exemplified in the statement of a top executive in one of the Jewish national intergroup relations agencies: "In order for us to make a meaningful contribution to the security of the Jew in the U.S., we must likewise be concerned with the security of all minorities." It is difficult to know to what extent this position is still held today in the light of increased tensions among various ethnic groups. Much of this pragmatism and broad-based consideration can be illustrated by two instances in recent decades.

As is described in Chapter 9, the financial support which a national Jewish intergroup relations agency gave to the American Federation of Labor (AFL) and Congress of Industrial Organizations (CIO) (when they were still separate) in initiating their civil rights programs in 1948 was a "pump-priming" approach, an expression of a universalist concern with civil rights for the benefit of the entire American community.

The second instance of universalist motivation occurred when Kenneth B. Clark testified before the Supreme Court in connection with the 1954 decision on public school segregation. In his testimony, he utilized a study he had previously made on the effects of separation on school children, a study financed by the same national Jewish intergroup relations agency. Four years after the study was made, the evidence cited by Professor Clark became one of the pillars on which the Supreme Court rested its decision to outlaw segregated public schools (*Brown* v. *Board of Education of Topeka*, May 1954).

Women, the new "minority" category, actually constitute the majority of the population of the United States. They remain a minority group with respect to equality of opportunity, although this condition is rapidly being rectified. The evolving women's movement is digging deep into all areas of American life where women face discrimination—from employment to the disposition of court cases involving women as plaintiffs or defendants; from education to the ability to obtain financial credit in their own right.[25]

Prejudice and discriminatory practices (which are discussed in later sections) have been for many years, and still are, directed against other ethnic groups. Hispano-Americans, Chicanos, and native Americans (Indians) are extreme examples. The blacks dealt with as a race are still the classic American victims of discriminatory practices and prejudicial attitudes.

As already indicated, a basic aim of intergroup relations is to devise approaches and methods that would bring members of the various groups in our American population to an appreciative understanding of the differences that characterize them. The goal is to prevent and ameliorate misunderstandings and intergroup hostilities.

At this point, some definitions of intergroup relations terms are in order:

Sociopsychological definition—"Whenever individuals belonging to one in-group, collectively or individually, interact with another group or its members in terms of their group identification, we have an instance of intergroup relations."[26]

General and goal definition—To bring about social change in the American society so as to improve the conditions of government and conditions generally as they pertain to minority groups in particular.

Functional designation (the objectives of intergroup relations activity):

1. To remove those limitations and restrictions on legal and civil rights, economic, educational and social status and opportunities which, based on racial, ethnic, or religious differences, the larger society inflicts upon some of its constituent groups and their members.

2. To introduce compensatory procedures and institutions in all the above areas, assuring de facto as well as de jure equality of opportunity for those disadvantaged groups whose historical experience has made it difficult for them to benefit from removal of restrictions.

3. To reduce intergroup tensions and hostilities, whether based on group competition for limited facilities or upon existing stereotypes, attitudes, or prejudices.

4. To build positive relations between groups and their members based upon mutual understanding of their diverse cultural backgrounds and identities, and the consequent differences of their separate needs.

Differentiation between the designations *human relations, intergroup relations,* and *community relations* can perhaps best be considered in historical perspective. In earlier years, the term *human relations* referred to individuals rather than to the community.[27] *Intergroup relations* came into more general usage in the 1950s and 1960s when the emphasis shifted from the purely individual psychological approach to consideration of the individual as integral to his group (ethnic, racial, religious, and the like). With the entry of the federal government into the funding of community relations projects, emphasis shifted to communities, and the term *community relations* came into increasing use. In general, this term is a broader one, since it encompasses both human relations and intergroup relations, embracing problems in social welfare and education, problems of poverty, and matters pertaining to child care, in addition to relations between different ethnic, religious, and racial groups within the community. *Community relations* offers a much broader notion of the systems approach and emphasizes the role of community resources as an instrumentality for obtaining the desired results. *Community relations* is the process for realization of goals spelled out above under "functional designation."

One's philosophy of society expresses itself in the methodology one favors in coping with intergroup relations matters. An elitist philosophy favors a methodology that is focused on the few showing the way to the many—a pyramidal approach. The thinking is done by the few for the many to follow. In both the Jewish and black groups, this approach was utilized in the early stages of the organized "defense" and "civil rights" organizations. In the recent past, however, the philosophy of "participatory democracy" has gained ascendancy, resulting in greatly increased group participation and mass action.

Similarly, one's philosophy of worldwide interdependence will determine the relative values given to universalist and particularistic approaches in intergroup relations, even domestically.

Notes

1. Amram Scheinfeld, *Your Heredity and Environment* (Philadelphia: J. B. Lippincott Co., 1965), p. 634.

2. Robert K. Merton, *Social Theory and Social Structure* (Glencoe, Ill.: Free Press, 1957, enlarged edition), pp. 475–90.

3. T. W. Adorno, Else Frenkel-Brunswik, D. J. Levinson, and R. N. Sanford, *The Authoritarian Personality* (New York: Harper Bros., 1950).

4. *Harvard Encyclopedia of American Ethnic Groups*, Preparatory Study (Cambridge, Mass.: Harvard University Press, August 1976).

5. *The World Almanac & Book of Facts / 1977* (New York: Newspaper Enterprise Association), pp. 348–49.

6. The U.S. Office of Bilingual Education reports that federally aided programs serve 165,000 students in sixty-eight languages (David Vidal, *The New York Times*, January 30, 1977).

7. *The State of Black America* (New York: National Urban League, 1977), p. 50.

8. John Slawson, "Mutual Aid and the Negro," *Commentary* (April 1966): 43–50.

9. Murray G. Ross, *Community Organization: Theory, Principles and Practice* (New York: Harper and Row, 1967), pp. 79–80.

10. Alex Haley, *Roots* (New York: Doubleday and Co., 1976).

11. The concept of relative deprivation was introduced by Samuel A. Stouffer in *The American Soldier* (Princeton, N.J.: Princeton University Press, 1950): "Deprivation or disadvantage measured not by objective standards but by comparison with the relatively superior advantages of others, such as members of a *reference group* whom one desires to emulate." Source: George A. Theodorson and Hilles G. Theodorson, *A Modern Dictionary of Sociology: The Concepts and Terminology of Sociology and Related Principles* (New York: Thomas Crowell Co., 1969), p. 343.

12. Gordon W. Allport, *The Nature of Prejudice* (Cambridge, Mass.: Addison-Wesley Publishing Co., 1954), p. 281.

13. Martin Meyerson and Edward C. Banfield, "Politics, Planning & Public Interest," in Fred M. Cox, et al., *Strategies of Community Organization* (Itasca, Ill.: F. E. Peacock Publishers, 1970), p. 32.

14. Christopher Jencks, et al., *Inequality: A Reassessment of the Effect of Family and Schooling In America* (New York: Basic Books, 1972), p. 4.

15. Ibid., p. 262.

16. "Report of the National Advisory Commission of Civil Disorders," Washington, D.C.: U.S. Government Printing Office, March 1, 1968, p. 1.

17. This challenging suggestion was made during an interview in 1971 with the director of the Institute on Pluralism and Group Identity of the American Jewish Committee.

18. Alexis de Tocqueville, *Ancien Regime et La Revolution* (Oxford: Clarendon Press, 1933), p. 223.

19. J. Milton Yinger, "The Reduction of Discrimination: Problems of Strategy," in Cox, et al., *Strategies of Community Organization.*

20. Jack Rothman, *Planning and Organizing for Social Change: Action Principles from Social Science* (New York: Columbia University Press, 1974).

21. J. Allen Williams, Jr., Clyde Z. Nunn, and Louis St. Peter, "Origins of Tolerance: Findings from a Replication of Stouffer's Communism, Conformity and Civil Liberties," *Social Forces* (December 1976): 394–408.

22. Ann G. Wolfe, in a presentation to the Annual Meeting of the Chicago Chapter of the American Jewish Committee, June 8, 1971, estimated the Jewish poor "at 700,000 to 800,000 in the United States" (out of a Jewish population in 1971 of 6,059,730).

23. Charles Y. Glock and Rodney Stark, "Christian Beliefs and Anti-Semitism," University of California, Anti-Defamation League Study, 1966, p. 205.

24. Bernhard E. Olson, *Faith and Prejudice: Intergroup Problems in Protestant Curricula* (New Haven, Conn.: Yale University Press, 1963), and his introductory essay in Jules Isaac's, "Has Anti-Semitism Roots in Christianity?" (New York: National Conference of Christians and Jews, 1961).

25. Nancy Seifer, "Cultural Diversity and the Women's Movement: Two Parallel Forces for Change," Institute on Pluralism and Group Identity, American Jewish Committee, October 25, 1957, p. 3.

26. Muzafor Sherif, *Groups in Harmony and Tension* (New York: Harper and Bros., 1953), p. 2.

27. The term *human relations* itself was used in earlier years in the field of labor-management relations with a somewhat different connotation. George Henderson, *Human Relations* (Norman, Okla.: University of Oklahoma Press, 1974), p. 59.

2

Historical Perspective

Changes in the total socioeconomic environment or important segments of it have had their effects upon intergroup tensions and have brought about corresponding changes in the overall priorities of intergroup relations practice. In turn, changes in agency objectives have affected the major strategies and techniques employed by intergroup relations agencies in their day-to-day activities. The success or failure of these strategies and techniques in reducing or eliminating undesirable practices has demonstrably affected our thinking about the nature of discrimination or bigotry.

To the extent, then, that we can trace the effects of such changes, we must necessarily concern ourselves with history. Certain major "events" of the last four decades have directly influenced the intergroup relations field. The first of these events is the New Deal.

The Roosevelt era (1932–1945) has often been regarded as an historical watershed in many areas of political, economic, and social life. Not the least of these is the area of intergroup relations, which has its roots and branches in all aspects of social life. Broadly speaking, the Roosevelt era marked the conscious entry of government into economic and social spheres which had been generally reserved to private enterprise, individual initiative, or private philanthropy. At the same time, the extended role of government broadened the general concept of individual civil rights to include employment, education, housing, and access to public accommodations. The central tenet of civil rights—i.e., that such rights may not be denied to any individual or any group on religious, racial, or ethnic grounds—was given the force of official sanction, if not law, by means of a series of executive orders.

In the economic field, the steady succession of New Deal regulations and orders signaled the acknowledgment by the body politic that private enterprise had been unable to solve the immense problems which beset it, especially with the economic depression and its attendant evils. So, too, in the civil rights field, Executive Order 8802 and its successors constituted acknowledgment that the efforts of private and voluntary agencies to deal with instances of discrimination and bigotry, as well as with many intergroup tensions and hostilities, needed massive and powerful shoring up by governmental decree and material help from government agencies.

To be sure, Executive Order 8802 specifically tied its prohibition of discrimination to the need for workers in defense industries. The order states:

Whereas it is the policy of the U.S. to encourage full participation in the national defense program by all citizens of the U.S. regardless of race, creed, color or national origin . . . [and] Whereas there is evidence that *available* and *needed* [our emphasis] workers have been barred from employment in industries engaged in defense production as well as within government agencies themselves solely because of considerations of race, creed, color or national origin . . . .

The order was hardly a civil rights manifesto, but it was of considerable historic significance. Only five years later, at the end of World War II, Executive Order 9808 establishing the President's Committee on Civil Rights could base itself more directly on constitutional grounds. It begins: "Whereas the preservation of civil rights guaranteed by the Constitution is essential to domestic tranquility, national security, the general welfare, and the continued existence of our free institutions." Clearly, President Truman believed that civil rights for all races no longer had to be justified on grounds of economic necessity or national defense requirements. These rights, he felt, were not only expressly guaranteed by the Constitution but were of vital importance to the nation's tranquility and welfare.

The entry of the federal government into the civil rights arena did not immediately end employment discrimination as most of its proponents would have wished. Nonetheless, its moral effect and its influence upon the subsequent course of discriminatory practices were far-reaching.

The National Recovery Administration and the National Labor Relations Act of 1935 are probably the most significant examples of government's abandonment of the accepted laissez-faire philosophy. In no sense, however, did they imply the abandonment of the private enterprise system as such. They were in fact an affirmation that this system had to be maintained. At the same time, if the system was to survive, measures for ameliorating some of its major defects had to be taken by the only agency which could effectively do so—the government itself.

The deemphasis in the 1960s and 1970s of the sociopsychological methods used in the 1930s and 1940s to deal with individual bigots and bigoted groups—methods which were almost universally accepted by most intergroup agencies—can be traced to the Roosevelt era. To be sure, the currently accepted views of the politicoeconomic bases for discriminatory practices and bigotry go back much further, at least to the middle of the nineteenth century. However, it was the Great Depression of the 1930s which gained them more general acceptance.

The difficulties experienced by the agencies in the 1940s in effecting changes in individual attitudes gave rise to a growing realization that the very magnitude of the problem called for a broader all-societal attack. This realization coincided with growing pressure from the disadvantaged groups themselves, primarily the blacks, who would no longer live under conditions they rightly considered intolerable. They demanded governmental intervention to end discriminatory practices. At the same time, the American economy, barely out of a major depression, was faced with a burgeoning demand for skilled and unskilled labor to produce the war material needed by the United States and much of the Western world. The very abundance of job opportunities overcame what might in other circumstances have been an active opposition by whites to the influx of black workers—opposition based upon a real or fancied threat to their jobs and livelihood.

Here then was a concatenation of events. A major depression with its inevitable accompanying human miseries—unemployment, poverty, and evictions whose effects were most severely felt by minority groups, especially blacks—followed by a sudden rise in the demand for workers, skilled and unskilled. The pressures of the disadvantaged for their just share thus combined with the demands of the economy and industry for the labor needed to produce essential goods. This combination of demand for and need of change in employment practices resulted in the promulgation and acceptance of government intervention and regulation.

At much the same time, another series of events culminating in World War II affected the intergroup situation. The war itself and the subsequent American entry into the conflict against the Axis brought the U.S. government, and in a very real sense the American people, into the arena of intergroup relations. During the 1930s there had been an exacerbation of anti-Semitic and racist propaganda, incidents, and demonstrations, some of them violent. Many of these activities were inspired, organized, and financed by paid and unpaid Nazi agents in this country, the German American Bund being among the best known. These activities alarmed many Americans and led some intergroup relations organizations to institute a series of countermeasures (some of these are examined later), some of which might even be called counterintelligence operations.

Subsequent to America's entry into the war came the discovery and exposure of the full horror of Nazi racism and its inhuman implementation in the death camps. It would seem that knowledge of the atrocities should have resulted in concern for the victims of persecution and perhaps in better attitudes towards minority groups, especially the Jews, at home. After all, it could be argued, the United States' entry into the war against Nazism put the official stamp of government disapproval on Nazi racial theories and acts, making it unacceptable, or perhaps even unpatriotic and un-American, to parade such sentiments in public. The intergroup relations agencies hoped for this effect, but in vain. For the most part, Americans held on to their prejudices. Sympathy for the victims was scant. Most people even opposed sanctuary for the victims.[1]

Nonetheless, many intergroup relations agency people began to feel that their activities against bigotry had become part of the mainstream of American life and purpose. Even though no specific legal sanctions against prejudice existed, they could bring moral pressures to bear on the bigot. The nation was at war with Nazism and all it stood for—world conquest, racism, anti-Semitism. It was an affirmation in which the whole nation participated and for which an army of 12 million men and women had been mobilized. More than ever before in recent memory, Americanism was equated with opposition to antihumanism. Already in the early 1940s, it was considered un-American to be racist.

The task of relating historical events to the changing ideologies of intergroup work, and even more specifically to the changes in strategies and techniques employed in corresponding periods of time, is not an easy one. One essential difficulty is that of time lag. Social actions rarely produce immediate effects. For example, in the decade or so immediately following the end of World War II, racial and religious prejudice did indeed decline dramatically and significantly, if the public opinion polls can be taken as reasonably accurate indicators of such trends. Jews, for example, were no longer rated a "menace" to America. In 1962, only one in a hundred Americans agreed that "Jews are a threat to America." Only sixteen years earlier, in 1946, the year of President Truman's establishment of the President's Committee on Civil Rights, one in five Americans interviewed concurred with such a statement.[2]

Prejudice against blacks also seemed to have fallen dramatically in this time period. A poll taken in 1942 revealed that only 35 percent of people interviewed would not object to a black neighbor. By 1963, however, the figure had risen to 63 percent.[3] While the two questions were not phrased in strictly comparable terms, the magnitude of the drop in prejudiced responses is unquestionably significant.

During the postwar years, the main thrust of intergroup relations work gradually shifted from the area of religious prejudice—Protestant against Catholic, Christian against Jew—to that of racist attitudes and racial discrimination. Simultaneously, the end of World War II marked the end of the uneasy friendship between the capitalist and communist worlds. Churchill's "official recognition" of the Cold War and the Iron Curtain in his 1946 Fulton, Missouri, speech was followed by the proclamation of the Truman Doctrine in 1947. The United States, the doctrine declared, was now ready to fight communism anywhere it threatened "democratic regimes." At nearly the same time, as a parallel to his announced position on international communism, President Truman created the Government Temporary Committee on Employee Loyalty to deal with subversives within our national boundaries.[4] The later indictment of eleven communist leaders in 1948, the much publicized hearings held by the House Committee on Un-American Activities, and the susequent "accusations" and "investigations" by Senator Joseph McCarthy signaled a new hierarchy of public enemies; Jews and blacks were summarily relegated to lower rungs on the hate ladder. The attempts by some of the more intractable bigots to equate Jews with communists had relatively little effect upon the general public, which wholeheartedly embraced the Truman Doctrine at home as well as abroad. The extent of American support for and acceptance of the Truman policy has been amply documented.[5]

President Truman established the Committee on Civil Rights in December 1946, only one month after he set up the Committee on Employee Loyalty. To see this as a political strategy would attribute greater astuteness to Truman than even he, master politician that he was, possessed. Nonetheless, he must certainly have realized that the coming together of the two proclamations eased the task of the supporters of racial equality.

The report of the President's Committee on Civil Rights recommended a number of sweeping reforms in the governmental setup. It also recommended that Congress enact a series of laws protecting the rights of suffrage of all citizens, eliminating segregation based on race, color, or creed and providing for the Federal Fair Employment Practice Act which would prohibit all forms of discrimination in education, housing, health, and public services. Finally, the report recommended the enactment of similar legislation by the states.

In 1948 came the Supreme Court ruling making restrictive covenants unenforceable in the courts. In the same year, President Truman's Executive Orders 9980 and 9981 created a Fair Employment Board in the Civil Service Commission and a broadly similar body in the armed services. The Civil Service Commission was ordered to make merit and fitness the sole valid criteria for appointment or promotion in government employment. Similarly, the armed services were asked to implement a policy of equal treatment of all personnel without regard to race, color, religion, or national origin.

Coinciding with the Truman administration's positive acts in the realm of civil rights were the negative, many-pronged attacks on civil liberties that began at the end of World War II and continued through the 1950s. These included the activities of the newly established "loyalty" boards in governmental departments and their offshoots in private industry, and the nationwide "hearings" of the House Committee on Un-American Activities. Most damaging to the nation were the "investigations" and widely publicized, largely unsubstantiated, charges of Senator Joseph McCarthy against various public figures, the State Department, and even the Army. These charges were trumpeted before public forums, before McCarthy's own Senate Permanent Sub-Committee on Investigations, and on the Senate floor. Even President Eisenhower did not escape the senator's wild attacks.

The atmosphere of fear and suspicion generated by McCarthy and his associates did much to mute the struggle for civil liberties which some intergroup relations agencies were beginning to see as a legitimate extension of their universalist concern for the general welfare. At the same time, many professionals in the field began to see that there was a dangerous relationship between McCarthy's attacks upon civil liberties and the racial and religious bigotry which was the prime target of intergroup relations workers.

The McCarthy era also gave rise to the so-called silent generation of the 1950s. The majority were apolitical, fearful of speaking out on any controversial issue or of coming to the defense of any of the senator's victims, lest they themselves be accused of being "soft on Communism." Not all were silent, however. There was much forceful opposition to the McCarthy smear tactics among many groups. Among these, the National Council of Jewish Women (organized in 1893 and numbering some one hundred thousand members in 287 branches) launched a campaign against the senator from Wisconsin. "The greatest domestic problem," the council charged, "is not Communism but McCarthyism." Their slogan was, "Speak-up, Freedom Needs Exercise."[6]

In some measure, the student campus revolts of the 1960s were a direct reaction to this period of repression of all freedom of expression and to the "silence" of the previous generation in the face of the concerted campaign against civil liberties.

Thus far, only some of the national "events" which can be easily and directly related to the intergroup scene have been mentioned in this chapter. During the same postwar decade, a number of other events, of international scope, occurred. Although their immediate impact upon American intergroup relations was probably less direct and certainly less visible than that of the national events mentioned, their long-term effects should not be underestimated.

There was, first, the defeat of Hitlerism, signifying the total victory over the forces of overt racism and anti-Semitism. Second, there was the establishment of the United Nations and its Commission on Human Rights, with the attendant overtones of peace on earth and the universality of human rights—rights which were not to be anywhere denied on grounds of race, color, creed, or national origin. Third, there were the emerging new African states, each and all affirming the end of white overlordship and exemplifying the newly won power of the black man. Fourth, there was the creation of the state of Israel. This, to most Jews at least, meant the reassertion of their dignity as equal members of the family of man.

To many intergroup relations professionals, and to people of good will everywhere, the occurrence of so many historic events asserting the freedom of man in the space of only one decade constituted proof that both international and domestic relations among the peoples of the world were improving. It was hoped that the trend would not be reversed.[7] By some process of social interaction, however, the white supremacists' weakened image was accompanied by increased black mobilization in furthering their claims to social and economic justice. At the same time, the new-found acceptance of Jews in America that followed the final defeat of Hitlerism and the subsequent creation of a Jewish homeland facilitated the transfer of much of the energy of Jewish intergroup agencies to the civil rights arena. While this transfer of emphasis had been in the making before the war, it was made easier by the victory over Nazism, which could easily be interpreted as a victory over anti-Semitism and bigotry in general.

Many factors, then, were involved in making civil rights the main theater of operations for intergroup relations agencies, including the rising discontent of black Americans and their new-found militancy; the evident reduction in overt religious prejudice against Catholic and Jew; and finally, the official proclamation of a new and easily acceptable public enemy and "menace," the communist threat. All of these factors combined to effect the shift away from the previous concentration upon prejudice alone as the principal barrier to good intergroup relations. Discrimination, social and economic, was now becoming the principal target. In line with the emergence of this approach was the concomitant proliferation of agencies, for the most part public (federal, state, municipal, and even community) rather than private, which entered the field in the postwar decades.

For the most part, the problem of attitudes remained the province of private "defense" organizations, while administrative enactment and enforcement of existing antidiscrimination laws became the chief concern of government. During this period, there was considerable cooperation between the public and private agencies and much overlapping in activities, especially in the "compliance" area, where governmental agencies saw their function as largely educational. Some even regarded the hearings held by various state commissions on civil rights as educational rather than "enforcing" in nature and the attendant compliance, when it was forthcoming, as resulting from genuine persuasion rather than from coercion or fear of consequences.

The 1950s witnessed three major events in the battle against discrimination. The most monumental of the three was the Supreme Court decision in 1954 that segregated schooling was a denial of the equal protection of the law and a violation of the due process clause of the Fourteenth Amendment. Of somewhat lesser import, but still one of the great antidiscrimination rulings, was the decision a year earlier which outlawed segregation in Washington restaurants. This ruling was followed by the extension of its nonsegregation provisions to other places of public accommodations by the Washington District Board of Commissioners. Then four years later came the Civil Rights Act of 1957. It established the Commission on Civil Rights and a Civil Rights Division in the Department of Justice. At the same time, it gave the federal government the right to use its power of injunction against any attempt to deprive citizens of their right to vote. The Department of

Justice was also broadly empowered to act in cases where more general civil rights were threatened or violated, such as the right to attend unsegregated schools.

The 1957 act, long overdue (it was the first national legislation of its kind in over eighty years), represented a major congressional recognition of the new imperatives current in the United States. The executive branch of the government, as was perhaps natural, had been the first to react to the demands of the civil rights movements and the pressure from the disadvantaged groups among others. The Supreme Court had followed with its historic rulings of 1953 and 1954. Congressional response came shortly thereafter, and while it was still minimal, its significance as a trailbreaker was large. Subsequently, the 1960 Civil Rights Act authorized the courts to appoint referees who would help those blacks who needed assistance to register and to vote.

During the 1940s and 1950s, the major strategies employed to combat bigoted attitudes and prejudices were educational and sociopsychological ones. Pamphleteering; school and religious textbook revision to eliminate slurs, insults, and just plain ignorance; and use of the mass media to project a correct image of minority groups, were all part of the educational armament of the intergroup professionals. Interracial summer camps, sensitivity training groups, and rumor clinics were among the most popular sociopsychological techniques.

The 1940s and 1950s also marked the appearance of some major scientific works on prejudice and methods of overcoming prejudiced attitudes. Among them were Gunnar Myrdal's *The American Dilemma* which focused national attention on the plight of blacks in America and *The Authoritarian Personality* which remains a landmark in scientific investigation of prejudice. In general, the employment of research and research findings as tools in the fight against bigotry was especially useful in the decade which witnessed the historic antisegregation rulings of the Supreme Court.

Pressures for more direct social action had already begun to build up in the 1930s. As the changeover in emphasis and direction of intergroup activities became more pronounced, they became well-nigh irresistible. It was in the summer of 1941 that A. Philip Randolph organized and successfully held over Roosevelt's head the threat of a mass march on Washington unless something were done about unfair employment practices. (For Randolph's full statement, see Chapter 8.) Randolph's threatened march was a concrete manifestation of belief in the use of confrontation and of organized power. Its "success" increased the militancy of the NAACP and the Urban League in their effort to achieve equal opportunity in housing as well.

The newborn insistence on the utility of social action had many forerunners. Tens of thousands of blacks denied employment because of their color exerted mass pressures. Joining in their struggle were the Jewish intergroup relations agencies which had for some years advocated alliances with other groups to achieve common goals. Although self-interest played a role, these groups also realized, supported by extensive research, that bigotry was indivisible and omnivorous in its choice of target, that bigotry against one group was very easily directed against another. The obvious conclusion was that it must be fought wherever it reared its head. Equally productive of such alliances was the fundamental belief in the democratic ideal of equality of opportunity for all—a belief which could be regarded as a charter provision of all intergroup relations agencies. It was an idea whose time had come.

In the 1930s and 1940s, the fight for fair employment practices as well as the struggle to ensure to all citizens the free exercise of their constitutionally guaranteed right to vote held the center of the social action stage. Fair employment practices and voting rights also became the focal points of alliances among intergroup agencies of all persuasions. In the years which followed Randolph's threatened march on Washington, confrontation strategies, coalitions, and mass action generally were to spread to all areas of social life, wherever discrimination or prejudicial acts were to be found. The historic 1955 Montgomery bus boycott which brought Martin Luther King, Jr., to the leadership of the black protest movement, the lunchcounter sit-ins throughout the South in 1959 and 1960, the Freedom Rides of 1961 organized by the Congress of Racial Equality (CORE), the nonviolent direct action demonstrations in Birmingham of 1963, the 1963 March on Washington for jobs and freedom that brought out more than two hundred thousand people from all parts of the country, and the Selma demonstration for voting rights in 1965 were dramatic evidence that the new strategies of social action, entailing the use of social pressure and mass power, were firmly entrenched in the arsenal of intergroup relations work.

It is generally believed that the wave of demonstrations and sit-ins were instrumental in insuring the passage of the Civil Rights Act of 1964. The fact that the bill which was passed was a broader version of President Kennedy's 1963 proposal to Congress and that it contained stronger provisions for enforcement is also in large measure attributable to the pressures of the disenfranchised and disadvantaged blacks. The bill was unquestionably a sign that the times had changed or were changing rapidly. The fact that Senator Everett Dirksen, never a champion of civil rights, was one of the principal organizers (with Senator Hubert Humphrey) of support for the civil rights bill was in itself a remarkable indicator of a change in national opinion.

The 1964 act filled in many of the gaps left by the 1957 bill. It spelled out in detail the prohibitions against discrimination in public accommodation, in public education, and in employment; it added clarification of voting rights and forbade verbal literacy tests; it provided for federal assistance to state programs; and it established a Community Relations Service in the

Department of Justice to provide assistance to people and communities with civil rights problems. It also set up the Equal Employment Opportunity Commission (EEOC), charging it with investigating infractions of the anti-discrimination statutes. At the same time the bill extended the life of the Civil Rights Commission and added to its functions the duty of acting as clearinghouse for civil rights information, incidentally providing such information to governmental and private organizations as well as to the general public. The commission was also assigned the duty of investigating allegations of voting fraud.

Despite the broad provisions of the 1964 act, violations of civil rights continued. Some states and municipalities still denied blacks the right to vote, laying down various and spurious registration regulations, delaying enforcement by long-drawn-out lawsuits and the like. The Civil Rights Act of 1965, by requiring states and counties to establish uniform standards of voting registration, was designed to combat this evil.

The 1960s were to be remembered as a time of struggle for compliance, for enforcement of enacted legislation. The combined action of the federal and state civil rights agencies (by 1967, twenty-five states and twenty-four cities had established Civil Rights Commissions or agencies of their own),[8] while of considerable effectiveness, was still not nearly enough to compel compliance. Direct mass pressure, this time by alliances of all races and creeds (as in the case of the fifty thousand people from many walks of life who converged on Montgomery from all parts of the country in 1965 after the violent suppression of the Selma demonstration) was still needed to make it abundantly clear that further violations of the laws of the land would not be borne peaceably.

In the mid-1960s, the civil rights agencies, federal, state and local, were almost swamped with complaints and charges of discriminatory practices and violations of civil rights. In its first year of operation, the EEOC reported having received nearly nine thousand individual complaints,[9] while state agencies reported nearly half that many.

The long-overdue Civil Rights Acts of 1957 and 1964 and the Voting Rights Act of 1965 could not have stemmed the rising tide of discontent among blacks, even if total compliance could have been enforced. As it was, 1965 witnessed riots in several cities, the largest and most destructive of them in Watts. In the South, die-hard bigots murdered black and white civil rights workers who had come to their communities to see that the new laws were carried out. The accused assassins were quickly acquitted, adding to the fires of disillusion and hate.

The same year, 1965, marked the beginning of the breakup of alliances and coalitions which had been so effective in pressing for the passage of civil rights legislation. Black organizations influenced by the newly arisen black power movement began to adopt separatist approaches. Even the older organizations like the National Association for the Advancement of Colored People and the National Urban League could not altogether resist the pressures for going it alone. Jewish intergroup agencies, Catholic and Protestant groups, and labor unions, antagonized by the more extreme black separatist groups, also retreated from the old alliances, while continuing to affirm their faith in equality of opportunity for all; and in civil rights, now firmly and legally enunciated, for all Americans.

During the last years of the 1960s, a number of serious black ghetto riots took place. The riot at Watts, the most violent and costly, was followed by riots in Chicago, Cleveland, Jacksonville, New York, Detroit, Newark, and some sixty other cities throughout the country. They signaled the ghetto's refusal to tolerate the slow pace in eliminating employment and education discrimination, and its protest against continuing poverty, substandard housing (where there was housing at all), bad sanitation, and poor health facilities. The 1968 report of the National Advisory Commission on Civil Disorders (the Kerner Report) warned that American society was becoming split into two separate and unequal sectors. More significantly, it blamed the white majority for creating the ghetto and the consequent riots.

By the end of the 1960s, it was clear that intergroup relations activity in the years ahead would emphasize racism and racial discrimination. Ghetto poverty and minority unemployment increasingly became the focus of the intergroup relations effort. Both absolute and relative deprivation were involved and obvious to all; both combined to compound the problems of governmental and private communal agencies.

Of perhaps greater significance at the time was the nation's involvement in the Vietnam War, a war which has rightly been called the most divisive in American history. The long-term effects of the frustration and disillusionment generated by the war and its aftermath upon intergroup relations have still to manifest themselves completely. Likewise, its impact upon the economy and upon governmental poverty and welfare programs, though concrete enough, needs further study. Of more direct concern to intergroup agencies was the fact that the U.S. war machine was manned in significant measure by black soldiers, who, for the first time in the experience of the American military, formed a large proportion of the combat and service troops. As might be expected, this fact had both positive and negative consequences for the black participants themselves and for American society as a whole. Some of these effects, such as unfulfilled expectations of future security, and the returning blacks' hostile or violent attitudes toward white society, have already made themselves felt. The Vietnam War has left its mark both upon the content and the process of intergroup relations programs, particularly in the racial area.

Also of significance for intergroup relations was the Yom Kippur War in the Middle East and the continuing Arab-Israeli struggle, which took their own toll in the form of divisiveness within the American community, this time in the area of Jewish-Gentile relations. Although America's sympathies, by and large, were with Israel, there was a residue of uneasiness about Jewish occupation of Jerusalem and about the dispossessed Palestinians which to Jews, at least, seemed to augur renewal of old and supposedly buried anti-Semitic attitudes.

Complicating the picture even further by 1965 were some of the directions taken by the newly found black militancy, this time in open black-Jewish conflict in a number of areas, chiefly economic and educational. Old canards of specifically Jewish rather than general white exploitation of blacks by slum landlords or extortionist shopkeepers were revived. At the same time, pressures for community control of schools in black neighborhoods brought black aspirants for supervisory jobs into conflict with Jewish incumbents. In the Ocean Hill district of New York City, the conflict took on major proportions, resulting in 1968 in strikes of some fifty thousand teachers and in community violence directed against the teachers. Feelings between blacks and Jews were bitter, and the struggle developed anti-Semitic overtones before the dispute was settled. As a result of heightened black-Jewish hostilities, Jewish intergroup agencies in the 1970s began seriously to differentiate between white and black anti-Semitism and to accord the black manifestation greater space on their action agendas. For the time being, all "alliances" were to be held in abeyance.

Black separatism also contributed to the revival of the pluralistic theme in intergroup relations. Questions regarding ethnicity and ethnic rights to survival in a pluralistic society received new impetus from the black power movement, even though many blacks continued to insist that ethnicity had little if anything to do with the matter. Black separatism and black power were held to be the "natural" answers to white power and white ghettoization of the blacks. They implied no automatic assertion of a black ethnicity. (Even the recent movement among blacks for proportional racial representation in all walks of American life does not necessarily imply the existence of, nor does it advocate, a black ethnic community.)

The events of the past few years which have influenced intergroup relations are still too recent to allow evaluation of their impact. Some of them, like the Nixon and Ford administrations' moratorium on federal assistance to housing, or the overall downgrading of various other federal assistance programs with their attendant budgetary cuts, may still be reversed by congressional action or the new Carter administration. Here then only a few of those events which have had direct or indirect influences on intergroup relations are listed.

The obvious negative effects of cutbacks in federal assistance programs by the Nixon administration, justified on the basis of a so-called return to the "values" of private initiative and reduction in governmental spending, need little elaboration here. The resulting increase in unemployment among minority groups, the inevitable lowering of an already dangerously low standard of living, the attendant frustrations, and the disappointments of many social and economic expectations have only served to exacerbate already strong tensions.

Coupled with the inflation and recession of recent years, the governmental retrenchment programs aggravated the already difficult problems facing intergroup relations workers. There are some indications, however, that President Carter may restore some of the cuts instituted by the previous administration.

With regard to effects in the area of anti-Semitism, Arab embargoes (threatened and actual) on American firms dealing with Israel, as well as the international furor created by the Arab-sponsored anti-Zionist resolution passed in the United Nations General Assembly in 1975,[10] have aggravated Jewish fears of a newly burgeoning anti-Semitism here and abroad. There was fear, too, that the support given by many African states to the anti-Zionist resolution might further heighten black anti-Semitism in the United States.

The actual effects of all of these related "actions" on anti-Jewish feelings within the general population are still unclear. Without doubt, however, the actions themselves have led all Jewish intergroup agencies to renew their program emphasis on Israel and on specifically Jewish problems. Among these problems is that of the emigration of segments of Soviet Jewry, which has occupied many Jewish communal agencies for some years.

In the wake of these events, there has been a discernible trend to parochialism (already in evidence at the height of the black power movement) within the intergroup relations field. Although all private agencies, whether Catholic, Jewish, or Protestant, have continued their efforts on behalf of general antipoverty programs, full housing and full and fair employment practices, desegregated schools, and the like, they have placed a greater or renewed emphasis on the concerns of their own constituencies. There are some signs, too, of insistence on reciprocity: mutual support of each other's programs.

Notes

1. In response to a question asked in November 1938 "Should we allow a larger number of Jewish exiles from Germany to come to the United States to live?," 71 percent said "no." Charles H. Stember, *Jews in the Mind of America* (New York: Basic Books, 1966), p. 148.

2. Stember, *Jews*, p. 128.

3. Ibid., pg. 379.

4. Executive Order 9835 (March 12, 1947) created a loyalty-security program for

the federal government and established loyalty review boards in each government department.

5. Samuel A. Stouffer, *Communism, Conformity and Civil Liberties* (New York: Doubleday, 1955).

6. Robert St. John, *Jews, Justice and Judaism* (New York: Doubleday, 1969), p. 392.

7. See also Chapter 1.

8. Burton Levy, "The Racial Bureaucracy 1941–1971," *Journal of Intergroup Relations* (July 1972): 11.

9. In fiscal 1974, the EEOC reported that 56,953 individuals had filed charges of employment discrimination with it. ("The Federal Civil Rights Enforcement Effort," U.S. Commission on Civil Rights, 1974, p. 510.)

10. On November 10, 1975, the U.N. General Assembly passed a resolution declaring "that Zionism is a form of racism and racial discrimination."

3

Role of Government and Law

The entry of the state as an active agent in the intergroup relations field entailed essential changes. The introduction of formal sanctions against discrimination in education, housing, employment, public accommodations, and most other social areas was a giant step forward. In addition, the establishment of governmental agencies to finance and implement programs designed to promote civic equality significantly affected the roles and functions traditionally reserved for private agencies. In turn, contacts with private agency workers often tempered and sometimes changed the approach of public officials on methods of carrying out their legal responsibilities.

Government in America may be said to have entered the intergroup relations field in the early nineteenth century with the repeal of state laws which had deprived certain rights of citizenship from a given religion or color. The true beginning of governmental activity, however, was President Roosevelt's Executive Order 8802. The right to discriminate or segregate had hitherto been held to be inherent in or natural to the ownership of a given property. Employers and hotel or property owners often refused employment, or denied access to their property, to persons whose color or religion was not to their liking. These discriminating practices were gradually curtailed through a series of laws, executive orders, and court decisions, and through the establishment of government agencies and bureaucracies designed to implement and enforce these laws and decisions.

The law as it applies to the civil rights aspect of intergroup relations is the frame of reference within which human relationships are cultivated and expressed. It establishes the limits and boundaries of social behavior. However, the law itself operates within the framework of social custom, social beliefs, and attitudes. So long as it prohibits or circumscribes universally condemned behavior, there are no obstacles to compliance or enforcement. But when it goes beyond these limits and proscribes behavior which, though morally wrong, is favored or practiced by some members of the community, resistance develops. It is at these outer limits that problems of enforcement and compliance arise.

By and large, our informants, both public and private, agreed that without attitudinal or motivational support within the individual and his community, law is greatly handicapped. A former head of the Civil Rights Division of the Justice Department stated emphatically:

Well, I can tell you one thing, I do not limit myself to the purely legal aspects and I doubt that my men do. I happen to have a personal philosophy that if equal opportunity in this country is going to depend purely on the law, we will never get the job done on enforcement. (1970)

He asserted that if the law is clear as to what is required, and voluntary compliance is generally practiced, many of the legal steps which would otherwise be necessary become superfluous. However, he added that this approach works only when an effective enforcement procedure exists.

An article published some years ago expresses similar views:

The effectiveness of any law, as is generally known, depends for the most part on three elements: First, it must set a standard which the community regards as right and desirable. Second, it must provide for enforcement procedures. Third, it must provide for an administrative agency to take the initiative, if need be, in enforcement; and more important, to engage in social engineering in order to generate willingness to abide by the law.[1]

Legislation and litigation, then, constitute the frame of reference for social action. Law is a basic framework for the protection of the rights of individuals. Furthermore, the spirit in which law is interpreted directly affects the quality of the human relationships that the specific law intends to safeguard. This is especially true when a meticulous and alert enforcement and compliance procedure has been instituted and accountability has been established in a well-organized administrative agency.

The real value of law in intergroup relations, according to our informants, is the law's ability to serve as a model for behavior and to help codify existing mores. It does not take the place of negotiation and conciliation, nor of the social engineering needed to prepare people to comply with the law. However, as one of our informants stated, "we cannot wait for attitudes to change before we enact laws, but we can prepare the people to be receptive when the law is enacted or even applied." There was a definite difference in emphasis on the use of law and litigation among the professionals interviewed in this study. (Some of these differences are explored later in the chapter.)

The interviews explored what impact the federal government's entry into the field has had on private community relations agencies, as well as some of the developments that grew out of this important thrust—primarily as it affected those outside of government service. During the Kennedy and Johnson administrations, the federal government forcefully entered the intergroup relations area with civil rights legislation and implementation of civil rights measures and constitutional provisions. It also became involved in service and preventive programs, such as the creation of the Community Relations Service (CRS) through Title X of the Civil Rights Act of 1964. This unit of the Department of Justice was set up to deal with problems of intergroup tensions and conflicts among local racial and ethnic groups, either directly or through local and state organizations.

The CRS is both structurally and functionally fitted to the study of process. In the first place, it has relationships with the local communities and with many private and public agencies, and second, it is frequently called upon to handle crisis situations requiring special skills.

Interviews with representatives of the CRS revealed many of the same insights encountered in other areas of group relations. (1) If contact in communities is to be effective, it should not be limited to prominent leaders; ordinary people can be important links in obtaining a meaningful appraisal of significant aspects of community dynamics. (2) Two types of professional skill are required: generic community-relations expertise and specialization, such as education, the law, or economic development. The generic intergroup relations worker utilizes the services of the specialists as needed.[2] The process is primarily that of catalytic action. In all indigenously launched confrontation activities, the task of the CRS is to keep the conflict as civilized as possible and to encourage both sides to be constructive. Another task is to develop leadership.

At the time of the interview, the director of the CRS stated that 80 percent of his work was preventive and 20 percent crisis-oriented. More recently, however, at an Interracial Colloquy[3] meeting in 1975, he indicated that most of the work had become crisis-oriented.

According to the CRS, compliance is not enough, for "if you depend solely on compliance in a case by case adjudication of disputes, it might take 25 years to effect social change." Moreover, according to CRS interviewees, few local and/or state commissions, even if they have compliance power, have the strength of will to engage in class action or to challenge patterns of discrimination.

Another problem which continues to plague intergroup relations workers, both public and private, is that of police relations with minority groups in communities. Mutual hostility and distrust have occasionally led to ugly incidents and have even sparked riots. The informants by and large agreed on what ameliorative measures and plans are needed in this sensitive area. Executives in both a large private agency and a key federal agency concurred that police relations must be handled within the context of the administration of justice—a broader universe in which community relationships are focal. Good police-community relations require close contact with a wide range of minority community members—from moderates to the most intransigent militants.

The informants emphasized that efforts should be made to help the police develop greater sensitivity to minority group problems. Some of the carefully planned training sessions for key men in police departments have proved helpful by giving them greater awareness of their responsibilities as peacemakers and community workers—as people with preventive as well as enforcement obligations: "The policeman needs to be involved in the preventive aspect of meeting problems, rather than just operating on an ad hoc basis."

As would be expected, different regions of the country require different types of training. For instance, police training in Georgia primarily involves specific problems of the Southern constabulary. In all regions, however, successful training demands that the emphasis be shifted from the policing function to the service function since nearly 90 percent of an officer's time is spent on what might be termed services. England and other countries have long been familiar with this concept and have implemented it in their work.

Still another major problem encountered in the enforcement of compliance with civil rights statutes can be subsumed under the term *backlash*. Backlash occurs when a group which has occupied a privileged or superior position in the community feels threatened by the demands, achievements, or "encroachment" of newcomers to the scene. Such a situation can lead to open violence, usually initiated by the hitherto entrenched group. The reaction of Boston whites to the busing of their children is an outstanding example.

Some black leaders were concerned that strict enforcement of the laws might result in white backlash. White leaders too were concerned with the same problem. According to a prominent white professional in a national public enforcement agency:

I am concerned that there are some real benefits that whites have gotten in the past from discriminatory systems, and nobody likes to give anything up; very often they don't give it up voluntarily.... All that backlash means is a reaction, so we'll see some strong reaction when some entrenched groups find that the real enforcement of the law means that some of the advantages they have had in the past will be eliminated.

This prediction, made at the end of 1970, has indeed come true. Our informants believed that most Americans are willing to obey the law if it is clear, reasonable, and definite. One informant, however, indicated that "on the human level there needs to be some understanding of the state of mind when after enjoying a benefit for 350 years, it is about to be taken away." Effective enforcement is certainly preferable to disorder in the streets.

Some informants felt that the government's entry into the field has enabled private groups to concentrate on community-relations services and has relieved them of their legal concerns. This was not a unanimous opinion, however: "I don't believe that entry of government into the intergroup relations field does in any way reduce the burden," said one executive.

The private agencies have been able to expand their services by utilizing government resources and government grants for specific functions. City and state agencies serve as mediators between various community groups. The government's entry on both the local and national level has helped the community at large to recognize the importance of intergroup relations in its everyday functioning.

Government resources have facilitated the progression from "fairness" in the use of facilities to "fullness," i.e., actual expansion of resources in housing, education, and employment. The government has been pivotal in establishing a concern with intergroup relations and in promoting the idea that equality of opportunity is a basic public responsibility. It has also helped reduce the gap between the haves and have-nots. In addition, the federal government has broadened the role and concern of state and local governments in the human relations field. One informant opined that without federal intervention "states would simply go the usual way of people in the state and would be tardy to respond to the ills of those in need." Another informant put it even more strongly: "For local municipalities to respond to the ills of society, it would have to be a cold day in hell."

Through both laws and subsidies, the federal government has elevated the quality of performance of workers in the intergroup relations field. It is generally conceded that John F. Kennedy and Lyndon Johnson did most to get states and municipalities to respond to obviously existing needs. Some believe that of the two presidents, Johnson made the more significant contribution in this area.

According to the informants, certain programs financed by public agencies but conducted by private agencies have yielded satisfactory results. One of these is the training program conducted by CORE for dropouts and for young men with criminal records. Training as mechanics, printers, and gas station attendants were cited as successful public-private ventures.

The interviews also revealed that the roles of the private and public agency were changing. At that time, the private organization stressed the advocacy function; i.e., it supported and promoted policies leading to better intergroup relations. The public agency mediated between contending groups and regulated community policy. An additional distinction was that the private agency tended to be the developer of community policy, while the governmental agency was its implementer. Several of the interviewees maintained that the public agency intergroup relations worker was obliged "to be responsive to his political situation and to his superiors in the bureaucratic framework." In the interviews, the broader issues confronting society appeared more central to the private than to the public agency worker. However, the public agency worker had a greater obligation to master the workings of the institutions in the areas in which he operated than the worker in the private agency. Finally, the private agency was said to help the community understand how to make the best use of government facilities and to give effective support to those public agency programs consistent with its own policies.

As the affirmative action programs of the public agencies gained momentum, the distinction between the equipment and skills required by the private and public agency worker, respectively, narrowed to a marked degree. Now, both have to plan, both have to formulate, and both have to initiate; in general the public agency worker remains the implementer, however.

At the time of our interviews, the prevailing view was that the private agency worker was primarily the "thinker" and the public agency worker the "doer." This view, too, is rapidly changing as the federal departments and state and municipal human relations commissions begin to assume the functions formerly considered the special domain of the private sector. Today, both are formulators and doers, although the private agency worker retains greater flexibility and facility for exploration.

Officials in a number of federal agencies, such as the Department of Housing and Urban Development (HUD), believed that the extent of involvement of local private organizations in a public agency's national program can be a determining factor in the magnitude of federal funds obtained for special projects.[4] They maintained that a goodly number of resources available at the local level are to be found in the voluntary (private) institutions and that they influence much of the thought at the local level generally. In fact, unless the private agencies are involved, committed, and convinced of a program's worth, large portions of national resources will not be utilized. Therefore, some federal public agencies encourage cities to involve local private organizations in intergroup relations programs.

This view also holds for work with private enterprise. According to a top HUD official:

It's not enough to work in New York with the Human Relations Commission. It is also important for us to work with the black contractors. It's important for us to work with the black Mortgage Bankers Association. It's important for us to work with the Real Estate Brokers Association—all the way down the line. In other words, we're not only concerned with the socially oriented organizations. We're also concerned with the organizations that are economically oriented.

The EEOC keeps abreast of the situation in industry with respect to the problem of discrimination. For example, the New York State Division of Human Rights supplies the EEOC with information. In addition, the EEOC has its own research operation which, via spotchecks of industrial corporations, obtains additional detailed information about the representation of different races in specific industries.

On the whole, at the time of the interviews, federal departments had experienced very little negative pressure from the administration. Little or no attempt was made to soft-pedal the implementation of decisions with respect to grievances. Pressures that did come were in the positive direction from minority groups, and these were on the increase. Some negative pressures came from contractors and from certain unions accused of discriminatory practices in connection with the implementation of the Philadelphia Plan.[5] Both the unions and the contractors claimed that the plan violated the Civil Rights Act of 1964.

Employer groups also put pressure on the EEOC, especially when a pattern rather than an individual case was involved. A June 1975 congressional investigation of government agencies responsible for enforcing laws on employment opportunities for minorities and women indicated that apparently employers are confused by the plethora of enforcement agencies. The increase in agencies and protected classes (racial, religious, and ethnic minorities, as well as women, handicapped persons, and veterans) was said to have had an adverse impact on affirmative action since strict compliance with all regulations would affect work productivity.[6]

At the time of the interviews, the EEOC did not regard discrimination as isolated instances involving specific, identifiable individuals. Rather, it defined discrimination as a broad pattern of inequality. Whites were treated differently than blacks; among other things, they were given different tests and were required to meet different standards. The EEOC was concerned that a pattern was emerging. For the pattern approach is concerned not with the single person but with a class and an entire group. The courts have been supporting this pattern approach. Even a promotion system that follows seniority where workers were put into various classifications in the past, on a discriminatory basis, and where today they can transfer between those categories on an equal basis, may still be illegal, the Courts have said.[7]

In July 1975, the Labor Department and the EEOC became involved in a controversy arising out of "last hired, first fired" layoffs. The EEOC had supported minorities and women; but changed its position to conform with the policy of the Labor Department favoring the seniority system. It was anticipated by our informant that controversial cases would be turned over to the courts for determination of the meaning of "bona fide" seniority system as it appears in the Civil Rights Act of 1964.[8] The NAACP has called on federal and state authorities to insure that recently hired or promoted blacks not be among the first to be laid off or demoted.[9]

As far back as 1970, both the pattern and the practice with respect to resistance to and evasion of the civil rights acts were factors in determining violations. In recent years, especially since the application of affirmative action in the fulfillment of equal opportunity goals, the pattern itself—what the situation is actually like—has been used to determine the degree of compliance with the law. Is the violation typical or atypical? Or as the interviewees were asked: "Is it an isolated, discriminatory incident in the midst of dozens of non-discriminatory events?" One of our informants believed this to be the basic issue. Some informants also pointed out that another general criterion is employed in initiating enforcement procedures, i.e., setting in motion a desirable practice or stopping an undesirable one. This criterion is whether a racial situation, of general public concern, such as "blockbusting,"[10] has developed.[11]

Joint charges may be filed in the case of fair housing and fair employment violations. Many cases do not reach the courts, however, for federal enforcement agencies do negotiate and many cases are settled out of court. There are many sources of complaint referrals. Some cases that come to enforcement agencies, such as the Civil Rights Division of the Department of Justice, originate in a rather unusual manner. For example, a white prospective tenant may be told by a leasing agent: "Oh, you don't have to worry about niggers here. We don't allow niggers." At the time of our interviews, this was a rather frequent occurrence and, of course, it constitutes evidence of a violation. Today such information is usually conveyed indirectly, not overtly.

The head of the Housing Section in the Civil Rights Division of the Justice Department pointed out how "cases," i.e., complaints, are brought to the attention of some of the enforcement bureaus or units of federal departments: "We try to develop our own. We send people to cities, deal with fair housing groups, civil rights groups, blacks and other minorities who become leads. At times, the newspapers are employed" (1970). He called the elimination of restrictive racial covenants from all major title-insurance policies "one of our best accomplishments." He indicated that the newspapers were the principal source of information for instances of this kind of violation. Of course, restrictive racial covenants had been unenforceable since 1948; the 1968 statute, however, prohibited title insurance companies from even copying racial restrictions from deeds. Oral statements indicating restrictions on the basis of race in the context of a commercial transaction are also now illegal.[12]

Today the priorities in enforcing civil rights housing legislation are to protect the rights of minorities and to promote open housing in both urban and suburban areas, especially where industrial jobs are available.

The practice of "steering" needs particular watching. This practice works as follows: A white person contemplating the purchase of a house in an integrated community may be told by the real estate agent, "You don't want to live there with a bunch of blacks." But the same agent, discussing the purchase of a home in the same area with a black client, will be enthusiastic over the house and the neighborhood. In this way, the area becomes resegregated—all black.

Blockbusting is another evil that the legal and enforcement agencies must prevent and eliminate. It is a violation of the law to induce a white person to sell his house because "blacks are moving into the neighborhood." To establish that blockbusting is practiced, it must be shown: that the defendant, for profit, induced or attempted to induce any person to sell a dwelling by representations regarding the entry or prospective entry into the neighborhood by person or persons of a particular race, color, religion or national origin.[13]

Patterns of discrimination in employment are established by obtaining statistics on the number of blacks (or other minorities) employed by a company relative to the total number of employees. Next, the volume of minority applicants over a given period is determined, and rejections are analyzed and related to acceptances. Finally, racial identification from the files based on the enforcement agency's knowledge of the geographical area or of the schools in the area, or perhaps on other factors, is made. An official of the Civil Rights Division said that when a number of qualified blacks have applied for a job and either none or very few have been hired, a pattern of discrimination in hiring has been established.

Even as late as 1970, it was possible to identify "Negro jobs" in an industry—laborer, bus boy, and similarly menial occupations (especially in the South). To what extent have the discriminatory practices of former years persisted?

Until 1964, the stated policy of many factories was to hire on the basis of race. To what extent have the seniority or transfer practices of earlier discriminatory periods been perpetuated? In the past, when blacks were consigned to what was known as the "labor department," they enjoyed job seniority in that department, but if they transferred to the so-called white jobs, they received no credit for the time spent in the "labor department." The Civil Rights Act of 1964 removed the division between "black" and "white" jobs, but employers often substituted other barriers, such as tests or education.

The practice of assigning blacks to the least desirable jobs and denying them seniority if they transferred to a "white unit" has been severely discouraged by the U.S. Labor Department. In 1973, offending employers such as Bethlehem Steel were ordered to permit black employees to transfer to better jobs with no loss in seniority status.[14] Other companies, such as Detroit Edison, were assessed large sums in punitive damages by the courts.[15] In another case, American Telephone and Telegraph agreed to give $15 million in back pay and $23 million a year in raises to women and minority males against whom it had allegedly discriminated in job assignments, pay, and promotions. This settlement embraced a principle that had never before been accepted: financial restitution—even though applications for better-paid jobs had not been filed because minority workers and female employees knew that company policy excluded them from those jobs.

The enforcement powers of the various federal departments differ. In the field of employment, the legislation of 1972 has considerably strengthened the enforcement of the EEOC provision.[16] If conciliation attempts fail, the

EEOC may bring a civil action in a federal court. When state governmental agencies are respondents, the Office of the Attorney General is responsible for enforcing laws against discrimination in employment.[17]

Seventeen agencies now carry out compliance functions in the employment field for the federal government. The Department of Labor, principally through the Employment Standards Administration, has overall responsibility for the administration of Executive Orders 11246 and 11375.[18] At the same time, each government agency bears responsibility for affirmative action compliance of those companies with which it has contracts. Thus, each federal agency through the Department of Labor's Office of Federal Contract Compliance (OFCC) is engaged in affirmative action efforts. The compliance officer who determines whether or not an industrial corporation is following an affirmative employment policy is generally the person who negotiates with the industrial corporation if noncompliance is found to exist.

In the case of housing, perhaps the most delicate area because of its privacy aspect, HUD may assist an individual in instituting a civil suit. The court may appoint an attorney, and if a pattern of discriminatory housing practice is found, it may issue an injunction. In dealing with a complaint of housing discrimination, Title VIII and the HCDA of 1974 require HUD to refer the case to the Justice Department. HUD cannot go directly to court.[19]

The enforcement power of the Department of Health, Education and Welfare (HEW) lies in its right to withhold funds from a project, cancel it, or terminate or suspend the contract.[20] About 10 percent of the average school district's funds come from federal sources.[21]

The Labor Department, through its Contract Compliance Division, has the power to withhold money from the state. It can hold up a contract until the contractor has spelled out his timetable for achieving the civil rights objectives.[22]

The Justice Department can, of course, bring suit on behalf of any federal department involved in a dispute over violations of agreements.

An official in the Civil Rights Commission observed that laws are by no means self-executing:

After a law is passed, a lot of the people that fought for the law feel that the battle is over and those who fought for its enactment can retire to the sidelines. This is a grave error. In 1970 only a little more than $100 million was available for all Federal enforcement work.[23]

From our interviews, it appears that when an agency is responsible both for developing a program and for civil rights enforcement, enforcement tends to suffer because the agency is primarily concerned with expanding the program.

For example, the guidelines of the OFCC now call for an outreach and positive recruitment program to give members of religious and/or ethnic groups fair consideration for job opportunities.[24]

At the time of our interviews, only two needs were indicated with respect to expanding legal provisions, but with regard to enforcement and implementation. Of the two felt needs for expansion, one related to sex discrimination. "We've got a whole rash of complaints from some of the women's groups lately about the assignment of faculty and the entire problem of equal opportunity for women on the U.S. campuses in various academic departments," said an HEW official. Since then, new legislation has been enacted.[25] In addition, Executive Order 11246 as amended by Executive Order 11375, constitutes a legal foundation for the advancement of rights of women not just on the campus but in all employment. The process has been rather slow on the college campus, but there are indications that it is gaining momentum. Because of long-standing exclusionary practices in academe, the remedy will require more time than in the general employment field.

The second need for legislative expansion was in the area of state and local governments. Civil service employees were excluded from the stipulation of Title VII of the 1964 law. One reason given for this exclusion[26] was that since Title VII was based on interstate commerce, it would be anomalous to include the states in this formulation.

Additional legislation, for example, improvement in the housing law, was recommended by the then assistant secretary for equal opportunity of HUD:

In the fair housing law, if HUD had the authority to go out and initiate complaints that would be an improvement. If we had the authority to issue cease and desist orders against real estate brokers, mortgage bankers, when they discriminate, I think that would be an improvement. I think that if there were laws prohibiting a community from screening out minorities on economic grounds, that would be an improvement. So, I think that there are a variety of improvements that can be made in the laws, but on the other hand I would also have to admit that all of the current laws have not been fully implemented.

I would say that the fair housing law, to be really effective, should give us the authority to issue an order to say—you are compelled to cease and desist from the practice that you're now undertaking.

This power to initiate complaints appears to be similar to the power of the National Labor Relations Board to issue cease and desist orders. The head of the Civil Rights Division of the Justice Department expressed a similar need for authority to issue a formal complaint. He believed that information on the existence of a specific violation should suffice for initiating action.[27]

An HUD official pointed out one interesting evasion of the housing law.

Upon joining a private association, a realtor becomes eligible to subscribe to the multiple listing service. "Undesirable" brokers are denied participation in the service; "undesirable," in essence, means ethnic and racial groups. Information as of August 1976 indicated no change in this practice.

The preponderant view on enforcement among the HUD staff was along the following line: first increase the supply of housing, and then make certain through the enforcement of law that the housing is marketed fairly.

The administration of a law is basic to its effectiveness. If an illegal act has been committed and legal action has been taken, one informant asserted, "you do not make vital progress in achieving the desired goal even if you obtain a change in the particular individual situation through a court order." What is required for a lasting impact is a commission which can take automatic action whenever a law has been violated. This would eliminate the need for elaborate court procedures to establish guilt; the determination would rest with the commission. Its decision would, of course, be subject to legal appeal, but a basic principle on the violation of civil rights provisions would thus have been established.

An educational process can follow, but it was the view of our informants that meticulous enforcement should precede the educational effort. As one informant, the New York State commissioner on human rights, stated: "I think history has taught us that education by itself is not sufficient. You've got to enforce the law and then, hopefully, people are going to observe the law."

There are sixty-two Human Rights Commissions in New York State. The only local commission that has concurrent jurisdiction with the State Division is the New York City Commission on Human Rights. The New York State Division of Human Rights has fourteen offices at which complaints can be filed, including two in Manhattan and one in each of the other boroughs of New York City. The Division of Human Rights has the power to set up local, regional, or statewide advisory councils to serve without pay, but the division provides technical and clerical assistance. The authority vested in these councils is discretionary with the commissioner of human rights, who said that he has given them as much leeway as possible consonant with his own responsibilities.

The New York State commissioner of human rights described the relationship of poverty to intergroup tensions as follows:

...You cannot look upon human rights as a purely legal matter. This point is a new philosophy we are trying to develop in the State Division based upon my previous experience that human rights consists of a host of other social problems....if he doesn't have a meaningful job, you are denying him his inalienable rights as an American citizen. Life, liberty and the pursuit of happiness...refers to the quality of man's life and the delivery of services that government must provide to all of its citizens. Therefore, human rights is more than the complaint process. It is the totality of man's existence. I'm speaking of economic rights, health rights. A man has a right to expect the State to give him good health services.

In the early 1970s, the New York City Commission on Human Rights, in an attempt to expedite the disposition of complaints which had been piling up, requested that its general counsel be named a special corporation counsel. This enabled him to go directly to court and eliminated the long wait for the disposition of a complaint, since it was no longer necessary to refer cases to the corporation counsel's office.

The Federal Communications Commission (FCC) receives many complaints against radio and television stations charged with antiblack or anti-Semitic or anticivil libertarian actions. Frequently, large coalitions of civic, church, and intergroup relations agencies are formed to lodge these complaints. At one time Philadelphia had twenty-nine such groups. A landmark decision was rendered when the FCC refused to renew the license of a radio station in Philadelphia on the grounds that it was anti-Semitic and antiblack.

As indicated previously, the enactment in 1972 of legislation covering the rights of women in federally assisted education programs and the 1972 amendment to Title VII of the Civil Rights Act of 1967 removing the exclusion of civil service employees met the two major needs for legislative action. While others remain, it is probably true to say that today the emphasis must be on the improvement and strengthening of enforcement and compliance procedures.

Notes

1. John Slawson, "Intergroup Relations in Social Work Education," *Education for Social Work Proceedings* (Council on Social Work Education, 1958), p. 110.

2. See "Professional Preparation" in Appendix B. This material was not included in the text because, while of possible assistance to the professional, it was not of sufficient depth to justify inclusion.

3. The Interracial Colloquy (sponsored by the National Conference of Christians and Jews, the National Association for the Advancement of Colored People, the American Jewish Committee, and the National Urban League) is an association of member organizations dedicated to intergroup understanding.

4. The Housing and Community Development Act of 1974 specifies "citizen participation" as one criterion for the funding eligibility of a community.

5. The Philadelphia Plan called for a 25 percent increase in non-white employment over a period of four years in the construction industry in Philadelphia. See Chapter 11 for a fuller description of the Philadelphia Plan.

6. *The New York Times*, June 20, 1975.

7. In *Quarles v. Phillip Morris, Inc.*, 279F. Supp. 505 (Ed.Va), January 4, 1968, the court held that "a departmental seniority system that has its genesis in racial dis-

crimination is not a bona fide seniority system." [*The United States Law Week*, 5–31–77. (45LW4511)]

8. In its June 16, 1977, ruling, the Supreme Court held that "bona fide" seniority systems may not be set aside to permit employees to observe particular religious days of rest.

9. *The New York Times*, July 5, 1975.

10. The meaning of blockbusting, including its legal basis, is considered later in the chapter.

11. Sec. 813 of the Civil Rights Act of 1968 (Title VIII) prescribes:

Whenever the Attorney General has reasonable cause to believe that any person or group of persons is engaged in a pattern or practice of resistance to the full enjoyment of any of the rights granted by this title, or that any group of persons has been denied any of the rights granted by this title and such denial raises an issue of general public importance, he may bring a civil action in any appropriate United States district court by filing with it a complaint setting forth the facts and requesting such preventive relief, including an application for a permanent or temporary injunction, restraining order, or other order against the person or persons responsible for such pattern or practice or denial of rights as he deems necessary to insure the full enjoyment of the rights granted by this title.

12. See Title VIII of the Civil Rights Act of 1968, Sec. 804C.

13. Refers to Title VIII, Civil Rights Act of 1968, Sec. 804(e).

14. *The New York Times*, January 22, 1973. In 1973, a federally appointed panel found that Bethlehem Steel had discriminated against blacks for years by assigning them to the dirtiest, least desirable jobs and keeping them there by a company policy that forced anyone transferring to another unit to give up seniority and pay status and start over at the bottom rung of the new unit.

15. *The New York Times*, October 3, 1973. A federal judge ordered the Detroit Edison Company to pay $4 million in punitive damages to blacks who had been victims of "deliberate" and "invidious" racial discrimination by the utility.

In addition, United States District Judge Damon J. Keith assessed $250,000 in punitive damages against Local 223 of the Utility Workers of America for what the judge said was the union's part in helping to maintain Detroit Edison's discriminatory practices in hiring and promotion.

16. Equal Employment Opportunity Act of 1972, Public Law 92–261, March 24, 1972. To enforce the law, the EEOC may bring civil action in the federal court against private employers, a government agency, or a political subdivision. The General Counsel of the EEOC may issue cease and desist orders.

17. Equal Employment Opportunity Act of 1972, Sec. 706(f).

18. See "Toward a More Cooperative and Productive Relationship Among Civil Rights Agencies and Officials," *Proceedings*, Regional Civil Rights Conference I, U.S. Commission on Civil Rights, St. Louis, Mo., February 11–13, 1974.

Executive Order 11246 of 1965 remodeled the compliance program requiring each federal agency to include in its contractual agreements with contractors an equal opportunity clause, as follows: (1) not to discriminate in employment on the basis of race, color, sex, religion, or national origin, and (2) to undertake affirmative action to ensure that equal employment opportunity principles are followed in personnel practices at all company facilities, including those facilities not engaged in work on a federal contract. Executive Order 11246 was amended by Executive Order 11375 (1967) to include affirmative action compliance in Federal agencies administering contracts.

Hearings are presently underway for consolidation of all federal equal opportunity and contract compliance programs to be consolidated within the Department of Labor. If passed, the OFCCP would have full enforcement and administrative authority for Executive Order 11246, Sec. 503 of the Rehabilitation Act, and Section 402 of the Vietnam Era Veterans Law.

19. Civil Rights Act of 1968, Title VIII.

20. Civil Rights Act of 1964, Title VI.

21. Interview, acting director, HEW, Public Affairs.

22. Interview, assistant secretary of labor, Workplace Standards.

23. Interview, staff director, U.S. Commission on Civil Rights.

24. Guidelines on Discrimination because of Religion or National Origin, Part 60-50, 1/17/73 (U.S. Department of Labor, OFCC).

25. Title IX of the Education Amendments of 1972 which prohibits "sex discrimination in all federally-assisted education programs and amends certain portions of the Civil Rights Act of 1964."

26. Note: On March 24, 1972, this exclusion was removed by the Equal Employment Opportunity Act of 1972. This amendment to Title VII of the Federal Civil Rights Act of 1964 broadened coverage of the title expressly to include "State governments, governmental agencies, political subdivisions and Federal government employment."

27. In accordance with the Fair Housing Law of 1968, after conciliation, conference, and persuasion on behalf of an individual complaint, HUD can subpoena witnesses and examine necessary records. Failure to respond to subpoena or produce records makes the individual liable to a fine up to $1,000 or imprisonment up to one year, or both. If there is reasonable cause to believe that "a pattern or practice of resistance" under the Fair Housing Law exists, the attorney general (Department of Justice) may take action. Such litigation in a federal district court may lead to the issuance of a permanent or temporary injunction against the person or persons responsible for a "pattern or practice of resistance" to the law (Civil Rights Act of April 11, 1968, pp. 36LW93-94, Sec. 809-819).

4

The Factor of Ethnicity

Most of our informants agreed that the maintenance of group identity within an environment of cultural or ethnic pluralism was an important determinant of approaches to the treatment of intergroup relations problems.

With possibly one exception, both black and white informants agreed on the increasing role played by ethnic group identification. The concept of black power, for example, was considered basic to the advances made by the blacks in the past decades. There was also ample evidence that the quest for black identity served to encourage Jewish group identity strivings and to promote ethnic consciousness among other white groups.

In the past, the attitudes of blacks and other ethnic groups on the question of group survival differed markedly. For blacks, group identity meant a state of separation from the mainstream of society—a form of social injustice. However, the persistence of white community nonacceptance resulted in a turn toward the opposite view. Generally, blacks now no longer want to be lost in the mainstream, i.e., melt away; they wish to retain their identity. Most other ethnic groups in American society—the Jews, Poles, Chinese, and American Indians—have for the most part always wanted some form of group identity. Among all such groups, of course, are assimilationists who consider such "ethnic" identity a burden, partly because of the discriminatory attitudes and behavior of the larger society. It is probably true, however, that the 1960s and 1970s witnessed a considerable strengthening of ethnic consciousness among most minority groups, including blacks.

The executive director of CORE told us in the early 1970s: "A lot of what we push gets picked up a year later or six months later, two years or three years later." Blacks did not have the same resistance as whites historically had to the intensification of their group identity. The melting-pot concept was off limits to blacks even in more recent days. Nor were they obliged to shed the melting-pot ideology in order to foster ethnic group identity. The melting-pot, a pre-World War II concept, was fairly prevalent among whites but not among blacks. A. Philip Randolph's position on ethnic identity is as follows: "Yes, I believe in group ethnic consciousness. I doubt that there is any other way for survival...(however) no single group in a democratic system can win its fight for its cause without the help of public opinion." He therefore condemns separatism, although he appreciates the reasons for black mistrust of whites who espouse black liberation.

As late as 1970, a professional executive of an extremist group expressed a somewhat different position: "Clearly we are not going to live together in harmony, so let's live apart in peace." He further asserted: "The blacks now want to be black."

Irving Levine, director of the Institute on Pluralism and Group Identity, reminded us that America has not finished with its migration problems: "Each year we now have more immigrants, both legal and illegal, coming in than we have had in the past few decades... We had them coming from a wide variety of nations. The reform of the McCarren-Walter Act has created new East European pockets in our cities."

In the early 1970s, a black power Catholic movement took form. It was felt that unless black Catholics assumed a positive and aggressive attitude toward self-determination, the exodus of blacks from the Catholic church would accelerate. Through the urging of black priests and Catholic religionists, the National Office for Black Catholics was created. It is currently contributing toward a greater unity of purpose among black Catholics. With their common backgrounds and cultural experiences, black priests can better relate to black constituents. Because of a shortage of black priests, white priests are being taught by their black colleagues how to relate to black parishioners.

The informants emphasized that while group identity—white as well as black—is wholesome, it can also lead to defensiveness and may perhaps even be harmful. And while such identity contributes toward group stability, it can become a liability if it serves merely as a basis for negative or antagonistic attitudes. In the process of enhancing wholesome group relations, group identity can be an asset in negotiation, but it can be destructive if it assumes an ethnocentric dimension or involves an exclusively self-interest goal with little or no regard for overall concerns.

Ethnocentrism, an outcome of overstressing group identity, can result in greater conflict between ethnic groups. This effect is produced when ethnic group boundaries, formed by differing characteristics of group identities, are allowed to become barriers between them. This need not be the case. On the contrary, recognition of the uniqueness of each group can become a fertile field for productive competition.

A negative outcome of ethnocentrism recently surfaced in black-Puerto Rican conflicts, particularly in connection with antipoverty programs. It also developed in a black-Jewish controversy about educational matters—jobs as well as desegregation programs—and in interpretations of affirmative action programs bearing on the use of "quotas" as a device for desegregation.

Polarization deepens when competition for social status and position exists. New groups cannot fit into the meritocracy or the credentialism system created to protect the life-styles and the power of the older groups. The older groups find that they have to change standards as well as rules. "Polarization," said Irving Levine, "comes in when the group that is emerging [from below] tries to change the rules." One governmental official felt that the imbalance of "racial leadership" in "biracial" or "interethnic" decision-making committees tends to contribute to polarization. The ultimate goal of the depolarization process is to develop reforms for the credentials system and at the same time not devastate it or threaten those who made it through this system. Implied in this process is a sharing of power or privilege by the older and newer groups; this is a difficult task indeed.

In *Strangers in the Land*,[1] John Higham points out that racism became a factor in the life of the Jewish community when Jews began to compete for place and position with established majorities. In turn, Jews are now being challenged by members of minority groups who want "a piece of the action," since Jews now occupy many middle-management and top positions in teaching and other professions.

As early as 1971, a Jewish community relations worker in New England conceded that "there has grown a deep degree of anti-black feeling among Jews in my area." He did not feel that it was reciprocated, but developments since that time indicate increasing anti-Semitism among blacks. There certainly is a great deal of antiwhite feeling in the Boston area, as witness the tragedy of a young white girl who in the fall of 1973 was forced by a group of young black men to douse herself with gasoline; she was then set on fire and died from third-degree burns. Her attackers said "she didn't belong in our neighborhood," although she had chosen to live in an integrated environment.

A number of our informants suggested that Jewish attitudes toward blacks have become negative largely because of the blacks' acts of violence against Jews, especially attacks of elderly Jewish men and women. Most recent additions have been the clashes between blacks and Hassidic Jews in Crown Heights, a section of Brooklyn, New York. Another source of Jewish-black conflict is in the employment arena: middle-income Jews resent the fact that blacks are promoted ahead of them.

Such rivalry notwithstanding, considerable material aid and some joint action continue. One example, given by a representative of a Jewish communal agency in Cleveland, is illustrative. The Jewish community of Cleveland considers the inner-city requirements a continuing part of its responsibility even though the number of Jews residing in that area has declined steadily. In fact, the city of Cleveland proper is for all practical purposes "without Jews." Jewish businesses in the central city are being liquidated. Despite this development, and even though the Jewish community relations setup is now an integral part of the Cleveland Jewish Community Federation, once concerned exclusively with "Jewish" welfare problems, the Jewish community fosters extensive inner-city programs. This social action certainly cuts across ethnic boundaries and deeply involves the Jewish community—its financial resources, its personnel, and its constituency.

One top community leader (professional, white, and Christian) interpreted the Jewish proclivity for communal service as follows:

My observation about the Jews creating the Community Chest was that they became civic in direct proportion to their own strength of identity. When they knew that they could cope with their own community problems—their social, welfare, and communal needs—they said to themselves: "We'll take this same dynamic idea to the broader community."

This informant did not touch on the motivation for the Jews' sharing of strength, but it is obvious: it derives from the universalist belief that the civic problems in one area are ultimately bound to affect all others. In the case of Cleveland, those living in the more desirable section of the city are responsive to the needs of the depressed portion.

The director of a local Catholic intergroup relations agency concerned with urban affairs observed:

If they [the minority groups] are just a lost kettle of fish and they have no identity, no feeling, then it is more difficult to sell them on the dignity and worth of another minority person or a person who is not a part of their group. The more consciousness of group that people have, the better they are.

"Ethnic competition," he continued, "is good. I think it is great, as opposed to the old kind of thing, which is one ethnic group getting all the attention and another ethnic group winding up with nothing. I think we can see this with the American Indian in the negative." He added that competition strengthens: "I think it is easier to form coalitions of strong groups than it is with weaklings."

A professional executive with wide experience in governmental and private voluntary intergroup relations activities stated that the strength and self-confidence derived from the consciousness of group identity reinforces the capacity to compromise.

Weak people don't compromise; only strong people compromise. I think you have to have a strong base from which to say, "I see the equity of this relationship. I think it's good for me. I'll compromise to get along. If I'm in a weak position with weak identity and no understanding at all that I might have some influence on the circumstance, I am forced to say either—"I'll go along and do so subserviently," or "I hate the———secretly." I think weakness engenders tremendous feelings of hatred and hostility, and I think that strength, if it has any virtue at all, has the capacity to relate effectively to other people.

According to one outstanding professional leader in the intergroup relations field, the concern with group identity in the United States is not confined to blacks. Indeed, this concern is worldwide.

I think you can see it in almost any group where there still exists a strong potential sense of group identity. Partly, I suppose it's a reaction to anxiety, a lost feeling, the feeling of alienation and confusion, resulting from so many of our problems and complexities as the society gets bigger, as our institutions get more complex and harder for the individual to reach. As nothing seems to work anymore, confidence in the big institutions seems to decline. People need something to hold on to, and identity, for the moment anyway, enables people to feel something solid underneath them.

Overemphasis on ethnic and racial identity may lead to a failure to consider that actions taken for certain groups, such as blacks and Puerto Ricans, may affect the thinking and feelings of other groups. One top leader in a national civil rights agency (the then director of the Civil Rights Division of the Justice Department) stressed the importance of fully representative membership on biracial committees on all major decision-making matters. He also felt that effectiveness increases as "official" (governmental) dominance decreases.

Enormous civil rights progress has been made in the last two decades, however unpopular such an interpretation might be. In 1965, there were 20,000 black registered voters in Mississippi; in 1973, there were 307,000, as well as 191 elected black officials. About half the black population in the United States lives in the North. As of April 1975, blacks served as mayors in about 120 communities.[2] Nearly 4,000 blacks currently hold elective offices (out of a total of 500,000 such offices).[3]

Much remains to be done, however. Some believe that while we have made progress, the inequity in our society is the same or worse than ever before. For example, black unemployment in June 1975 stood at 14.2 percent, as compared to 8.5 percent for whites; 41 percent of black teenagers were out of jobs in February 1975.[4] The actual rate of unemployment is much higher than the official figures would indicate since there is also a great deal of underemployment.

One of our black respondents stated that while in recent years the proportion of middle-income black Americans has increased in relation to the total black population, the gap between the median income of black and white middle-Americans is much wider now than before. The improvement on top has no bearing on the condition at the bottom. "It hasn't even begun to trickle down. The situation has worsened down there."

In Kenneth Clark's view in 1970, the Kerner Commission's conclusion that we are becoming two separate societies was wrong: "We are not *tending* toward two societies, side by side but unequal. We were always there. We never had one society. This is what we have been suffering from. This is why we had to do some of the rioting." The prevailing view among the informants, both black and white, however, was that the gulf between blacks and whites is narrowing and that during the past fifteen years America has faced its racial problems more directly and honestly. Gunnar Myrdal's study in 1944, *The American Dilemma*,[5] was the beginning of a catharsis that made the problem of racism part of the public consciousness. Regressive developments have also occurred, such as black separatism and white backlash. On numerous recent occasions, Myrdal has expressed himself affirmatively on the progress blacks have achieved since his 1944 study, particularly in the area of voting rights.

Misunderstandings seem to occur when members of the majority make statements about minority advances. No matter how careful the phrasing, the accusation is often heard that "better" is the equivalent of "all is well." Many whites have been told that "we give the impression that the job is well-nigh done."[6] Discussions in this area often reflect the minority group's great sensitivity, and even paranoia.

Among Jews, the top priorities in local Jewish community relations councils with regard to the group identity factor have been and still are Israel and Soviet Jewry. With respect to Israel, the time is long past when local Jewish community relations councils merely responded to overtly anti-Semitic statements by Arab propagandists. As one respondent said, "Today the Jewish Community Relations Council isn't involved in this ethnic approach from the point of view of self-defense so much, but as an advocate for Jewish interests and Jewish causes." Israel is paramount among these causes; the plight of Soviet Jewry dominates the thoughts of many Jewish youth. As several local Jewish community relations workers revealed, civil rights and civil liberties are no longer their major concerns.

Another fundamental problem facing American Jewry, one intimately related to the question of group identity, is the unsatisfactory state of Jewish education of the young. In spite of the increasing attention given it in recent years, Jewish education in the United States has not been adequate. Many Jewish youngsters, even those who receive both Jewish religious and secular education, grow up with insufficient understanding of the meaning of Jewishness—its traditions, its precepts, its vast storehouse of ethical and moral values. Furthermore, many are confused about their group identity. According to some of our Jewish interviewees, this confusion often leads to feelings of insecurity and alienation from the Jewish community and from its communal, religious, and cultural goals. The Jewish community is giving this problem its concentrated attention.

The then head of the National Conference of Christians and Jews, an intersectarian agency focusing on interreligious group relations, stressed the growing ethnic group consciousness, not just of blacks but also of Puerto Rican, Chicano, and American Indian groups. The deep ethnic group consciousness of Jews, he observed, has become more intense since the Holocaust and the establishment of the state of Israel and considerable public attention has been focused on these matters. He believes (1970) that "over the conflict in Israel has come the only rupture I think we have had in recent years of a serious nature between Christians and Jews." This break has temporarily interfered with the continuing improvement in Christian-Jewish relationships in the United States that began in the mid-1960s when the Vatican Council Declaration on Christian-Jewish relations was issued.

Another group for whom ethnic identity is a critical factor in their adjustment to American life is the Spanish-speaking American. This group includes people of diverse national origins—Mexican-Americans, Puerto Ricans, Cubans, and Latin-Americans, among others. The many-sided historical and cultural differences among them make it difficult, if not impossible, to treat them as a single group. The problems each group faces are quite unlike those of the others. The common denominator among them is that all are subject to the usual varieties of dominant group discrimination and prejudice meted out to other American minority groups.

Although Spanish-Americans were among the earliest settlers of the United States, they have only recently entered the intergroup relations scene in earnest. Only in the past decade or two have they really begun to voice their demands for equal treatment under the law. The surfacing of these demands has undoubtedly been accelerated by their increasing consciousness of their diverse, though related, ethnic identities. It is highly probable, too, that the character of their activities in the intergroup field has been strongly influenced by the fact that the time of their "arrival" as minorities coincided with the emergence of the government as a prime mover against discrimination and the new role of law. This development, as we have noted elsewhere, changed many of the basic rules of the game. Some of the more obnoxious discriminatory practices of the dominant groups in American society have been outlawed. Others are falling into disrepute and disuse. Government agencies now offer help with intergroup problems. Financial and other help with language adjustment, employment, housing, and education have become standard practice, however inadequate they may sometimes appear to be.

On the other hand, on the intergroup scene, Spanish-Americans have also been faced with the necessity of competing with other ethnic groups, especially with urban blacks, for a share in political and economic power.

The then head of the New York City Commission of Human Rights indicated his great desire to build bridges between the various ethnic groups by

attempting to get across "the simple message that pride in oneself, recognition of one's worth, is not inconsistent with the recognition of all people—
all mankind." Within the Puerto Rican community there has been a development similar to that which took place in the early stages of Jewish immigration from Eastern Europe. Jews employed the *Landsmanschaften* (fraternal groups based on geographic origin) as the intermediary between themselves and the outside world. Puerto Ricans coming out of small Puerto Rican
villages entered the mainland and settled in precisely the same kind of large
centers,[7] huddled together for a while until they were strong enough to begin to reach out. This was the observation of one Puerto Rican informant.

One method of dealing more effectively with the human relations problems in the Southwest was developed by the National Conference of Christians and Jews. It set up an institute in collaboration with the University of
the Americas in Mexico. The Human Relations Institute in American Culture was initiated in 1968 and (except for 1975) has continued as an annual
training experience during the weeks of July 28 to August 19. In addition to
lectures and discussion, participants are taken on educational field trips into
Mexico. The ethnic factor was found to be focal in dealing with the group
relations problems of the Chicanos. The institute has helped teachers in the
major schools of southwestern United States obtain first-hand experience
and insight into the culture of Mexico. School people in the Southwest, both
teachers and administrators without a Mexican background, have found the
experience helpful. The question arises whether it might not be useful to
establish a similar facility in Puerto Rico for school people working with
Puerto Ricans in the continental United States.

Spanish-speaking groups, including the Mexican-Americans, the vast majority of whom are Catholics, have placed great pressure for services on the
Catholic church. They believe they have not captured the public imagination as the blacks have been able to do. They are convinced that many of
their problems with racial discrimination in housing, employment, and education, and in the area of social recognition, are as severe as those of the
blacks. To cope with these problems, they want to develop leadership in
their own ranks, and even to create separate institutions if necessary, as an
interim step to full entry into the mainstream of society.

Probably 90 percent of Mexican-Americans reside in the Southwest. Kansas also has a significant Mexican-American population, many of them railroad workers who came from Mexico two or three generations ago. According to a Chicano worker in the Community Relations Service of the
Department of Justice, it would be erroneous to think of all Chicanos as
migrant workers. He thought that Cesar Chavez,[8] who captured the imagination of the Eastern media, was partially responsible for this misconception.
As a result of the publicity given Chavez, a good portion of the American
public has gained the impression that most Mexican-Americans are mi-

grants and that most of the issues affecting Chicanos concern the migrants. The fact is that while most migrants are Mexican-Americans, not all Mexican-Americans are migratory workers; some are professionals and in industry.

According to the same worker, integration is not now a Chicano objective:

> I don't think that that's an issue. I was thinking of assimilation as opposed to integration because integration in the schools at one time was a very hot issue. Integration is an issue in various parts of the Southwest at this time. As an example, the school district in Sonora, Texas, was just recently—through a court order—forced to desegregate their facilities. They had three separate school systems there by custom—one for whites, one for blacks, and one for browns.
>
> Sonora is not the only one.... There are still areas in Texas where Mexican-Americans cannot get a haircut in a white barber shop. They can't eat in certain restaurants. A lot of people in the East find that hard to believe because they generally don't picture Mexican-Americans as suffering the kind of discrimination that blacks have suffered. (1970)

The housing problem has been severe for the Chicano in the Southwest, but it has not been the same as for the black:

> I don't know whether Mexican-Americans have had the same kind of problems in the Midwest, but our problems in housing are not similar to the blacks. By and large Mexican-Americans don't live in tenement houses or row houses. They mostly live on a little plot of land. It may be a shack....
>
> In the cities, if you go into the slum areas of San Antonio, you'll find it may be a shack made out of cardboard, but it is sitting on a plot of land.

In large urban areas, however, Chicanos have the same housing problems as blacks: "But in a place like New York City, they would have to [live in apartment houses]. They would have a problem in New York City" (1970).

The benefits derived from ethnic group identity can be observed in the case of Chinese and Japanese groups. In the early years of migration, the Chinese chose more passive roles of adjustment to their new environment. While the older generations accepted their ghetto existence and minor roles in the economy as imposed upon them by the exclusionary practices of American society, the native-born Chinese-Americans[9] and many of the newly arrived immigrants from Hong Kong and mainland China[10] have begun to break down the walls of the old Chinatowns in San Francisco, New York, and other cities. Increasingly, the Chinese are becoming part of the larger communities surrounding them.

At the same time, the old family associations with their worldwide ties still serve as the principal sources of aid to immigrants and other needy Chinese.[11] They may finance the education of their children, furnish loan capital to start a small business, or obtain a job for a newly arrived immigrant. They may even act as an unofficial extraterritorial "court" for settling disputes among members.

Like the Chinese, the Japanese-Americans led a largely segregated existence[12] until the last decade. They are unique among all minority groups, however, in that during World War II they were labeled enemy aliens and interned in concentration camps. That many believed their internment to be unjustified and largely attributable to the agitation of some bigoted West Coast groups did not make the experience any less onerous or less costly.[13] Despite the bitter experience of evacuation and confinement, the Japanese-Americans, especially the younger Nisei, have made a remarkable recovery since the end of World War II. So complete has this recovery been that Marden and Meyer even question "whether they are still a minority in any other sense than numerical."[14] Their educational achievement is now far ahead of all nonwhite groups and even exceeds that of the white population as a whole.[15] Their income level is among the highest, and their unemployment rate among the lowest, of all minority groups. The acculturation of the new generations, Nisei and Sansei, is proceeding with equal rapidity. It is difficult to assess the role which ethnic group-identity consciousness (as distinct from family loyalties) has played in the "success" stories of the Chinese- and Japanese-American minorities. Certainly the distinctive cultural values of the two groups have had a major part in their developmental histories.

There is some evidence that the younger Chinese- and Japanese-Americans are beginning to make their demands upon the larger society in ethnic terms —the "Chinese share of the pie" so to speak. New community organizations are attracting the young Chinese. Efforts to enlist government aid for community projects are proliferating. Group identity perspectives give them an ethnic pride that contributes to personal security and individual status.

Perhaps the most disadvantaged[16] group in all American society is the American Indian. The median income of the Indians is lower than that of any other disadvantaged groups; their unemployment rate is among the highest. They are only now beginning to gain the attention of the American people and of governmental and private agencies. In large part, this awakening of the public conscience has been the result of a renewed militancy, now expressed in "ethnic" terms, which has succeeded in dramatizing the Indian plight. Among the most dramatic examples of the Indians' use of confrontation in recent years were the occupation of Alcatraz in San Francisco Bay for more than a year and a half, the sit-down in the offices of the Indian Bureau in Washington, which forced the reinstatement of Commissioner L. Bruce, who had been dismissed in 1973 in a personnel shakeup, and the affair at Wounded Knee. A resurgence of long-smoldering ethnic grievances, now expressed within the framework of the new cultural pluralism, has revitalized Indian demands for civic and economic justice.

The interviewees, especially the blacks (and these included those of all political persuasions—extremists, moderates, and middle-of-the-roaders) placed considerable emphasis on intragroup strengthening. Their view was that in the larger society the pressure for required improvements and basic social change must continue, and that within the black community, within the ghetto, there must be persistent emphasis on the development of leadership and on assembling resources to enable the black community itself to recover from the damage inflicted upon it for almost three hundred years. Only in this way could blacks be expected to move more decisively into the mainstream of American society. In order to achieve the peer status needed for this upward mobility, the acquisition of economic and political power was considered essential.

Our interviewee at CORE described his efforts to acquire economic and political group strength on a level with peer groups outside of Harlem. In July 1968, his group had gained sufficient leverage to introduce a Community Self-Determination bill in the ninety-first Congress. The stated purpose of the bill was to

establish a community self-determination program to aid the people of urban and rural communities in securing gainful employment; achieving the ownership and control of the resources of their community; expanding opportunity, stability, and self-determination; and making their maximum contribution to the strength and well-being of the Nation.

The bill also called for "community development banks and other supportive programs."[17]

CORE also supported the view that health services should be controlled by community groups. During the 1969 session of the State Legislature, control of New York City's public health facilities was transferred to the Health and Hospitals Corporation; a rider to this act provided for a Harlem Health Corporation whose stated objectives were to further "define and demonstrate the specific and logical options for community control and participation" and offer "the development of local machinery" more responsive to the interests and needs of the Harlem community.[18] Although the rider exempted the Harlem group from the required two-year waiting period for its formation as a subsidiary corporation under the act, the group was unable to take advantage of the authority mandated to them by the legislature because it lacked adequate facilities.

A community spokesman from the Cleveland area spoke of "a massive movement of blacks into the middle class." In addition, he reported what he considered to be a new phenomenon. Unlike a generation ago, when, according to this informant, blacks who were advancing economically cut their ties with the people they had left behind, many new middle-class blacks did not now turn their backs on the problems of the inner city. Other informants did not seem to feel that the dimensions of the problem were any greater among blacks than among whites who had "made it": some turned their backs on the problems and others did not.

The late Whitney Young stressed the basic right of blacks and other groups to choose whether to live within or outside the ghetto. An important HUD official also expressed this idea of freedom of choice:

Today you find many black middle-class people who feel there is nothing wrong with living in an all-black neighborhood.... There isn't any question in my mind that the bulk of the black people say the main thing we ought to be seeking is the privilege of choice, it's not an "either-or."

A number of our black informants emphasized that the "victims" need to be organized to produce the required social change, for while men of good will, black and white, assert principles, relatively little happens. However, the search for allies was not ruled out, although some felt that there are times when allies tend to "tire out" the demand and to weaken the inner motivating force of the group concerned.

Other pertinent views from black professionals emerged. One informant, the head of a national intergroup relations agency, stated:

I do not see a salt-and-pepper society in which a black man lives next to every white man or a black man lives at every five blocks, or some proportional thing like that. I also do not see an integrated society in which black enclaves are entirely eliminated.

Perhaps the strongest support for black group identity came from the black director of a national community relations service in the public sector:

Just as other ethnic groups have held on to a certain cultural heritage—voluntarily because they want to, without suffering—I think blacks should be able to do that. I feel very, very strongly that for our immediate goal we should put greater emphasis on the development of the black community—black control of schools, of business, even police departments! We should take this route first as a transition.

Similar strivings for inner-group strengthening were evidenced within the Puerto Rican community. Louis Nunez, then the executive director of Aspira, a national educational counseling and leadership development agency devoted to promoting leadership among Puerto Ricans, especially among the youth, spoke of one method employed by his organization. Potential Puerto Rican leaders, generally young people selected from the Aspira clubs, are taken for a two-week visit to Puerto Rico. There they see a Puerto Rican government, a Puerto Rican legislature, a Puerto Rican police force, Puerto Rican business people—in short, a progressive society run by Puerto Ricans. They see an entire range of class structures, not just the bottom one. According to Nunez, this experience gives them a new perspective, heightening their sense of identity and enhancing their pride in their heritage. Nunez stated: "What is unique about the [Aspira] program is the kind of leadership-training process we employ and the fact that it is a Puerto Rican agency established for the benefit of Puerto Ricans by Puerto Ricans."

Nunez also emphasized the importance of stimulating creative self-help by placing the responsibility for such support on the membership groups themselves; by encouraging the group itself to determine its goals and strategies; and by expecting members to go out to get the needed funds— from the city, federal government, foundations, corporations, and individuals. However, he added emphatically, "We don't believe that any group can depend completely on the government."

Aspira was born out of the desire of the Puerto Rican people to develop an organization that would service their unique needs. It was not imposed from the top; it was not the product of the sentiment usually expressed as "Well, we have to do something for these poor, misbegotten. . . ." The statement which sums up Nunez's basic philosophy on community organization among the Puerto Rican people is: "Ours is a program to integrate into the community from a position of strength at the same time retaining our individual identity."

A quite different organization of the Puerto Rican community was the Young Lords (which has faded from the local scene since the time of our interviews). Luis Alvarez, national director of Aspira since 1972, characterized their tactics as comparable to those employed by the Black Panthers and the Jewish Defense League, their reactionary counterparts in the black and Jewish communities. Alvarez indicated that, although the issues which prompted the growth of the Young Lords are still viable, the group disappeared because the Puerto Rican community rejected their tactics.

It is of some interest to note the views of Kenneth Clark on the rhetoric associated with the concept of black power. According to Clark, the rhetoric of black power as distinct from its real essence is not a symptom of inner strength. Rather, failing to achieve social change, its adherents escape into verbalism. "The frustrations are great." Of these frustrations, one prominent housing specialist we interviewed stated: (1970) "There is a greater depression in the impacted racial ghettos than we encountered in the Great Depression of the Thirties."

An emphatic statement on the necessity of inner-group strengthening came from A. Philip Randolph: "Negroes like other groups should develop inner-group business establishments and they should prepare themselves by developing the educational qualifications successfully to compete in all areas of American life. They must master the various areas, and that can be done."

Despite the emphasis on group identity, several black informants expressed a coolness toward "black studies." They believed that rather than treat black history and culture as a separate entity, it should be integrated into the larger history of America. At the time of our interviews, the mass media's misrepresentation and underrepresentation of minority groups was still of concern to our informants. They suggested that minority groups be taught the skills required for working effectively with the communications media. These increased skills, they thought, will eventually result in the media's allotment of more "available" time to meet group needs constructively.

As we note elsewhere, in the past much of the news reports pertaining to minority groups consisted of disasters, criminal activity, and sensational items. Few reports dealt with their normal lives and activities; hence, the public was given a distorted image. Fortunately, this situation has been rectified somewhat in recent years. The media, television in particular, have made a conscious attempt to portray the real life and experience of minority groups, especially the blacks and Spanish-Americans. But much remains to be done.

Notes

1. John Higham, *Strangers in the Land* (New York: Atheneum, 1963).
2. *U.S. News & World Report* (April 7, 1975): 34.
3. *Statistical Abstract of the United States*, 1976, p. 466.
4. The National Urban League, in "The State of Black America: 1977," reports that while the number of black unemployed has remained constant at 1.5 million, the *rate* of unemployment has declined somewhat, from 14 to 13 percent. However, no such improvement was recorded among black teenagers.
5. Gunnar Myrdal, *The American Dilemma* (New York: Harper, 1944).
6. Ben J. Wattenberg and Richard M. Scammon, "Black Progress and Liberal Rhetoric," *Commentary* (April 1973), p. 35. See also the tilt between Philip Perlmutter and Gregory D. Squires in *Journal of Intergroup Relations* (Summer 1973, p. 21, and Summer 1974, p. 45).
7. Karl Wagenheim and Olga Jiminez de Wagenheim, eds., *The Puerto Ricans—A Documentary History* (New York: Praeger, 1973), pp. 246-47.
8. In 1965, Cesar Chavez, organizer of the National Farm Workers Association, led the Delano Grape Strike (San Joaquin Valley of California) and maintained a lengthy fast to keep the strikers from violence. In addition, Chavez obtained AFL-CIO support in organizing farm labor (Leo Grebler, Joan W. Moore, and Ralph C. Guzin, *The Mexican-American People: The Nation's Second Largest Minority* [New York: The Free Press, 1970], pp. 464, 532, 548, 549).
9. By 1970, there were almost as many native as foreign-born Chinese in the United States: 167,000 as compared with 172,000, or a total of 339,000 (*Statistical Abstract of the United States*, 1973, p. 35).
10. 109,771 in the decade 1961-1970 (*Statistical Abstract of the United States*, 1973, p. 95).
11. H. Brett Melendy, *Oriental Americans* (New York: Hippocrene Books, 1972), pp. 74-77.

12. By 1970, there were 274,000 native-born Japanese in the United States and 120,000 foreign-born, or a total of 394,000 (*Statistical Abstract of the United States,* 1973, p. 35).

13. Charles F. Marden and Gladys Meyer, *Minorities in American Society,* 4th ed. (New York: Van Nostrand, 1973). (Marden and Meyer estimate the net losses to the Japanese at $367 million.)

14. Ibid., p. 401.

15. Ibid.

16. Grebler, Moore, and Guzin, *The Mexican-American People,* p. 24, describe the "disadvantaged group" as follows: "A category of people, then, can be defined as disadvantaged, if society at large has acted by omission or commission to hinder a disproportionate number of its members in the development of their individual abilities." (Or, we might add, hindered them in the exercise and enjoyment of the normal rights, privileges, and benefits of citizenship in the society at large.)

17. "Community Self-Determination Bill," CORE, p. 2. (An inquiry in 1976 indicated that the bill never got off the ground.)

18. Harlem Health System Organizing Committee, "Planning for a Harlem Health Corporation," New York, 1969.

5

Faith and Prejudice:
Interreligious Relationships

Of the three major forms of group prejudice in America, racial, ethnic, and religious, at the time of our interviews, religious prejudice seemed to be most responsive to the strategies and techniques employed by intergroup relations agencies. Anti-Semitism had retreated into the background of concern, while racial and, to some extent, ethnic problems, occupied center stage. Nonetheless, relations between Christians of all denominations with each other and with Jews continued to claim a large share of intergroup agency attention. While Jewish-Christian relations had always been at the center of Jewish agency activity, they were now (with the Holocaust experience still fresh in all minds) becoming of increasing concern to Protestant and Catholic religious groups all over the country. Shortly after the Ecumenical Council, the National Conference of Catholic Bishops established a permanent Secretariat for Catholic-Jewish Relations, and in 1974, the National Council of Churches (a group of thirty-one Protestant and Eastern Orthodox churches) set up its Office on Christian-Jewish Relations. Both have full-time directors. In addition, an increasing number of Christian conferences on the Holocaust have been held, some of them on college campuses.

Following the historic statement on the Jews by Vatican Council II (1965) and the statement on anti-Semitism (1961) by the World Council of Churches (Third Assembly), forceful declarations against anti-Semitism have been made. Thereafter, many Protestant, Evangelical, Roman Catholic, and Greek Orthodox groups issued condemnations of anti-Semitism. For example, the Southern Baptist Convention of 1972, attended by more than 13 million members, unanimously passed a resolution condemning anti-Semitism. It said in part: "The Convention goes on record as opposed to any and all forms of anti-Semitism; that it declares anti-Semitism unchristian...we pledge ourselves to combat anti-Semitism in every honorable, Christian way....Jews, along with all other men, are equally beloved by God."

These declarations no doubt led many Christian bodies to respond to the plight of Soviet Jews and to announce more balanced positions on the legitimacy and security requirements of the state of Israel. In addition, they have made clear to their members that the use of Biblical or theological teachings as a basis for prejudice against or hatred of Jews is without justification and is to be condemned. Lutheran, Episcopalian, Methodist, Catholic, and Southern Baptist church councils have openly repudiated the deicide charge which has plagued Jews for almost two thousand years. Concomitantly, the councils have called for improved relations between Christians and Jews on community levels, for active interfaith meetings, and for cooperation in resolving social problems. Unfortunately, these strong positions have not always had their intended effects. Much Christian religious teaching material continues to present Jews and Judaism in ways likely to "foster hostility against Jews, their religion and experience."[1] Nevertheless, substantial progress in Christian-Jewish understanding has taken place in the past two decades. One factor which helped pave the way for this understanding was the experience of World War II. After the war, Christianity, hitherto regarded as the predominant world religion, was recognized as primarily the religion of the Western world, which comprised only one-third of the world population. This recognition led to a more realistic view of the role of Christianity, as well as the position of the Judeo-Christian tradition among the religious traditions of the world.

In the 1970s, the Roman Catholic church, for one, no longer exercised as great a central control as formerly. As a result, local collaboration with other religious groups and communal organizations on behalf of social justice, human betterment, and mutual understanding became more feasible. Such cooperation has improved greatly since the pronouncements of the Ecumenical Council in Rome in the mid-1960s and the 1961 New Delhi meeting of the Protestants (World Council of Churches).

The Ecumenical Council also helped clarify the relationship of Catholicism to other Christian religions as well as to Judaism. The Council's pronouncements gave birth to a Joint Commission of Catholic and Jewish representatives whose objective was to facilitate mutual understanding and regard between Catholics and Jews.

In our interviews, in the interreligious field, a multilevel approach to effect constructive change in intergroup relations was generally found to be effective—the theologian and academician as sources of altered basic views and ideas; the religious educator for the transmission of these views; and the clergy to communicate the altered thinking of their parishioners. We must keep in mind, however, that the power of religious leaders over their congregants, while significant, is limited. Getting the desired points of view across to the people also requires work with labor, industry, business, education, and other groups.

In Protestant denominations as well as the Catholic church, collegiality has been replacing the former authoritarian structure. Since the central religious body no longer exercises the power it once did, movement of the religious institutions into the community arena has been accelerated. The trend toward closer cooperation between the local community services and religious institutions has spread to Jewish groups as well. The church's own resources are increasingly being channeled to the local level; as a result, an ambivalence toward national bodies, often bordering on suspicion, has become evident.

Clear evidence of the trend toward decentralization emerged in late 1975 in response to the anti-Zionism vote of the United Nations General Assembly. The strongest Christian condemnation of the U.N. action came from local and regional church councils and associations; the reactions from national and international Christian bodies were more muted. Clearly, the daily contact between Christians and Jews on a community basis helped build a deep sense of trust and respect.

At the time of our interviews, it was predicted that Israel would soon be the dominant concern in Christian-Jewish relationships. That has happened. It is interesting to note, too, that Christian scholarship is becoming increasingly more Biblical (Old Testament) and, hence, more Jewish-oriented. At the same time, the political influence of the Third World on Christian groups continues to grow. The World Council of Churches (the Protestant and Eastern Orthodox groups) can no longer be considered primarily a Western Christian body.

One important outcome of the Vatican II was its concession of the "right to error," as suggested in the Council's enunciation of the concept that underlying the various faith-inspired differences is a common humanity. This and similarly broad views led to the convening of the Council by Pope John XXIII.[2] Another early sign of ecumenism was seen in 1961 at the Third Assembly Convocation of the World Council of Churches when all forms of bigotry, particularly anti-Semitism, were condemned.[3]

Although differences on specific issues (e.g., abortion, church-state relationships, aid to parochial schools, or the Middle East situation) remain, intergroup activities, whether under secular or religious auspices, are much the same in goals, substance, and form. However, there is a difference in motivation (as between spiritual and social bases for the actions taken). The task of the worker in the interreligious area is to help channel religious impulses into minority and intergroup relations problems, including poverty and world hunger.

In general, Jewish-Christian relations improve when the broad common values of Judeo-Christian tradition are taken as the basis for collaboration; Jewish as well as Christian concerns can then be dealt with individually within that context. The dialogue is an important means of achieving collaboration between different religious groups. An interesting illustration is the "Christian-Jewish Consultation" held in New York City beginning in 1964. It originally included approximately ten representatives from the National Council of Churches and an equal number from Jewish organizations, among them synagogue and rabbinic groups. The Jewish group was brought together by the then program coordinator of the National Jewish Community Relations Advisory Council (NJCRAC). The total membership of the consultation was thirty-five, but attendance averaged twenty for both groups. The consultation lasted seven or eight years, and during this period the group met about once a month except during the summer. The meetings were unstructured and generally lasted the entire morning. Social issues of common concern such as poverty, the Middle East, and civil rights comprised the agenda.

In April 1975, the former program coordinator of the NJCRAC interviewed two leaders of these religious groups in order to obtain their reaction to these consultations. One of the leaders was a former top official of the National Council of Churches and the other an Orthodox rabbi and executive vice-president of the Rabbinical Council of America. Both men thought these meetings were beneficial. Both noted that the consultations had widened the social views of the participants and that they themselves had gained greater understanding of their "difference," which did much to help dissipate their mutual prejudices. Substantive theological matters were not discussed during the meetings, but attitudes on social issues were debated with great candor; while an awareness of the different theologies was present, the essentials of theological commitment were not debated. The Protestant representative had hoped that the consultations would produce an "evaluation of bases of agreement on concerns with the social fabric of our life which demand action by our citizens." He stated that this anticipation had been met; in addition, he acknowledged that his own prejudices against both Jews and Catholics had been shattered.

In contrast, the Jewish participant had at first doubted that the dialogue would reduce intergroup suspicion and hostility: "Well, let's put it to you this way. Psychologically most of us . . . have in our genes a suspicion and a fear of Christians and Christian theology." After the consultations, however, he observed that the dialogue experience had created a genuine understanding of Christian thinking and Christian attitudes on issues of vital concern to Jews. He also indicated that a useful relationship had been set up between the members of the two religious affiliations. Furthermore, he felt that he had convinced several Christians in the group that "orthodox Jews don't wear horns under their yarmulkas." As for his own attitudes: "I was convinced that most of the people in this discussion group whom we met were decent human beings who wanted to do the right thing." For him, this group dialogue, by forcing him to defend his views, helped crystallize his own thinking. During the meetings, the impact of the Third World on Christian leadership became clearer to him and his colleagues. His one great caution was that to achieve success in interreligious dialogue, "a peer-to-peer basis" is necessary with respect to substantive knowledge of one's religious doctrine and one's religio-ethnic affiliation. He summed up his reaction to the consultations in these words: "I would say that definitely, at least these dialogues were worthwhile."

Both respondents felt that continuity was just as important as content. The dialogue made no attempt at exhaustive treatment of the subjects considered. Christians and Jews communicated on issues that mattered very much to them and on a fairly regular basis; according to these interviewees, sensitization to each other's problems was achieved.[4]

Christian groups, both Protestant and Catholic, must of course deal with relationships among their various denominations, as must the Jewish groups with relationships among their Orthodox, Conservative, and Reform bodies. With the current emphasis on ethnicity, the ethnic entities within the religious groups have also become an important concern. Ethnicity is especially relevant among Catholics, whose constituent groups include Poles, Italians, Puerto Ricans, and Irish. Other areas of mutual concern to Christians and Jews are issues such as abortion and church-state relationships; they require great patience, cautious handling, and skill in negotiation.

The church-state relationship has historically been a source of disagreement between religious groups in America. The disagreement for the most part has been between Catholic and Jewish groups, but in recent years many Orthodox Jewish groups have tended to side with the Catholic position, as have some Evangelical church groups. This disagreement generally takes on a sociopolitical aspect, and it is often played out in divisive terms on a community level. It stems from different views on the interpretation of the "establishment clause" of the First Amendment of the Constitution, especially in the area of public support (tax funds) for religious (parochial) education. It is argued that a "wall of separation" must be maintained between church and state in order to preserve complete freedom of religious expression, freedom of conscience, and the principle of pluralism. Jews who hold this position have often been supported by Southern Baptists and mainline Protestant groups. The issue has been joined in court on a variety of specific cases, including religious services and Bible reading in public schools, financial aid to parochial schools, and religious symbols erected on public property. The heart of the issue, however, remains the use of public funds for private and/or religion-sponsored schools.

The prohibition of public support for such schools is producing great financial hardships for parents, mostly Catholic and orthodox Jews. However, direct aids to the child, such as lunches and medical and dental services, are now legal. The law also allows textbook loans and support of remedial educational services (therapeutic and welfare) on parochial school premises. Experiments in dual enrollment (shared time), when strictly interpreted with respect to exclusive jurisdiction of the public school on public property, are also permitted, as are release-time programs for religious education conducted off public school premises.

The church-state issue will likely continue to exacerbate intergroup relations in the forseeable future. Hence, the best minds and talents must be employed to solve this problem creatively. It is hoped that a legal solution within the framework of the Constitution will result in quality education for all students and a minimum of intergroup discord.

When such issues arise, they can be dealt with more objectively if, preceding such consideration, consultations on less highly charged social issues have already been held. This approach tends to reduce the suspicion and fear which often accompanies a first meeting or one held on a crisis basis.

An established periodic consultation, such as the Jewish-Christian consultation of 1964 described above, requires meeting certain conditions for successful outcome and durability. Protestant and Jewish representatives at this particular consultation agreed on some of these conditions:

(1) Each religious group should possess sophistication and have knowledge of its own tenets, practices, and value commitments. This is especially true for the representatives of the minority group.

(2) The representatives of the different religious groups should, as far as possible, be of similar cultural status.

(3) No one group should predominate either in numbers or in amount of input at the meetings.

(4) The representatives of the religious groups should avoid debates on matters of belief or theology.

Some, specific problems that have to do with issues affecting both Jews and Christians, however, cannot be avoided. These problems often involve dealing with the Christian roots of anti-Semitism.[5] When these issues arise, the Jewish community enters into dialogue with the Catholic and Protestant communities primarily, but the Eastern Orthodox group and, increasingly, the black churches are also brought in.

The deicide charge, for example, has caused much Christian hostility toward Jews for almost two thousand years. In the United States, Christian groups are increasingly probing theological attitudes toward the permanent value of Judaism as a faith. Included in these fundamental considerations are such specific factors as conversion and proselytizing, as well as general matters pertaining to the theory of religious and cultural pluralism.

Another important area of interreligious concern has been the treatment of each other's religion in textbooks and lesson materials. By analyzing this treatment, Christian religious leaders have gained insights into how such texts influence attitudes toward other religions. This material has for the most part been analyzed by Christian scholars. Their studies have uncovered frequent misrepresentation of Jews and unfavorable portrayals of

Judaism and have resulted in extensive textbook revisions and the removal of some objectionable passages. Stimulated by these studies, some Christian educators have pursued the training and sensitizing of religious teachers to the intergroup relations factor.

Conflicts between Christians and Jews have at times assumed catastrophic magnitude. The Holocaust—the extermination of six million Jews under Hitler—is probably the cruelest episode in all of human history. This barbarism was, of course, anti-Christian; yet, several of our informants reminded us that "the Nazis' anti-Jewish legislation found many of its precedents in canon law."[6] The idea that the centuries-long denigration of the Jew in Christian thought and teaching culminated in the Holocaust is well summed up by the Jewish theologian Emil Fackenheim:

While Nazi anti-Semitism is, of course, anti-Christian in essence, both this anti-Semitism and the attempted genocide in which it culminated would have been impossible except for centuries of Christian anti-Semitism; indeed without considerable cooperation of Christians not all of whom were nominal. I trust that I am not uttering a Jewish view only when I assert that the confrontation of this grim truth, begun in some Christian quarters, is one of the major tasks of Christian thought in this generation.[7]

Only in recent years, however, have Christians confronted the probable connection between the denigration of the Jews in Christian texts and elsewhere and the cruel and inhuman acts perpetrated against them by the Nazis. Hence, the study of the treatment of Jews in Christian texts assumes enormous importance. Some progress has been made by certain denominations—largely in the "mainstream" Protestant (in contrast to the "conservative") group and in a number of Catholic dioceses, but "there is no evidence so far that these painful yet essential issues are being adequately dealt with in Christian teaching."[8]

Some Christian groups such as the Lutheran Church-Missouri Synod have set high standards for the improvement of their religious teaching content. Nonetheless, "the Yale Study has not had the long-term effect which the initial reception seemed to promise."[9] With respect to these teaching materials, there appears to be a vast gap between declarations of intentions to modify the content of religious texts and actual implementation. One important outcome attributed to the Yale Study,[10] is that prejudice is dealt with in lesson materials not morally, but also cognitively.

This is not to say that there are no encouraging developments. One of the more significant changes is that the Crucifixion story, which has generally been dealt with in a manner prejudicial to Jews, is now treated with much greater objectivity. On the negative side, the informants reported that the Holocaust is still inadequately treated. A general problem with regard to interreligious relations is that religious teachings do not present a full picture of the multireligious and multiracial nature of American society, even though racial and ethnic hostility as such is condemned.

Our informants stated that mainstream churches tend to deal with prejudice in psychological terms and as a social phenomenon. The conservative churches, however, still treat prejudice as a theological concept, rejecting the scientific explanation.[11] The rationale of religious differences is inadequately treated.

The head of the interreligious department of a national Jewish intergroup relations agency has stated that certain missionary approaches "are frequently based on a stereotyped and caricatured depiction of Judaism as a dessicated fossil which has been replaced by the 'new Israel' of Christianity."[12] Furthermore, we were informed that only a small number of teaching texts "acknowledge that Judaism still exists as a living meaningful religion in the modern world." The existence of the modern state of Israel is almost completely neglected.

What Jewish attitudes toward the majority (Christians) are conveyed by Jewish educational texts in Jewish schools? As part of the religious textbook project, a study of Jewish religious texts was undertaken under the auspices of Dropsie College in 1965 in order to determine "how Jewish textbooks visualize the Jewish community in its relations with non-Jewish groups."[13] This study showed that the Jewish schools generally emphasize the transmittal of Jewish heritage. Approximately 60 to 80 percent of the time is spent on subjects not ordinarily involving intergroup relations matters, such as language (Hebrew and Yiddish), customs, history, Bible, Hebrew classics and literature, and ceremonies.

One important difference between the bases underlying Christian and Jewish education should be noted. Since Christianity stems from Judaism, "it is impossible to expound Christianity without reference to and comparison with Judaism."[14] Hence, Christian education is obliged to enter into theological desiderata of a clarifying nature as to origin and to make comparisons and to engage in polemics, with the likelihood of conscious or unconscious derogatory characterizations of the religious source from which Christianity grew and developed. Judaism, on the other hand, has no need to make theological comparisons and thus is less likely to be derogatory. It is concerned largely with historical and sociological phenomena. However, the age-long persecution to which Jews have been subjected may engender an unbalanced view of the oppressor in the victim's eyes. Therefore, Jewish educators and Jewish texts need to guard against sweeping generalizations.

As much as possible, the negative should be balanced by the positive without sweeping the negative under the rug. The history of suffering and the countervailing factors of achievement and contributions to society have perhaps been overplayed in Jewish texts. They should be balanced by citing instances of social justice and helpful behavior of majority groups, such as Danish help to Jews during the Hitler era. The "difference" between Christians and Jews should be presented as a valid difference, and every attempt should be made to inculcate a "respect for difference." This advice, of course, applies to Christian education as well.

The researchers at Dropsie point out the strong possibility of reducing the small number of prejudiced references to non-Jews, since many of these appear to be "the result of careless editing or thoughtless selection rather than ingrained or persistent negative attitude."[15]

Thus, social science has been instrumental in creating special educational (insight-producing) programs to enrich Christian and Jewish religious teaching methods. The use of social science as a tool in analyzing subject matter pertaining to Jews in both Catholic and Protestant religious texts has made an important contribution to the improvement of religious educational programs.

The aim of Jewish and Christian interfaith workers has been twofold: to make all religious groups aware of the general human relations problems facing society, and to remove any content from religious teaching materials that produces group hostility. Frequent contact with members of religious persuasions other than one's own was generally found to be an effective approach in positive attitude modification in the interreligious sphere.

Mutual understanding is also brought about by the communications media such as the *Religious News Service*, published by the National Conference of Christians and Jews (NCCJ). In addition to reading about themselves, each group learns about occurrences, problems, and approaches among other religions.[16]

Ideally, the church group with the means of effecting change should itself take the necessary steps to produce this change, whether it be on the level of an ecumenical council for policy change or promotion of an educational program for implementation of such policy. It has been frequently necessary to cut across denominational lines to effect social change.

Perhaps one of the greatest developments in intergroup relations during the past twenty years has been the increase in interreligious understanding and cooperation. In the Catholic-Jewish segment, for example, especially with respect to the matter of Israel, there has been much progress. Of the effectiveness of interreligious group cooperation, Senator Hubert Humphrey asserted that "if it had not been for the fact that the three groups—the synagogue, the Catholic and Protestant Churches—worked together and made this a moral appeal, the chances of the 1964 civil rights legislation going through might have been placed in considerable jeopardy."

Notes

1. Gerald S. Strober, "Portrait of the Elder Brother," American Jewish Committee and National Conference of Christians and Jews, 1972, p. 12.

2. See Appendix A for Statement on the Jews by Vatican Council II, 1965.

3. See Appendix A for Statement on Anti-Semitism by the World Council of Churches, 1961.

4. Warm thanks are due to Philip Jacobson, former program director of the National Jewish Community Relations Advisory Council for suggesting this approach of interviewing the two representatives of the two faiths and for volunteering to conduct these two interviews; and to Reverend David H. Hunter, former deputy general secretary, National Council of Churches, and to Rabbi Israel Klaven, executive vice-president, Rabbinical Council of America, for agreeing to serve as the two interviewees.

5. One of the Jewish community relations executives viewed the roots of Christian (orthodox) anti-Semitism in the following manner:

"An ingrained ingredient in Christianity which hasn't been overcome yet is one which makes the rebirth of Israel somehow a strange phenomenon within the framework of Christian theology and the Christian perception of the Divine Drama of Salvation. According to that part of Christian theology, a Jewish people should have stopped being in existence a long time ago and Israel should never have been reborn. This is built in; this is present in the Christian doctrine of Christianity being the "New Israel."

In addition, he indicated that pro-Arab bias and Christian compassion for the underdog also play a role.

6. Raul Hilberg, "The Destruction of the European Jews," quoted in Strober, "Portrait," p. 39.

7. Emil Fackenheim, "On the Self-Exposure of Faith to the Modern Secular World: Philosophical Reflections in the Light of Jewish Experience," *Daedalus* (Winter 1967): 216n.

8. Strober, "Portrait," p. 39.

9. Ibid, pg. 12. The Yale study was a Protestant self-study of church school teachings in the area of intergroup relations. It was conducted by Bernhard E. Olson in 1958-1959 and sponsored by the American Jewish Committee. It resulted in the publication of a book by Dr. Olson, *Faith and Prejudice*, published in 1963 by the Yale University Press.

10. Ibid, pg. 49. See note 8.

11. Ibid.

12. Rabbi Marc H. Tanenbaum, "Christian Statements and Documents Bearing on Christian-Jewish Relations," Judith Banki, ed., American Jewish Committee, June 1972, pg. 3.

13. Bernard D. Weinryb and Daniel Garnick, "Jewish School Textbooks and Intergroup Relations," American Jewish Committee, November 1965.

14. Ibid., pp. 12–14.

15. Ibid., pg. 56.

16. The *Religious News Service* was initiated by the National Conference of Christians and Jews in 1933 for the purpose of distributing news items pertaining to all religions, on a daily basis, both domestically and abroad, to both secular and religious magazines, newspapers, periodicals, and the like. Daily circulation of the *Religious News Service* runs into the hundreds.

6

In the Community

At the time of our interviews, nearly all informants favored community control of both operation and decision-making where problems affecting the community were concerned. This was true of such organizations as the Urban League in the private sector and HUD in the public sector.

The late Whitney M. Young, Jr., then executive director of the Urban League, was especially sensitive to the idea that the minority community should select its own spokesmen and identify its own priorities. The Urban League did make available to the local community research and know-how bearing on confrontation procedures in particular situations. Young keenly felt that the Urban League had an obligation to help the disadvantaged and to avoid the view that conflict, even constructive conflict, was to be shunned.

In former years, as Young stressed, the Urban League had acted as the representative of the black community because the "big shots" would not talk to angry blacks. Now that blacks and whites were willing to talk to each other, this approach was less necessary than formerly. Care must nevertheless be taken that the discussions be constructive and creative. He also pointed out that negotiation would not be realistic unless "you set some short-range achievable goals; if you get a measure of success with these and win some victories then you can move on to the next level which may be more difficult." Outside force alone, however, will not produce results; victories have to come from within, "and you can't ask people to be responsible unless you give them responsibility."

Another executive of a black national group relations agency proposed that the local groups themselves, with some guidance from a central source, should make surveys of situations requiring attention—e.g., drop-out rates, reading levels, and grade levels in the education area. Black representation on the school board is imperative, she felt, even though the struggle for such representation may result in a political conflict which will temporarily deflect attention from the actual educational problem.

Nearly all black professionals interviewed considered it essential to develop expertise among potential lay black leaders to enable them to sit on planning boards. This point was made especially in relation to health planning services and community involvement in training programs dealing specifically with the health system.

While constructive change in the intergroup situation would be achieved largely through community organization processes—grass roots operations, local-level initiatives to bring together all the principal social forces in the community—it was observed that the white backlash incident to riots and other disturbances greatly interfered with the attainment of this objective. As an instance of "backlash thinking," an executive of one Jewish community relations agency observed that periodically the Anglo-Jewish newspapers received letters suggesting that his organization change its name to "Black-Jewish Community Relations Council."

In both the private and public sectors, local as well as national informants repeatedly indicated that the community agency representative "should not assume an active or personal leadership role" in the community organization process. He should be a stimulator, a catalytic agent who preferably works behind the scenes, as advocate, teacher, interpreter of facts and trends.

Working along these lines, an executive of a national nonsectarian private agency explained one interesting outcome:

The method was to bring together the diverse groups of the community around a common vital concern. There was an excellent representation, about 300 delegates. And a number of people in the community are of the belief that this experience may have contributed to the unusual outcome that we now have, a Jewish mayor and a black vice-mayor.

Perhaps the most ambitious attempt to achieve citizen involvement and participation in community program activities has been the Model Cities Program[1] sponsored by the federal government through HUD. Although the program was curtailed by the federal housing moratorium of 1973-1974, its objectives were retained in the Housing and Community Development Act of 1974.

In the original Model Cities Act, a "model neighborhood" was usually a section containing not more than 10 percent of the city population, the preferred size being approximately twenty thousand to twenty-five thousand residents. The federal statute required that the area selected be largely a blighted and deteriorated one containing an appreciable proportion of impoverished people. This provision has nearly always resulted in the selection of neighborhoods populated mainly by minorities. The project in the selected city began with the Model Cities planning process which called for the greatest possible citizen involvement.

Basic to this process is the theory that if all resources are concentrated in one residential area, a substantial impact can be made on many of its problems. First, the city authorities working together with its citizens identify the housing, education, and employment as well as health and welfare services needs. Then an inventory of all available resources is made, and the methods of coordinating these resources in all federal, state, and local agencies, public and private, are mapped out. All of these tasks are performed by the community officials in collaboration with the residents of the selected blighted area, including, of course, the poor and minority peoples.

Usually the realty and insurance boards are brought in at an early stage; these in turn recruit individuals from the area, predominantly members of minority groups, for training in real estate and insurance. Then, the construction unions and contractors are brought in; they collaborate on a training program for construction workers recruited from the model city neighborhood, mostly minority group members. In addition, the contractors' associations train individuals from the minority group to become contractors themselves. In one community, one informant said, a minority contractor (for the first time in that city's history) was brought in to build the initial housing units in the selected area.

The director of Assisted Programs at HUD made the following statement:

We believe we have an obligation under Title VI (of the Civil Rights Act of 1964) affirmatively to encourage participation on the part of the residents of the selected area because Title VI states that minority group residents "shall not be excluded from participation or denied the benefits of our program." One of the most effective ways we know that can assure that minorities are not excluded and denied the benefits of HUD programs is to encourage *citizen participation* to create a structure which would exist for the essential purpose of meaningfully involving minorities in our activities at the local level.

When the Model Cities Program was first organized, a citizen participation advisor was among the specialists placed in each regional office. His function was to give guidance and technical assistance to the "lead men" of the community in the development of the program.

From the very inception of ideas, the HUD programs in the Model Cities unit as well as the unit known as Assisted Programs aimed to involve citizens in planning and implementing local projects. Throughout, they were to participate in the entire decision-making process so that they could deliver their input while options were still open. They were also to evaluate project plans to determine whether the plans would in fact achieve the anticipated goals. If the plans did not measure up, citizens' groups were to be consulted in their reformulation and the readjustment of priorities. "If the project was to provide housing, local citizens including minorities and others, should play a role in determing what kind of housing it will be and deciding whether the housing selection would really meet local needs."

With respect to the kind of citizen participation envisaged, a HUD executive concerned with these Assisted Programs made a number of significant observations. As a demonstration, he cited the Baltimore project (1967-1968) known as the Model Urban Neighborhood Demonstration Program

(MUND),[2] where the black power thrust was quite evident. He indicated that the project evidenced more than just black pride; *Black Power* was manifested—i.e., black people were working to gain control of their lives and local institutions. In the beginning, many supported the exclusion of whites and giving up the notion of integration. Ultimately, a cross-section of all civic and civil rights organizations, including extremist groups, was represented. Community control was not interpreted in its limited sense of confining the project to those resources and solutions which existed solely within the local community. Advantage was taken of the expertise and technological skills available within private industry and elsewhere. For instance, Westinghouse was brought in because of its work in the aerospace field and its application of systems-analysis methods and techniques.

Since MUND was created as a program that would be controlled by the neighborhood, a neighborhood development corporation was formed. The corporation had a twenty-member board of directors who were to be elected each year from the community at large. The elective process gave all interested groups and individuals an opportunity to sell their ideas and plans to the public. In the election of officers in the neighborhood corporation, few of the more extreme segments of the community were elected.

In one review of the situation, our informant, who had been the project's manager from 1968 to 1970, found that the program involved both black and white residents and that it was being carried out by both groups working together. He was very happy to see the MUND system still working despite the heated rhetoric and polarization that, at the time of these interviews, had become so strong a force in American life.

According to the informant, the experience clearly proved that social, economic, and racial divisiveness is not inevitable. It also demonstrated that a neighborhood *can* seek outside technical assistance and expertise without losing its integrity and control of its own affairs. The basic honesty of the approach and the modesty of its expectations (the usual high-flown rhetoric was notably absent) helped to achieve success. Low-income persons were distrustful of programs that promised too much. He concluded his observations with: "Simply awakening the poor to their own potential isn't going to save our cities all by itself, but it is clearly a good and necessary beginning to that gigantic objective."

The Model Cities projects indicate that the other inhabitants of the city from which the particular area is selected must be taken into consideration. Even though there is concentration on the Model City area, the delicate balance between the attention being given a specific area and the rest of the city must be maintained. An interesting byproduct of the experiment was:

that while the attention was concentrated on this specific Model City project area and while the Model City project workers had only a small amount of experience with the execution aspects of the program, it can be confidently asserted that because these projects have been led through a very careful planning process [identification of the problems, development of goals and strategies for reaching those goals, etc.], these workers have been led to look at the whole question of community management and coordination in a manner that could develop into a sort of local management capability that did not previously exist.

Basic to Model Cities development is the need for urban renewal, which has met with considerable resistance largely because adequate relocation facilities are not always provided for the displaced, despite the law's stipulation that Model Cities must make housing available for those being displaced. In fact, HUD regulations prohibit cities from participating in this program until they have submitted a relocation plan to HUD for review and approval (1970).

The ultimate aim of the effort, as broadly stated by the executive of the Model Cities Program, is "to improve the quality of urban life." But, he continued, "The aim and goals in between are really tough ones. How do you get from here to there to improve the quality of life?"

The fact that the Model Cities concept survived termination by the federal housing moratorium of 1973-1974 is significant. Instead of being eliminated entirely, Title I of the Housing and Community Development Act of 1974 (HCDA) consolidated a number of programs, including Model Cities, into one "community development block grant" and set new application requirements and spending guidelines for these funds. In the tradition of federal housing acts since 1949, the HCDA was adopted to provide "decent housing and suitable living environment and expanding economic opportunities, principally for persons of low and moderate income."

As an example of the operation of the new act, the case of New York City is instructive. With the additional objective of offering "assistance on an annual basis with maximum certainty and minimum delay," New York City was projected to receive approximately $825 million over a six-year period (1975-1981). The first year's allocation from HUD was $102,244,000.[3] With these funds the city has been able to plan and expedite community development programs embracing the Model Cities concept established by the Federal Demonstration Cities Act of 1966. The selected program areas are Harlem-East Harlem, Central Brooklyn, and South Bronx. Ultimate responsibility for these programs rests with the central Model Cities Administration, but policies and programs are proposed and reviewed by the neighborhood's area director and locally elected policy committee.

The Model Cities Administration plans and coordinates programs and allocates federal and city funds. Actual functions are either carried out by the appropriate city agency or contracted out to public or private firms and institutions. Some of the supplementary programs in operation in the three model neighborhoods are Scholarship Awards, Paraprofessional and Career Opportunities, Treating Physicians, Dental Facilities, Summer Recreation, and Health Careers Training.

The American Jewish Committee, among others, has been especially active in the area of community rehabilitation. Outstanding among the examples of such activity have been the Coney Island, South Bronx, and Forest Hills projects in New York. The first and second of these are large-scale operations calling for full-time staff. In both cases, the central problem is the restoration and rehabilitation of acres of wasteland resulting from poorly planned urban renewal projects. The transformation of these large deteriorated areas into useful living, play, and commercial space calls for the cooperation of all forces in the community, including ethnic and religious groups. The success of the projects depends on obtaining financial and planning assistance from local, state, and federal agencies. But the driving forces behind the projected scheme are the communities themselves, organized in these instances by intergroup relations professionals.

Closely related to the community problems raised by urban renewal is the question of the relationship of the central city to its suburbs. According to several of our informants, this problem takes on two distinct aspects. On the one hand, the larger, older central cities have become populated largely by poorly educated, economically disadvantaged individuals. These cities have a high concentration of minority families—blacks, Puerto Ricans, and Chicanos—who are largely dependent on social services like welfare. The concentration of low-income, poorly educated population groups in the older central cities is in part responsible for their declining tax base and their consequent inability to meet the social and physical needs of these groups.

The other aspect of the city-suburb problem is associated with the rapid expansion of suburbia. Between 1940 and 1972, the number of municipal corporations increased substantially (from about 3,000 to 5,280).[4] These incorporated communities with a population of 2,500 or above are characterized by high expenditures for education, plant, roads, sewers, water, and hospitals. These suburbs are largely populated by middle- or upper-income groups (mostly white) who have already achieved or are trying to achieve a higher standard of living.

One perceptive policy-maker in a large midwestern community spoke of the possible consequences of the lopsided racial distribution of the population:

The suburbs may not be able to exist on a basis where the central city is in danger of being destroyed. There has been the dramatic out-migration of whites, lowering of the economic status of the population, a flight of industry and a narrowing of the tax base at the precise moment when the human needs in the central city are tremendous. In addition, in the rural dominated state, welfare support is generally inadequate. Therefore, the desperate problems of the central city together with the ultimate impact on the suburbs confronts us with the real possibility that the city can go down the drain carrying with it the suburbs.

Awareness of the serious and complex problems involved has stimulated the establishment of urban studies programs throughout the country. The Ford Foundation alone contributed about $36 million to urban centers and urban studies programs in the period 1959-1974. As William C. Pendleton, program officer of Urban and Metropolitan Development at the Ford Foundation,[5] points out, there are vast gaps in our understanding as to "how cities operate, what makes them grow or wither, what produces conflict or harmony and what the keys are to successful government, citizen participation and efficient delivery of services," and what is required for the training of urban specialists.

The agricultural colleges have had some success in training specialists in their field. But the vast shift in population from rural to urban centers demands new facilities devoted solely to the city, without competing interests in research, formulation, application, and interpretation of urban policies by other institutions. Hence, a university devoted totally to urban needs is the next important innovation required in our higher educational system.

The director of the League of Cities-Conference of Mayors characterized the situation as one of the new urban America versus the old urban America, since in 1970 about 55 percent of the metropolitan population was living in the suburbs.[6] At that time, the central cities were growing at a slower rate than the suburbs. People usually move to the suburbs in search of space, good health care, quality education, and personal safety. The suburbanite is an escapee from the city who looks back upon the central city as an aggregate of urban problems and a collector of taxes for "nonproductive" things. He is quite willing to pay taxes in his new community for better schools and a better quality of life.

Some efforts have been made to balance the needs of the suburbs and the central cities. In 1966, according to its executive director, the League of Cities adopted a policy resolution which stipulated that the federal government should stop federal aid for new growth areas (i.e., aid to the suburbs for water and sewer extensions, roads, hospitals, and schools) unless those communities were willing to commit themselves to the construction of housing for low- and moderate-income families. The 1966 Conference of Mayors felt that there was no justification for federal aid for suburban growth unless those suburban jurisdictions were willing to shoulder the responsibility of housing these families: "The people who have to work in the suburbs should have a place to live."[7] The adoption of the resolution was in the nature of a political arrangement because the suburbs needed federal aid for growth. As one central city mayor reported:

The central city mayors said, we don't think you should get it for growth unless you take care of your share of the burden that we are coping with. We have all the problems of welfare, dependency, problems of crime, problems of high concentrations of people in deteriorating housing. You fellows are taking all the "goodies" without taking any of the "baddies."

The problems connected with poverty, though national in scope, especially manifest themselves on a community level, for it is within the community that the diverse groups comprising our pluralistic society meet and make contact with each other. And it is within the community that the tensions between groups, brought about by perceived inequalities, develop. Economic hardship or economic opportunity falls unequally on different racial, ethnic, or religious segments of the population. Poverty[8] is integral to the whole black-white relationship. For one thing, as is noted earlier, the powerful effect of relative deprivation when poor blacks compare their plight with the situation of whites is aggravated by television presentations of nearby affluence and luxury.

In addition, Johnson's antipoverty program[9] raised expectations that could not be fulfilled. While about twice as many whites as blacks are in the poverty category, because of the absolute difference in numbers in the general population, proportionately there are twice as many poor among blacks as among whites. In spite of the close relationship of poverty to the racial issue, intergroup relations agencies have thus far been unable to make a dent in the problem. Nevertheless, they have supported income-maintenance and minimum-income legislation and have pointed out the need for clarifying welfare programs and policies.

Community relations workers are more and more focusing their concern on poverty. Hence, the welfare field and community relations have frequently coalesced. In many Jewish communities, especially among the Jewish organizations, general welfare aspects as well as community relations are considered. It is difficult to disassociate "fair" from "full"; very frequently the former depends on the latter. Without "full" or ample facilities or resources, the problems of "fairness" loom large indeed.

Intergroup relations agencies have helped stir up interest in welfare reform. Several agencies have endorsed the principle of a guaranteed annual income, also known as the Family Assistance Plan,[10] although with some reservations; a number have supported some kind of guaranteed income arrangement. Martin Luther King's famous statement—"What's the use of being able to sit down at a hamburg counter if you haven't got a dime"— aptly expresses the dilemma. The poor have a stake in civil rights, especially as related to economic justice.

Through its community activities, the antipoverty program—regardless of its inadequacies—has helped the poor to realize that they have potential power and that if they organize, they can make themselves heard. In other words, "There *is* something they can do at City Hall"; this new realization influenced the civil rights efforts of the intergroup relations agencies in the United States.

While the statutes do not expressly prohibit discrimination on account of poverty, they do prohibit discrimination on account of race, color, religion, national origin, and sex. Thus, intergroup relations action must be conducted through the economics channel, even though it may be basically concerned with race; this has been done in increasing measure in recent years.

Not surprisingly, our informants at the Civil Rights Commission indicated increasing involvement in the poverty area. The antipoverty programs frequently operate under the name of "poverty," even when their concern includes loans and housing programs as well as manpower development and zoning. Several informants observed that the participation of the poor in the Office of Economic Opportunity (OEO) programs improved their self-image. Some informants in the civil rights area were concerned by the failure to provide for citizen participation in a number of programs affecting their vital interests, e.g., urban renewal and displacement by highway projects.

Civil rights workers reported that even the best intentioned decisions have been made without consulting the people whose vital interests are at stake. As a result, these people feel powerless and discontented, and have lost faith in the aims of government. Informants from the Civil Rights Commission stated that they were exploring issues or concerns whose inclusion in the law would be desirable.

Irving Levine[11] observed that "we have made very bad errors in social policy in the last ten years" with respect to dealing with the poor:

We were confusing two things; we were confusing the organization of the poor—an essential step that had to be taken by means of advocacy and even agitation—with the mechanism of delivering services to the poor. You don't deliver through community organization; you organize through community organization. We have not learned how to deliver services to people so that our advocacy of the delivery of those services has turned off more people than the delivery of services has served.

During the late 1960s OEO's community action agencies became a source of controversy since they were grass roots organizations funded with federal antipoverty money and were often abrasive toward local government. President Johnson had signed the Economic Opportunity Act on August 29, 1964 to implement "the policy of the United States to eliminate the paradox of poverty in the midst of plenty." As the Johnson and Nixon administrations became more preoccupied with Vietnam, funds for antipoverty programs diminished.[12] The surviving community action agencies became primarily service organizations offering food, transportation, job training, health care, legal representation, and homemaker services; career ladders for minority group members were also made available.

After a series of temporary continuations, on January 4, 1975, President Ford signed a bill that abolished the OEO but continued its community action programs under a new independent agency called the Community Services Administration (CSA). The same legislation authorized a successor agency within HEW when the White House reorganization plan is approved by Congress. One successful OEO program, such as Legal Services to the Indigent, still operates as an independent agency with an eleven-member board of directors. The 1975 funding level for the nine hundred community action agencies under the CSA was about $300 million.

One particularly significant community problem stressed by some informants involves the near poor, the economically marginal who are in direct competition with the blacks and Hispanics for jobs, housing, and the like. These people feel they have been left out; hence, they carry a great many "ethnic prejudices on their back." This same group has also resisted social change. Their view is that they profit very little from social change and that any resulting betterment would go to the blacks and the Spanish-speaking poor.

In recent years, poor whites have not been making common cause with poor blacks. On the contrary, there has been appreciable hostility between them. During the Depression, there was a coalition among the "have-nots" which included labor and the poor—black and white. Today (1970), the majority of workers are no longer economically deprived, and relatively affluent workers do not have much empathy with the poor, especially with the large proportion of blacks in that category. Today, the "not-so-poor" are resentful that so much, as they see it, is being done for the poor and for blacks. This resentment has resulted in "backlash." Some time ago, in reply to a questionnaire handed out at a seminar conducted by a progressive union, 40 percent of the respondents felt that the government was doing too much for the blacks (as reported by one of our experienced and well-informed interviewees).[13]

The far-reaching effects of the continuing recession and inflation are not yet known. It may be that "increasing the pie" for everyone can become the dominant objective. On the other hand, interethnic and interracial friction may increase as competition intensifies to get as much as possible for a particular group from the "pie" we now have. As a matter of fact, the depolarization of white-black relations remains a central problem in the community.

An Urban League official made an interesting conjecture about the increasing hostilities between the lower white working-class ethnic groups and the black communities. He suggested that the roots of these hostilities may date to the time when Southern blacks were brought in as strike-breakers in large northern cities. He thought that some of the working-class resentment might stem from their beliefs, memories, and fears that black people were being used by the power groups to break the labor movement.[14] With an eye to this problem, the Urban League therefore considers itself an intergroup relations agency specifically concerned with relations between groups as well as with equalizing opportunities for black people. The New York Urban League, for example, has just recently added representatives from trade unions to its board and is attempting to acquaint people in Queens and Brooklyn with Urban League activities.

To counteract the increasing resentment expressed by lower class ethnic groups toward the use of their tax money for programs for the poor and blacks, as well as their resistance to social change, intergroup (community) relations agencies seek to develop programs which will stabilize intragroup and intergroup objectives. A basic goal of such a program is to enhance ethnicity; by fostering pride in group identity, it is believed that the differences characterizing each ethnic and racial group are more readily accepted. Another goal of the programs for ethnic groups is to defuse their tensions by making it possible for them to give expression to their feelings and needs. Toward these ends, the National Project on Ethnic America initiated by the American Jewish Committee in 1968 focused on the common problems of all groups to make Americans aware of their diversity while at the same time trying to avoid ethnocentrism.

In 1974, the AJC project eventually developed into the Institute on Pluralism and Group Identity. The institute attempts to bring the social sciences and humanities into closer contact with the needs and life-styles of America's diverse groups. It builds bridges linking scholars, intergroup relations practitioners, government officials, and community representatives; it formulates policies and programs related to group status, primarily to enhance group identity and to cultivate an accepting attitude toward group "differences"; and it produces and distributes appropriate literature designed to promote better understanding of self, the group, the community, and our pluralist society.[15] The aim of the institute is to depolarize ethnic tensions. It seeks to achieve the goal of integration by "recognizing and capitalizing on diversity rather than denying or ignoring it." An affirmative agenda for ethnic groups reduces defensiveness with regard to blacks. Their security is enchanced by the feeling that they, too, are receiving the social consideration due them.

At present, ethnics—those to whom ethnicity is a major concern—seem to be leaning to the right because liberal forces have not done very well for their particularistic interests. The question then is how to create a sense of community without fostering political reaction. Liberals tend to be universalists, and the creation of the community is a particularistic task.

During an interview, Levine asked whether the right wing or the progressive forces will become the guiding influence of America's ethnic groups. Consideration also needs to be given to the positive mental hygiene aspects of ethnic identity. At the same time, we need to be aware of the fact that divisiveness, hostility, and chauvinism can be the likely products of increased emphasis on ethnic identity.

Notes

1. Under Title I of the Demonstration Cities and Metropolitan Development Act of 1966, the Model Cities Program directed the Department of Housing and Urban Development "to improve the physical, social and economic conditions in blighted neighborhoods." Other objectives of the Model Cities Program were to improve the quality of life in selected neighborhoods over a five-year demonstration by means of "coordination and concentration of Federal, State and Local resources; development of innovative programs; involvement of local residents in the planning and development process" ("The Model Cities Program: Questions and Answers," Washington, D.C., HUD, 1969, p. 3).

2. MUND was a demonstration community-control program conceived in Baltimore, Maryland, with funding from the Office of Economic Opportunity. MUND evolved from Sargent Shriver's work at OEO, in which the business community was invited to become a partner in the nation's fight against social and economic ills.

3. The latest Community Block Grant Program, which provides more than $4 billion a year in federal aid to cities, includes the sum of $225 million for New York City (*The New York Times*, May 11, 1977).

4. In 1972, there were 5,280 municipalities and 3,170 townships with a population of 2,500 or more (*Statistical Abstract of the United States*, 1973, p. 430).

5. William C. Pendleton, "Urban Studies and the University—The Ford Foundation Experience," April 5, 1974 (New York: Ford Foundation), p. 9.

6. Current available statistics indicate that "more people now live in suburbs—37 percent—than in central cities or in rural areas and small towns" (*U.S. News & World Report* [November 26, 1973]: 53). *The Statistical Abstract of the United States* lists the findings of the 1970 Census as follows: central cities, with 31.4 percent of the population; suburbs (and other metropolitan areas), with 37.2 percent of the population (U.S. Department of Commerce, 1973, p. 17).

7. The Supreme Court's unanimous decision in *Hills vs. Gautreaux—Chicago*, April 20, 1976, ruled that HUD can be ordered to create low-cost public housing in suburbs if the government contributes directly or indirectly to segregation in the city through public funding programs.

8. The Bureau of Labor Statistics uses the federal definition of "poverty" ("poor" is considered synonymous with "poverty"). As of April 1976, the poverty level for a single person (nonfarm areas) was $2,800; for a family of four, it was $5,500. In 1975, 12.3 percent of the population (25.8 million) were in families with incomes below the poverty threshold of $5,500 for a family of four ("Poor in U.S. Rose by 2.5 Million in 1975, Most in Recent Decades," Eileen Shanahan report on Bureau of the Census annual survey, *The New York Times*, September 26, 1976). As of April 1975, unemployment statistics were as follows:

8.9 percent (8,167,000) of the total population
8.5 percent of the white population
14.6 percent of the black population
40.2 percent of black teenagers
(*The New York Times*, May 3, 1975).

9. The idea of the war on poverty was born in the summer of 1963, when Walter Heller, chairman of the Council of Economic Advisers, convened a meeting of officials to discuss how a strategy for fighting poverty could be made part of President Kennedy's 1964 program. Less than a week after Kennedy's death, Johnson ordered the plan accelerated. Thus, the Economic Opportunity Act of 1964 was born. It was temporarily extended through the Nixon and Ford administrations until January 4, 1975, when the OEO was abolished. Its community action programs were continued under the Community Services Administration, which was later transferred to HEW. Another OEO program, Legal Services, operates as an independent agency. See Mark R. Arnold, "The Good War That Might Have Been," *The New York Times,* February 28, 1974; William E. Farrell, "Poverty Programs Lag as Slump Intensifies Federal Aid Demand," *The New York Times,* April 10, 1975.

10. The administration's welfare-reform program (referred to as the Family Assistance Plan) was originally sent to Congress in 1969. It called for a minimum guaranteed income to qualified families. It was debated in the Congress through 1972 and formally abandoned on March 1, 1973, in Nixon's State of the Union message (*The New York Times*, March 2, 1973).

11. See Chapter 4.

12. Farrell, "Poverty Programs Lag."

13. Harry Fleischman, director, Labor and Race Relations, American Jewish Committee.

14. During the steel workers' strike of 1918, Negro workers were imported from the South to break up the strike. The steel workers were finally defeated by a combination of strikebreakers and employer-inspired violence.

15. See "Publications of the Institute on Pluralism and Group Identity," March 1975, p. 1.

7

Together or Alone

Allies

The coalition is a time-honored approach to coping with religio-ethnic and racial problems. Today, with most ethnic and racial groups turning inward, this method has diminished in importance. At the time of our interviews, however, it was widely used, and there is every indication that it will regain its former position in the not-too-distant future:

By the late sixties, white middle class rage collided head-on with black rage, with the women's movement adding to the instability of the times. Slackening of social progress in the United States had much to do with the breakdown in the traditional coalescing of these progressive groups. By 1975 there were new and healthy signs that they were again seeking each other out to construct new coalitions around economic and social problems that are less polarizing.[1]

Most of our informants acknowledged the desirability of joint efforts on the part of religious, ethnic, and racial groups. Three basic conditions for a successful coalition were set forth: a clearly discernible and easily articulated superordinate goal; an assurance that each member of the coalition group will benefit from the projected action; and a guarantee that the representatives of all the organizations involved will participate in the decision-making process.

The use of allies as a strategy in intergroup relations was prevalent in the decades preceding the 1960s and was especially employed by Jewish intergroup relations organizations. The technique has been vastly curtailed in recent years, for interethnic and interracial contentiousness—black versus Puerto Rican; black versus Jewish; black versus white; black versus Chicano—is no longer a rare phenomenon. Interreligious relationships are of a different order and will be treated later. Much progress has been made in this area since the convocation of Vatican Council II in Rome in 1965 and the World Council of Churches conference in 1961 in New Delhi, India.

With few exceptions, our informants yearned for the revival of the coalition approach. Some added that at certain times and in certain situations separate social action constituted a desirable method of accelerating the development of inner strength and group self-confidence. Separate social action, they felt, could later contribute to effective joint action on the basis of equality in power and know-how. For allies to be effective, our informants stressed, they must enjoy equal status within the coalition. An alliance cannot thrive unless each group in the coalition has a truly equal voice in decision-making both by right and in fact. Most of our Jewish informants urged vigorous efforts at coalition with black groups, even though black-Jewish confrontation was much more widespread than in former years. Even today (1970), they contended, when some blacks are openly anti-Semitic, the leaders of the black community must be called on to counteract this tendency.

Some black groups tended to have a more guarded attitude to collaboration than other ethnic groups. Black militants saw coalitions as devices of white groups to dominate black groups. They also saw white liberals predominating over black radicals in some coalitions.

Two diverse views on coalitions were expressed in the interviews. One informant, a veteran (a black) of the struggle for equality of opportunity, said:

I believe in the principle of the coalition because there is more power in the coalition than Negroes can mobilize by relying upon their power alone. In other words, a coalition of allies—including labor, the Jewish community, Catholic forces and liberal groups—represent more power and can achieve more objectives than can Negroes by themselves.

Another informant, an executive of a black extremist organization, expressed an opposite view:

It doesn't mean that I get trapped all the time in the last decades in Mickey Mouse alliances where whites got theirs out first and we end up holding the bag....It would be momentary associations. Those whites who see the wisdom of all this, those whites who feel that we have identified a solution to this very serious problem, in effect, for blacks and whites, who feel that they can't interfere; that we operate it, that they accept black leadership, black ideology, are welcome to work with us.

Some black leaders felt that the building of a black community, black organization structures, black leadership, and black symbolic structures was of primary importance. Hence, premature collaboration—especially collaboration at the community level—was held to impede the development of an autonomous black community. Therefore, for the time being, any intergroup collaboration should be confined to the leadership level and should not extend to the community level.

The leadership of the Jewish group whom we interviewed emphasized collaboration with other groups in many areas and tended to regret the current resistance to working together on a people-to-people basis. Even a temporary reduction in collaboration was harmful, they thought, because it was the only effective approach in certain situations, e.g., coping with black anti-Semitism.

Obviously, the weaker the group, the greater its need for allies to help it attain its aims. Yet, most of those interviewed revealed that the weaker the group, the stronger its resistance to allying itself with stronger institutions, for it feared being overwhelmed by its stronger colleagues. Those groups that seem to be (or feel they are) weaker are more likely to place greater emphasis on ethnic exclusivity, pride, and militancy. Full collaboration may not be possible until they develop genuine confidence in their group identity.

As already stated, to be effective, collaboration must be between equals and not between "superiors" and "inferiors." The Jewish group may have evinced greater desire for collaboration than any other group because of their communal structure, greater availability of resources, and long experience in community action.

Coalitions, our informants felt, should be formed around goals that are clearly stated and understood by all participants. Responsibilities should be clearly spelled out, and actions—joint and individual—concretely enunciated. All must be aware of the limitations of coalitions and agree not to go beyond the defined parameters without mutual consultation.

It is essential to set forth the situations in which coalitions can be set up; the conditions which favor them and those which do not. Incidentally, it is the stipulation of these conditions which helps to "professionalize" the field. An executive of the New York City Human Rights Commission pointed out that while it was highly desirable to get together on specific issues, black and white leaders must first establish the principles for more permanent and overall coalition purposes.

As already indicated, a common goal of a superordinate nature is basic to a successful coalition. When the coalition does not possess a clearly formulated goal, members of the coalition who have already achieved their own group objectives may cease to be concerned with the condition of their colleagues who may not as yet have achieved their aims. Without a common goal, then the reciprocity essential to a successful coalition cannot be achieved. In the early 1970s, for example, collaborative effort of American intergroup agencies on the Middle East question was merely a hope. More recently, collaboration has been more satisfactory, even though group attitudes continue to be influenced by specific issues and by pressures from both sides in the conflict.

One striking example of effective collaboration was the protest of religious, labor, racial, and communal groups against the resolution on Zionism adopted by the General Assembly of the United Nations on November 10, 1975. While the protest was largely spontaneous, it would not have been possible if the participants had not earlier engaged in mutual action in common causes. The resolution, passed by the combined vote of Third World, communist, and U.N. members beholden to Arab oil interests, equated Zionism with racism. The resolution was clearly anti-Semitic, aimed at Israel in particular and at Jewry in general.

Here are some sample statements:

The National Board of the Y.W.C.A...is...deeply disturbed that in the world political arena the ancient and historic longing of a displaced and persecuted people for a homeland has been equated with racism.... As Christians and Jews, sharing the same religious heritage, we totally reject the proposition....that Zionism is a form of racism and racial discrimination. This distortion of Zionist aspirations can only serve to encourage anti-Semitism. We support the conciliation efforts of the United States government in the United Nations and in foreign capitals and call on YWCA members and other Americans to play an informed and mediating role in the elimination of anti-Semitism.

The response of religious leaders was very clear. Archbishop Joseph Bernardine of the U.S. Catholic Conference expressed profound disagreement and disappointment with the resolution. He said it opened the door to harassment, discrimination, and denial of basic rights to Jews throughout the world. Several cardinals and archbishops issued similar statements, including Cardinal Cooke, who said:

Just ten years ago, we Roman Catholics hailed the declaration of the Second Vatican Council which stated unequivocally that the Church decries hatreds, persecutions and manifestations of anti-Semitism directed against Jews at any time and by anyone. This sentiment was repeated and emphasized at the beginning of this year by a Vatican statement concerning all forms of anti-Semitism. We must reject anti-Semitism just as much when clothed with seeming legality at the United Nations as when crudely exhibited on a neighborhood street corner.

Dr. Philip Potter, general secretary of the World Council of Churches, a black Methodist from Jamaica, sharply condemned the U.N. action. He called upon the world body to "reconsider and rescind" the resolution, and he declared the Council's "unequivocal opposition to the equation of Zionism with racism."

Claire Randall, general secretary of the National Council of the Churches of Christ, made the following statement:

The National Council of the Churches of Christ has consistently sought to support efforts toward reconciliation in the Middle East and has encouraged all parties to deal with the fundamental causes of the conflict there.

Our Executive Committee has called upon Israel and the Palestinians to recognize the right of the other party to the same self-determination which they desire for themselves.

I believe it is consistent with our positions, regarding the Middle East, now to urge the United Nations General Assembly not to approve the proposed resolution that declares "Zionism is a form of racism and racial discrimination."

Mutual recriminations will not help solve Middle-East problems nor contribute to peace. Furthermore, such an action on the part of this international body will undermine the struggle against racism, and has the potential for reviving an old form of racism, anti-Semitism, in many places in the world.

On the whole, separate group concerns are normally paramount, and a good deal of bargaining takes place to determine how much a group's special interests are served by united action. In a coalition process, the group-identity factor can serve a constructive role, providing each group works together from strength and at the same time considers its own needs in relation to that of all other groups in the coalition.

A coalition should comprise the full spectrum of American political thought, including the conservative right and liberal left. Allies are most useful in building up a strong middle because the cross-section coalition tends to produce a balance of views. Extremist and nonpermissive groups, such as the radical right, should be excluded because they often desire to achieve some goal other than the one for which alliances have been formed. Experience indicates that members of permissive groups have more wholesome and easier intergroup relations than those accustomed to the authoritarian pattern.[2]

Coalition efforts are still in evidence on church-state issues and in actions such as the "lettuce boycott" led by Cesar Chavez. In the California grape dispute, the U.S. Catholic Conference has at different times played a significant catalytic role.

An executive of the U.S. Catholic Conference recounted an interesting example of coalition effectiveness—Project Equality. The project was initiated in 1970 by a Catholic group in an attempt to limit institutional purchases by Catholic religious organizations to firms that have an affirmative policy with respect to employment. It has since become an interfaith enterprise.[3]

Catholic, Jewish, and Protestant institutions have at various times collaborated on social action programs. Black-Jewish coalitions, however, have become increasingly difficult to effectuate.

At the time of our interviews, the central Catholic religious agency concerned with human relations, the U.S. Catholic Conference, had instituted the Task Force on Urban Affairs for the purposes of fostering wholesome race relations and dealing with inner-city problems. At its disposal it had all the resources of the Catholic church—Catholic hospitals, Catholic schools, interracial councils, and lay Catholic civic organizations. The task force was sanctioned to oversee hiring practices in Catholic hospitals, with particular attention to upgrading doctors and other professional staffs without regard to race or color. Another concern was the Catholic school system, specifically the function of the schools in shaping the social attitudes of children. The roles of the priest and of the Catholic lay person in the inner city were other areas under the jurisdiction of the task force. A relatively large fund-raising program for the task force was approved by the bishops, both to obtain the required funds for the program and to educate the parishes and the schools as to their role in the intergroup relations area.[4]

Generally, the coalition process as an educational experience is far more effective for participants than the human relations workshop technique.

Some of our informants discussed the effects of "ethnicity" on coalition building. They saw ethnic pride as a positive factor in the use of allies as long as it did not become ethnocentric, as in the following examples: "We'll have nothing to do with white liberals and those phonies"; "We do our own thing in our own way." One informant asserted that group identity which is genuine and a source of strength, while requiring *boundaries* for the preservation of the identification process, should avoid the creation of *barriers* to group relationships. Thus, the Black Panthers in some cities of the West had been sitting in with black and even white community representatives to consider such communal problems as police practices. Inadequate resources, said one interviewee, may sometimes defeat the coalition objective. For example, because the antipoverty program did not have enough funds in a number of cities, an alliance between blacks and Chicanos became a practical impossibility.

Alliances are sometimes feasible by cutting across ethnic and racial group distinctions, primarily on a professional basis. The educator group in some states is a good example.

An important issue can bring diverse groups together; such was the case with Proposition #14 in the state of California in the 1960s[5] when, even though they failed, every responsible organization joined in the campaign to defeat the amendment. After the election, however, the coalition could not be held together; created to serve one purpose, and one purpose only, it promptly broke up.

The need to recognize the real problems and to take joint rather than separate action is becoming increasingly more compelling. The last great coalition movement was the March on Washington in 1963 "for jobs and equality," in which practically every important community group, including labor, the church, civil rights, and civic organizations, was represented.

A somewhat individual view of the use of allies by blacks was expressed by a high official of the Urban League. He asserted that real economic and political change can come about only through the white community: "The whites are obviously the overwhelming majority in the country and it is obviously up to them to set up an equal and equitable relationship between the various racial groups." In this sense, there really is no question about the use or need for allies. It is obvious that "whites can do it if they so choose."

With regard to the internal problems within the black community, the official was very skeptical about the use of allies. He thought that at this time (1970) it was better not to have white people come in to the black communities and that instead black people should develop some of their own institutions and their own self-image, and create their own leadership. In this sense, too, he felt the use of allies to be unwise.

His third point with regard to the use of allies was that "the real function today of the white man in the race relations field is to serve as a kind of missionary to the white community." Rather than get involved with the internal development of the black community, it would be much wiser for white people who wish to help to work among their "own" and attempt to change this country from what the Kerner Report termed a "racist country" into a country where all men are equal regardless of race, color, or creed.

Perhaps the broadest form of coalition that has a bearing on intergroup relations is that required of the economic classes. Unfortunately, bitter antagonisms exist today, especially between the working class and the welfare group. Another barrier is that industrial corporations continue to be almost exclusively concerned with their own economic interests and are reluctant to use their power sources for "non-directed economic concerns."

One informant suggested that reducing the economic differences between groups, instead of juxtaposing the welfare needs of one group and the amount of taxes from another, could facilitate the unification of all income groups. All could then consider themselves as recipients, and members of the working-class would no longer think of themselves as constantly "giving" to meet the needs of others—notably, paying taxes so as to sustain the welfare group, a large proportion of which is black.

The national health insurance plans now before Congress would help reduce polarization between the working class and the welfare group. At present the welfare group is eligible for Medicaid, while the working class is not because its average income is too high to qualify—although insufficient to pay the prohibitively high costs of private medical services in the case of prolonged illness. A national health insurance plan would provide medical service for all. The insurance premiums to finance the program would be related to income, with both the employer and employee contributing as they do now in the Social Security program.

Thus, the working class would not feel that the welfare costs of health services for the poor, including blacks and Puerto Ricans, prevent them from obtaining proper medical help. Medicare, a program for those over sixty-five years of age, constitutes the one true Social Security health system. Today, in the economic area, the only possible coalition seems to be one of the "have-nots," which is an unhealthy situation.

As important as coalitions through selective alliances are in coping with problems of intergroup relations, self-help and mutual aid among minority groups are of even greater significance in the long run. However, self-help movements, while developing at an increasing pace, are still relatively young.

Self-Help

The mention of "self-help" among blacks is no longer considered an unfriendly or even hostile act, as was the case about ten years ago. Blacks no longer view self-help as a diversionary tactic by whites, either consciously or unconsciously motivated by a desire to shift from the real issue of discrimination in employment, housing, and schools to the putative deficiencies and weaknesses of the black community in general and the black family in particular.

Gone too is the view that self-help is a covert implication that blacks bear an important share of responsibility for their plight. Moreover, the blacks' earlier objections that past self-help efforts foundered "on the shoals of ghetto life"[6] are seldom heard now. In fact, it is generally recognized that the black community has practiced self-help in the form of mutual aid since the latter part of the eighteenth century.[7] In the antebellum period, self-help took the form of associations of free blacks in the South. In the North, this effort was expressed in mutual aid and self-improvement societies. On the whole, it was a modest movement; moreover, many severe restrictions were placed on the association of blacks among themselves in the antebellum South. Assembly of more than four or five slaves was forbidden except when a white person was present. In the North during the post-Civil War years, competition with Irish and German immigrants was intense, making self-help more difficult.[8]

Today, in addition to the Urban League and the NAACP, there are numerous smaller black self-help organizations. One is a predominantly black job training program centered in Philadelphia (Opportunities Industrialization Centers—OIC) which is urging Congress to support a bill which would allow "community groups to train and provide jobs for a million unemployed persons in the next four years."[9] Others are the Savings and Loan Associations owned and operated by blacks; the National Council of Negro Women; and the National Business League.

One informant gave an example of the scope of such activity. In 1967, the Urban League, he stated, purchased thirty acres of land in Seattle and proceeded to construct housing units on that land. Here blacks were not simply appealing to white people to give them a share of what already exists; they were innovating and organizing on their own. More recently, the Urban League's Seattle Housing project became a separate corporation (the Seattle Housing Development Corporation) for the purpose of rehabilitating housing in Seattle's inner city. The corporation singled out white, middle-class neighborhoods and targeted them for black expansion. It provided funds to rehabilitate the existing housing so that such neighborhoods could be up-lifted and made attractive to middle-class blacks.

At the time of the interviews, one official of the National Urban League indicated that the organization was getting ready to evaluate the services they offered, including direct services, community action, consultation, and technical assistance. Discussion centered on the organization's moving away from "the business of being a recruiting, screening and selecting agency for white firms looking for the 'good nigger.'"

The late Whitney Young was responsible for the Urban League's new ap-proach to aiding blacks in the cities. Primarily economically oriented, he felt that the social and economic welfare and the material conditions of life formed the bases for an intergroup relations program. Until 1970, the Urban League tried to run its program by operating on contributions from private individuals and corporations.

The league's "new thrust" programs were in the areas of education, hous-ing, health, and economic and social welfare systems. In 1971 the Urban League had been characterized as a "social workers' group, active in re-search and program development for black communities emphasizing eco-nomic security."[10] For the first time, it undertook activities concerned with minority entrepreneurship, welfare rights, tenant groups, minority leader-ship development, police-community relations, day-care centers, and sum-mer programs for college youth. By 1977, the league indicated receiving federal support of about $8 million per year, mostly in the area of job train-ing through its LEAP program.

This author has previously commented on self-help in the black com-munity.

A true black community is now beginning to emerge out of the civil-rights move-ment. Northern, college-educated young Negroes, in their unique version of popu-lism, in their American-style "going to the people," are expressing solidarity with illiterate Southern black sharecroppers, not by rhetoric, but demonstrably by their presence in Alabama and Mississippi. Others are dedicating themselves to serving the black poor and outcast in the Northern slums. They are creating new traditions out of which authentic communal associations are developing—traditions as indige-nous to the black and as relevant to the special complexities of *his* particular condi-tion as immigrant-aid societies and hospitals were to the Jews.[11]

Blacks and Jews have had radically different experiences in their efforts to enter the mainstream of society. The Jewish family structure, religion, and centuries-old cultural heritage were important factors in the formation of self-help and mutual-aid facilities.

In nearly all the interviews, both black and white informants reiterated the self-help and mutual-aid themes. The Catholic prelate who heads the human relations activities of the Catholic hierarchy in the United States stressed the need to help people help themselves. He felt that the Catholic social service organizations in this country should assist inner-city people to get projects off the ground rather than themselves administering the programs.

The NAACP program director described one of its programs which was set up two years before our interview with the goal of "hitting the construction industry from two sides." He stated that the NAACP was actually organizing consortiums of black contractors with limited capital so that they could pool their resources and thereby qualify for bigger jobs instead of their usual small rehabilitation or renovation jobs. Specifically, a national consortium called the National Afro-American Builders, with sixteen local and regional groupings of contractors, was then in operation. Up to that time (1970), commitments of some $85 million in construction work were said to have been made available to regional groupings being created all over the United States. Of course, the problem of insufficient funds remained, especially for posting bonds guaranteeing performance on the contract.

One public agency, HUD, has developed an interesting device for assisting a minority group to engage in independent action. An executive of that agency, in order to offset the claim that the identity and whereabouts of minority group contractors were unknown, developed a regional directory of minority group construction contractors throughout the country. An arrangement with a consultant was made to seek out these minority group contractors. A listing of approximately two thousand minority group construction contractors throughout the United States was made available. He stated: "We can tell you where they're located, how many employees they have, what their area of expertise is, what is the biggest job they have ever done and what is their bonding situation."

On the other hand, the promotion of small black enterprises within the ghetto itself was not considered an effective step in the direction of upward economic mobility. Our informants believed that grocery stores in Harlem and little one-room business enterprises in the Bedford-Stuyvesant area would play an insignificant role in the upward mobility of the black people. They felt that what was necessary was the involvement of blacks in the mainstream of America's economic development and progress—"a piece of the action on Madison Avenue," not the inheritance of old, run-down small businesses, nor new ones in the older sections of town where everyone who could contribute to a viable community was fleeing as fast as he possibly could. The ghetto, nearly all of our informants contended, is a losing economic proposition.

The attempts thus far made to set up black business enterprises have made two basic errors. One is that the clientele has been restricted to blacks. This policy can be self-defeating. For example, Jews would never have played a leading role in the soft-goods industry if they had depended solely on a Jewish clientele in the manufacture and sale of clothing. The other error is an administrative one. Quite frequently, an industrial establishment under black auspices is headed on the operational level by a prominent black citizen—a professional person, a political leader, or even a businessman who often enough has not adequately mastered the fundamentals of the industrial enterprise that he is expected to administer. In most cases the head has neither grown up in the business nor has had sufficient experience in that particular area. Lacking the required background for a position of top responsibility in a corporation, such a person finds himself at a great disadvantage. Perhaps this explains why so many industrial ventures under black sponsorship—with or without financial aid—have failed. A. Philip Randolph most accurately characterized black capitalism:

Black capitalism is designed to encourage the development of business enterprise on the part of blacks. There is nothing wrong about its purpose, but in a period of the development of industrial and business conglomerates involving billions of dollars of capital, there is little hope for black capitalism. In addition to blacks not possessing the capital, they lack the economic expertise to survive as capitalists in this country of the highest form of business competition.

If blacks are to achieve the breakthrough needed to enter the mainstream of the business and industrial world, the "executive suite" of the larger corporations must open its doors to qualified young black executives. While blacks are finally being admitted into the corporate world, their progress remains slow, as is also the case for Jews who have been conducting a social action and educational program in this area for the past twenty years. The Cummins Engine Company, with headquarters at Columbus, Indiana, made a special effort in this direction at the time of our interviews largely through the efforts of its chairman and major stockholder, who in addition to being a top industrialist is a communal and religious leader of national distinction. Recently, a half-dozen black men were named to top posts in this corporation, including two vice-presidents. A black man was also named to the board of the corporation.

In the area of smaller businesses under black sponsorship, it is imperative to aim at a cross-sectional clientele, and not to be limited to any one racial or ethnic group. The leadership of the enterprise should go to black individuals qualified by experience. Furthermore, if at all practicable, not all the employees should be blacks, there should be an integrated employee group. It could be advantageous to place some whites on the boards of these corporations, although blacks should, of course, predominate.

As mentioned earlier, Aspira is the educational counseling and leadership development agency created by Puerto Ricans for Puerto Ricans in the continental United States for the purpose of developing leadership potential in the Puerto Rican community. Its primary emphasis is on youth. In January 1970, there were about fifty Aspira clubs in New York City high schools made up of over three thousand Puerto Rican youngsters between the ages of fourteen and nineteen.[12] Its program emphasizes the history, culture, and background of Puerto Ricans. Shy, uncertain youngsters tend to become confident, determined, and active participants as a result of this experience. The youngsters identify with the staff as models, for these men and women themselves went through the Aspira seminar on educational activities. "Madrinas de Aspira," godmothers of Aspira, was organized for women to engage in fund-raising activities and to develop skills in speaking and other leadership functions.

Programs are also conducted with Puerto Rican parents of junior high school students in order to expand the educational possibilities of the youngsters. The programs include meetings of small groups of parents at different homes. The case study approach is utilized with typical youngsters to determine how their difficulties might be resolved.

The then executive director of Aspira reported that institutions of higher learning now welcome Puerto Rican students, whereas before they did not. This change may largely be attributable to the ferment in our society, the current open enrollment policy, and related reasons. He observed that when Puerto Rican youngsters are involved in organizations sponsored by non-Puerto Ricans, the Puerto Rican's indigenous culture and mores are generally not understood. Hence, most of the youngsters feel alienated and uncomfortable. Aspira is an important uplifting agency for Puerto Ricans:

The very idea of having these clubs organized and administered by the youngsters themselves and by the Aspirantes (former participants of Aspira programming) is an important technique in uplifting a disadvantaged and deprived group to prepare them for adult middle-class responsibilities.

Despite all its advantages, Aspira has not escaped all criticism. Some claimed that to a degree the agency is selective. That is, youngsters at or near the bottom culturally and intellectually might not benefit from the program and that those youngsters who do succeed would have made progress even without the service.

A black informant suggested one means by which a wholesome relationship between blacks and Puerto Ricans, on the one hand, and whites on the other, could be effected. He stated that the disadvantaged groups should be assisted to do things for themselves and thereby gain control of some of the vital institutions of society that operate in their communities. The confidence so engendered in these and other minorities would contribute materially to a positive attitude toward other groups—majority and minority.

Something along these lines is being done by the Black Muslims. Recently, the Black Muslims, who have estimated business holdings of up to $70 million, announced their decision to dismantle their commercial holdings. Employees of the Muslim stores and shops were given the first opportunity to purchase businesses through the Small Business Administration.[13]

Notes

1. Daniel Elazar and Murray Friedman, "Moving Up/Ethnic Succession in America" (New York: Institute on Pluralism and Group Identity, 1976), p. 22.

2. John Slawson, "Intergroup Relations in Social Work Education," Council on Social Work Education Proceedings of the Sixth Annual Program Meeting, 1958, pp. 104–13.

3. More recent literature (February 1974) indicates that Project Equality is expanding as a national interfaith program for equal employment opportunity. *Project Equality News* lists the new sponsors and affiliates and the reorganized national offices and programs. It reflects the intensification of efforts to secure Equal Employment Opportunity commitments from major insurance companies, financial institutions and banks, and it publishes a *Buyers Guide* which contains the names of all participating organizations. *Project Equality News* (March 1975) reaches a national membership of religious bodies exceeding 50 million persons.

4. During 1970–1972, the U.S. Catholic Conference (USCC) awarded grants totaling $5.6 million to 264 self-help projects. In August 1972, the USCC announced grants totaling $1,004,450 to thirty-three organizations in twenty-two states. The thirty-three self-help groups include whites, blacks, Puerto Ricans, Indians, Chicanos, and Eskimos. The Campaign for Human Development is also known as the USCC Anti-Poverty Education/Action Program. Projects funded are primarily in the area of economic development, education, legal aid, communications, housing, transportation, social development, and health. Major programs in 1973 were in the areas of expanded communication structure, family policy, and a "Respect Life Program" which was a response to the 1970s "Improving the quality of life for all Americans."

5. "Neither the State nor any subdivision or agency thereof shall deny, limit or abridge, directly or indirectly the right of any person who is willing or desires to sell, lease or rent any part or all of his real property, to decline to sell, lease or rent such property to such person or persons as he in his absolute discretion chooses." (Proposition #14, 1964, statewide ballot. See *The New York Times*, May 30, 1967.) This provision obviously implies that actions contrary to civil rights prohibitions are protected.

6. Bayard Rustin, "From Protest to Politics," *Commentary* (February 1965): 25–31.

7. John Slawson, "Mutual Aid and the Negro," *Commentary* (April 1966): 43–50.

8. John Slawson, "Mutual Aid," p. 44:

. . .but after the Nat Turner insurrection of 1831, in which sixty whites were killed, a series of laws was enacted which struck the first major blow to the development of communal association among free Negroes. They were denied the right of assembly;

they could not hold church services without the presence of a licensed white minister; and they were prohibited from visiting or entertaining slaves and from convening meetings of benevolent societies and other organizations. In Maryland free Negroes could not have "lyceums, lodges, fire companies, or literary, dramatic, social, moral or charitable societies." In many slave states, they were enjoined from engaging in certain occupations and from trading in certain commodities.

9. *The New York Times*, September 1, 1976.

10. Gerald Fraser, *The New York Times*, July 24, 1971.

11. John Slawson, "Mutual Aid," p. 50.

12. In 1973, its twelfth year of existence, Aspira reported that a total of seven thousand high school freshmen, sophomores, juniors, and seniors took part in its counseling program at Aspira centers in New York, New Jersey, Philadelphia, Illinois, and Puerto Rico.

13. Paul Delaney, *The New York Times*, August 8, 1976.

8

Compulsion or Persuasion

Confrontation

Confrontation is not a new strategy in the field of international, intergroup, or interpersonal relations. It has been in use for centuries, perhaps millennia—war is the classic example of the extreme form of confrontation. The problem for contemporary intergroup relations is to determine the conditions under which it has been successful and those in which it has failed to bring about the desired result.

Confrontation is essentially a power struggle, and it may or may not be accompanied by violence. The position of a minority group on whether to use confrontation is sometimes determined by whether the group is ready to be seen as an "outsider" against the establishment. A group which considers itself nonestablishment has or thinks it has nothing to lose and much to gain by "confrontation." On the other hand, a group which sees itself as part of the "establishment," or desires to be so accepted, is reluctant to antagonize it and would oppose confrontation.

Confrontation either implies or openly states that established measures are no longer viable or that such measures will not bring about desired results soon enough. Confrontation therefore signifies impatience with the tempo of change. The approach generally (but not necessarily) calls for actual physical presence, at which time demands for immediate change are made. The demands are presented by persons who are convinced that the normal processes of negotiation are wasteful or useless. The action is frequently dramatic and precipitous.

The interviewees were queried as to the use of confrontation as an instrument in the struggle to achieve rights and improve conditions. Their responses cover the entire spectrum of opinion, although a slight majority favored its use. The interviewees also specified the conditions for success of the approach.

Only in one instance was violence (even when justifiable) sanctioned, and this minority view was expressed by a member of the one extreme group included in our sample. "To be frank," he said, "the use of any means is the pragmatic approach; if laws can do it, yes and fine." Or put another way, "He who has the power makes his own definition of violence."

A. Philip Randolph believed that under certain circumstances violence is inevitable, although he agreed with the vast majority that violence is neither a rational nor an effective means for achieving racial equality and "social freedom." Nevertheless, he stated that violence should be viewed as a social instrument which is good or bad according to the use to which it is put: "A knife which may be used to carve a steak can also be used to cut a man's throat." He went on: "It cannot be too strongly and clearly stated that violence is inevitable in the struggle of any people against racial and religious and social injustice. Many oppressed groups have taken up the weapon of violence when they could see no other way to throw off their oppressors."

Overwhelmingly, however, nonviolent confrontation was considered preferable to violence and was accepted as a legitimate, effective, and even necessary process to achieve desired goals. As an example of the value of confrontation, one public agency official in the civil rights area cited the demonstrations in Birmingham and Selma, Alabama (1955), which were important contributing factors to the enactment of the civil rights legislation of 1964 and 1965.

All informants, with the exception of a member of a national organization dedicated to the use of the educational approach in civil rights, believed that discriminatory practices or economic deprivation could be alleviated only through direct action by the minority groups, with the occasional help of outside forces. As they pointed out, blacks have achieved some measure of upward mobility mainly through their own efforts, and not through the good will of the majority population.

The contrast between the minority's use of "action" and the majority's preference for the educational approach was pointed out by the representative of the above-mentioned national agency which preferred the educational approach. He said: "I find it very difficult to distinguish at times between so-called education and so-called action." Action is itself an educational experience. Another executive of this organization told of an incident "which kind of jarred them" when a black writer observed: "Well now, let's see. As I understand it, you boys operate pretty much just on a verbal level."

On the basis of many years of practical experience, one executive of a well-known foundation devoted to the cause of human rights and equality concluded that it was almost useless to try to produce change in the white community. The only dependable route to equal rights, he said, was via the minority group itself in the form of direct action, protest, and other self-help measures: "Well, I think it [change] will come from the fact that people progressively indicate things they will no longer tolerate."

The informants stressed that nonviolent protest can work only when the vast majority embraces the fundamental moral position, even if not in its entirety. Bayard Rustin observed that "Southerners must say at least that they believe in the Constitution and in the democratic form of government." Martin Luther King was able to utilize nonviolent protest within the framework of democratic beliefs and compliance within the dictates of the Constitution. Obviously, nonviolence could not work as a framework in Hitler's Germany because Hitler excluded Jews from the human race and repudiated the Judeo-Christian tradition altogether.

One of our informants who is both an academician and an activist was convinced that the emphasis on confrontation by the late Dr. King produced definite movement in the direction of human equality, especially while there was still a lingering fear that some violence might occur as a result of such confrontation. Our informants believed that Martin Luther King's nonviolent and continuing protest action constituted a breakthrough in intergroup relations. On the other hand, one knowledgeable informant felt that Watts and similar riot situations produced more change in black-white relations than any other phenomenon. While he was not certain as to the durability of the gains made, he was confident that such events impelled those who have the power to produce change to reexamine their thinking.

The fear of material damage following a refusal to accede to protest demands does, of course, affect the outcome, e.g., the Montgomery bus boycott. The Rosa Parks[1] incident in 1955, with its attendant severe loss of income to the bus company (the blacks walked to work for approximately a year), finally led to the capitulation of the boycotted company. On the other hand, school boycotts, after initial success, have proved ineffective in the long run because as a rule parents cannot hold out for extended periods.

In certain situations, nonviolent confrontation is less effective. For example, if an industry such as building trades cannot hire any more blacks until economic expansion makes increased housing construction possible, then coalition politics, as suggested by Bayard Rustin, needs to be pursued: an alliance of blacks with progressive forces—trade unions, liberals, religious groups, and groups concerned with the pursuit of superordinate goals.[2]

The following statement by an HUD official elucidates the workings of confrontation:

Nonviolent confrontation appropriately conducted is effective because Americans are so accustomed to negotiating through committees, through studies, through research, that it really strikes into their guts to be confronted with the actual situation, including angry faces and language that frequently is highly offensive. And my experience has been that as a reaction, effort will be made to deal with the people who are confronting, concessions will be made, steps will be taken, planning will be initiated, power will be brought to bear to relieve the situation and conversation of a dialogue nature ensues.

You may have seen the black city councilman in Augusta, Georgia, talking to a CBS man after the explosion they had down there and the councilman was saying to him: "You know, it's unfortunate that this sort of confrontation had to occur, but these people have been living in very poor circumstances for years, and they have been petitioning, waiting upon the city and county, asking for increased help. I've seen it happen at this building here. I've seen welfare mothers and public housing tenant organizations come here and picket. And the reaction is quite interesting— increased guards; guards at the secretaries' doors, requirement that you show your pass going in and going out in the hope that the people would go away, but out of it comes increased grants of money to the local housing authority to paint and fix up, and so forth. It works, yes."

An important official in the Equal Employment Opportunity Commission also testified to the power of confrontation:

In the first place we get more money and more pressure through more laws that result from what goes on outside in the real world. The law we are enforcing here would never have been passed if there hadn't been demonstrations. The Congress and the President in 1963 and 1964 had been scared to death.... I think it's very clear that the Civil Rights Act of 1964 grew out of that confrontation down there. That's entirely different from saying whether I endorse it.

At the beginning of World War II, A. Philip Randolph, the dean of American civil rights activists, confronted President Roosevelt relative to the abolition of racial discrimination in industry, labor unions, and government itself. Because of the historic import of that confrontation, large portions of our interview with Randolph are quoted here:

J.S.: Mr. Randolph, you then came to the conclusion early in your career that a confrontation of some kind was an essential element in the strategy?

A. Philip Randolph: That is correct. I came to realize that mere statements by Negro leaders, while useful and necessary and proper, were not sufficient. It was evident that Negroes had met with top representatives in government who could do something about the problem of racial bias, but nothing definitely was done about many of the basic problems. I was able to involve, in our conferences with the President, prominent black leaders from different parts of the country. We made it clear to President Roosevelt that we intended to pursue our demands until we achieved some concrete and definitive concessions in the interest of abolishing racial discrimination in industry, labor unions, and government as a whole. Of course, we met with some hesitancy on the part of President Roosevelt. He was definitely fearful about 100,000 black people coming to Washington in a massive march, with possible resulting violence and perhaps death. In this respect the President also knew that there were no restaurants in which they could eat, few toilet facilities that were integrated and only one hotel in which Negroes were permitted to sleep.

He called in his entire Cabinet to sit with Walter White of the NAACP and myself on this question. We talked at length about it. The President said to me: "Now, Phil, I want to abolish racial discrimination in the defense industries as much as you do.

But the method by which this is to be done is important. I can't afford to permit you to bring 100,000 Negroes to Washington in a march because there is no way to manage a tremendous group of people such as that. You can never tell what might happen, nor can I."

The President had in the conference, in addition to the members of his Cabinet, Sidney Hillman, then president of the Amalgamated Clothing Workers Union, who held a top post in the President's administration. He also had a top representative from General Motors in the conference. He repeated rather constantly that he considered this matter extremely serious. He observed, "Now I want to assure you and Walter and Negro leaders in general, that I am deeply interested in the elimination of discrimination in all areas of industry, including the defense industries and government, but there is a limit to what I can do. Now I am not in the habit of issuing Executive Orders for anything. I don't know any other President who indulged in that method of dealing with various problems. But I can assure you that I will do something about this matter of racial discrimination with respect to defense jobs if you will permit me to do so. But you are going to block my effort in this respect if you insist on an Executive Order. We have here the entire Cabinet, and they are ready to contribute their judgment on this question. Negroes are American citizens and they have a right to share in employment opportunities along with other citizens of our country. So now I want to suggest, and I am going to appoint, a small committee out of this Cabinet to go into a conference room with you and Walter White to seek some solution to this problem."

He appointed Mayor LaGuardia to serve as Chairman of the committee. The committee spent quite some time discussing this question. At the outset of the discussion of the question by the committee, they attempted to make it definitely clear that they had no intention of going against the President's wish with respect to a march of 100,000 Negroes on Washington. Beginning with that position, they sought to persuade Walter White and myself to change our plan with respect to the march of Negroes on Washington for jobs.

I told them it was utterly impossible for me to change my position on this matter because I was reflecting the spirit of the masses of Negroes throughout the nation on this question of jobs in defense industries. I indicated to them that I neither had the right nor power to change this plan for a march on Washington unless the President issued an Executive Order banning racial bias in employment of Negroes in defense industries and government.

Mayor LaGuardia stated that he had known me a long time and he was rather confident that the committee would get nowhere in trying to get me to change the plan for the march on Washington unless the committee recommended to President Roosevelt that he issue the Executive Order requested.

The committee drafted an Executive Order and sent it to a group of government attorneys to put it in proper form. Among the group of lawyers was Joseph L. Rauh, who has an office in Washington. This group of attorneys worked up an Executive Order which they considered to be applicable to this problem. Walter White couldn't remain longer for the discussion of the question since he had to attend the convention of the NAACP in Houston, Texas. When the Executive Order was all properly prepared, it was presented to me. I read it and indicated that it was all right except for one thing. Immediately the question was raised, "What is that?" I said, "It doesn't apply to the government." The reply to me was, "You don't expect an Executive Order to cover the government, do you?" My answer was, "Well, we want an Executive Order which applies to the government because the government is guilty of racial discrimination itself with respect to jobs for persons of color."

The question was raised: "Where is this discrimination in the government? In what areas?" My answer was: "Racial discrimination is in practically all departments of the government."

While the committee was not convinced by my assertion concerning discrimination in the government, they presented the Executive Order to the President for his action. He wanted to know from the committee what I thought about it, and they told him I thought it was satisfactory except that it didn't apply to the government. Though the President had some reservations about including the government in the Order, he finally issued the Order.

I was called in to a conference with him and the committee, and he said: "Now, Phil, I want you to get on the radio and tell the colored people of this country that there isn't going to be any march on Washington for the elimination of discrimination in defense industries since I have signed and issued the Executive Order requested by you and the committee."

I replied: "I will be glad to do that, and in the name of the committee I want to express our great appreciation for the position that you have taken on this question." I also agreed to hold a public mass meeting in Watergate Park in Washington with some representative Negro leaders to speak on this question.

J.S.: You had set the date?

A.P.R.: Yes, we had set the date.

J.S.: How much time was there?

A.P.R.: Oh, well, the time was just about one or two days before the march was scheduled to take place.

J.S.: How did you get the message across to the entire country?

A.P.R.: We got this matter over to the entire country by way of the radio which had been suggested by the President. He also designated Mayor LaGuardia to arrange for radio time for me.

This was the year 1941. The order that Roosevelt issued was the historic and precedent-setting Executive Order No. 8802 abolishing all racial discrimination in defense industries—government and private.

Executive Order 9981 abolishing racial discrimination in the armed forces was enacted in 1948 by President Truman. A. Philip Randolph states: "In this case, it wasn't a threat to President Truman, but it was a definite statement to him on the mood of Negroes throughout the nation with respect to the manner in which they were treated in the armed forces."

A number of informants gave their views on confrontation. Several black professionals concerned with program development and execution pointed out that the strategy can sometimes harden resistance, result in polarization, and mobilize negative forces for counteraction. Even when successful, these agency executives felt that confrontation generally follows the law of diminishing returns. Bayard Rustin pointed out that except in an extreme revolutionary situation, real progress will not come through confrontation, for it strengthens rightist forces. And Roy Wilkins said that confrontation should be used only as a last resort, for "they snatch back what they were forced to give up."

Kenneth Clark also believed (in 1970) that the strategy has its disadvantages. He stated that confrontation has an initial dramatic impact, but is self-limiting. Its impact diminishes with each incident, until finally it loses all its dramatic content:

My feeling is that if you take a rigorously objective view of the consequences of the confrontation method, one finds that rarely do you have any sustained positive social change from it. You get a lot of words....You get some sort of emergency methods....Catharsis on both sides by the way...catharsis on the side of the victim and catharsis on the side of the establishment, but rarely do you get fundamental social change.

Clark may have arrived at his conclusion almost wholly on the basis of experience with the New York public school system. As mentioned previously, the school systems are least likely to respond to threats of confrontation because they know that parents will not hold out long enough.

Many respondents asserted that the confrontation strategy of the blacks as a method of producing social change stimulated in the 1960s the activist approach of other minority groups such as the Jews. This activist approach had not been as prevalent earlier. In this connection, the executive of a large (Jewish) national private intergroup relations agency observed: "Many of us are ashamed of our silence during the McCarthy period."

While Jewish agencies do not generally indulge in confrontation, they "do not stay out of the battle." Jewish agency professionals cited some illustrations of the efficacy of confrontation in the area of social discrimination, as, for example, in handling the discriminatory or exclusionary policies of recreational facilities. Let us say that a corporation decides to hold a golf tournament in a country club that engages in exclusionary practices. The undesirability of utilizing this facility for this purpose is pointed out in the form of a protest. This approach has frequently proved successful; in many cases, sponsors have canceled arrangements with such clubs.

Another Jewish professional with wide community relations experience maintained that confrontation moved the black problem to the top of the communal agenda.

Several Jewish intergroup relations executives pointed out that confrontation has frequently been employed prematurely. For example, in one case protestors staged sit-ins at public agencies in order to obtain information about the practices of certain landlords. The information, however, could have been obtained by a telephone call to an appropriate agency. Thus, the ultimate weapon was used before it was necessary. Some victories won by sit-ins at welfare offices, such as expediting the delivery of checks, are only short-term successes. Therefore, the technique should be used judiciously. An executive of a local Catholic agency concerned with urban problems unhesitatingly said that confrontation should be used only as a last resort to stave off "alienation and polarization." A local Jewish community relations executive stated that confrontation can be effective over the short run, but not over the long haul.

A revealing instance of successful confrontation was when in 1969 a group of Jewish college students picketed the annual convention of the Council of Jewish Federations and Welfare Funds, the central coordinating body of all local Jewish communal coordinating agencies in the United States. Their demands for increased funds for Jewish educational programs were met, but it should be stated that "a state of readiness" for this objective already existed. Previous dissatisfaction had been expressed by many groups with procrastination in granting the much needed funds. The protest for more and better Jewish education by the students themselves, actual and prospective, was unusual and highly dramatic.

In our total sample, one lay leader with many years of experience in educational and social welfare called attention to Kurt Lewin's principle that confrontational pressure generally brings on increased counterpressure. Hence, conflict is increased. But rather than increase the pressure, some of the factors responsible for the pressure should be reduced. The leader suggested making "sort of end-runs, rather than going right through the center of the line." Hence, the use of the negotiation process; settling one grievance after another might reduce the urgency of the need for confrontation, thus avoiding reprisal in the form of backlash.

The blacks' use of pressure tactics as an adjunct to negotiation began in the early 1930s, and they have become increasingly sophisticated in its use. This strategy, together with the emphasis on merging political and economic factors, has brought beneficial changes to the black population of the United States.[3] Even in the mid-1930s, black organizations were becoming involved in the united front movement of that period which strove to identify "the 'Negro cause' with the larger cause of human freedom and dignity."[4]

More recently, a study session of twenty-five intergroup relations professionals on May 17–19, 1968, referred to as the "Big Think" Conference, released the following conclusion with respect to confrontation: "One of the ways the power relationship between the ghetto and the general community may be changed is through encounters—if these are of the peer status."[5]

Confrontation has proved to be a legitimate and effective instrument for producing desirable social change under the following conditions: proper timing, avoidance of irrational personal hostility, focus on the issues involved, and avoidance of personal abuse. Avoiding violence and practicing confrontation as a process, and not as a goal, are basic requirements. If used as an outlet for "letting off steam," it has no real value and often results in harm. Effective confrontation requires careful planning and a reasonable amount of flexibility, together with a seriousness of purpose and persistence.

Exposure

One frequent method of compelling an individual, a group, or an institution to change or to end a discriminatory procedure is "exposure"—public revelation of an individual or institutional discriminatory practice. For many intergroup relations agencies, exposure is a basic method used to change the behavior of an offending institution or individual. Exposure has been practiced either by direct action or by implication, i.e., suggesting it as a plausible consequence of the undesirable act rather than as an actuality, or even as an overt threat.

Generally, exposure is not utilized in connection with disreputable or "crackpot" individuals or groups, for it would satisfy their main goal—to gain public attention. The technique of "going public" with respect to undesirable intergroup relations practices has sometimes proved effective. On one occasion, some interviewers revealed, New York City designated a committee to investigate black anti-Semitism in the schools. The findings released to the press were so general as to neutralize the purpose of the inquiry. Thereupon, members of the committee proceeded to expose groups and public officials responsible for the condition under investigation. Since this incident of exposure, overt abuse of ethnic rights has reportedly abated.

The long-range effects of exposure are not known, but occasionally the direct exposure of transgressions and/or ill-advised actions can be beneficial in the short run. Frequently, the exposure is in the form of a boycott—for example, the action in connection with the Japanese trade boycott of Israel in 1973. Discussions held by a group of businessmen with a large U.S. business enterprise dealing with Japan led to a threat by the company to cease its trade relations with Japan. As a result, Japan changed its stance on Israel. Of course, Japan's action was based primarily on enlightened self-interest.

In the 1960s, exposure was also responsible for producing a significant breakthrough in "executive-suite" discrimination by public utilities, a very bitter episode in the history of race relations in business. The names of the discriminatory utilities companies were released to the press, and as a result the companies decided to reevaluate their exclusionary employment prac- tices. Exposure was used only as a last resort, however, after other methods had failed. This was in line with the agency professionals' conviction that this strategy is best used as a last recourse.

There is much truth in Emil Durkheim's dictum that it is extremely diffi- cult to teach morality. Accordingly, the best approach is to restructure power relationships between groups; then a "moral action" might follow. Many confuse expressions of piety with moral action. As one of our infor- mants from academia asserted: "Major discrimination in this country is practiced by persons, presumably of good will, who lead personal lives of piety." They enjoy their unshared privileges for many years on a racially exclusionary basis, undisturbed by any moral compunctions.

Exposure of Soviet Russia's treatment of Jewish emigrants is another case proving the validity and relative effectiveness of this technique. It is gen- erally believed that this action resulted in an increase in the number of Jews permitted to leave the Soviet Union.

Some respondents believed that the threat or the likelihood of exposure is sometimes more useful than exposure itself, for it achieves the intended pur- pose without engendering the animosity which actual exposure provokes.

Who can use exposure? Public agencies cannot as a rule expose undesir- able practices of individuals or institutions, for their work is predicated on confidentiality. Therefore, the private community organization must assume this task. Such exposures may have beneficial side effects. Occasionally, re- sponsible citizens find themselves associated with an organization dedicated to spreading hostility and disunion. When the organization is exposed, the citizens will often sever connection with it.

In the early days of compliance, in many cases the technique of exposure rapidly eliminated discriminatory practices and instituted positive action. For example, the sizable Jewish community of a larger Eastern seaboard city maintained that, though no actual proof could be found, discriminatory practices prevailed in the staffing of its administrative positions—principals, assistant principals, and other administrators. A study of these charges was launched. The superintendent of schools was informed that officials of the Jewish community were planning a study, and this information was also released to the press. Having been put on notice, the superintendent of schools stepped in to improve the situation long before the results of the study became available. This is an illustration of an implied exposure, re- sulting in prompt elimination of an undesirable practice.

Questions which frequently arise with regard to exposure are: how essen- tial is the visibility of the organization or group representing the minority, and to what extent should the process be pursued through general channels? Obviously, an organization does not have to do the exposing in its own name; it can do so indirectly through the press and other mass media. It seems that while visibility was an important consideration in the past, the interviewees had little hesitation about speaking out openly. Speaking out does not rule out the formation of coalitions; today speaking out *and* being visible are considered speedier and more effective approaches to problems of discrimination.

Thus, in attempting to increase minority representation in banking institutions, one municipal human rights agency publicized the fact that a particular bank was "working with us." The human rights executive preferred to stimulate affirmative action by "working out agreements" that were fair and decent. He found "silent toughness" a more effective approach than filing a complaint that might become bogged down for "as much as two years." A number of large corporations, fearing publicity about their discriminatory employment practices, sought out the human rights executive to arrive at a settlement prior to the filing of an official complaint. An announcement in the press by New York City's human rights agency that x number of organizations had been "listed for examination" immediately brought inquiries from numerous organizations as to whether they were about to be cited. To avoid publicity, they eagerly took steps to initiate fair employment practices at their offices. In these and other instances, informants found the communications media, especially television and the press, powerful aids in achieving their goals.

Negotiation

Generally negotiation between contending parties precedes confrontation and the enforcement procedures of the public agency. Intergroup relations agencies in both the public and private sectors most frequently employ negotiation in their efforts to eliminate discriminatory practices. This approach is basic to implementation of legislative enactments and executive orders.

Despite appearances to the contrary, Jewish and black communities have relied mostly on negotiation. As one Jewish agency executive stated: "Our whole way of life has been historically countering violence without confrontation." As black groups achieve more experience in coping with problems of group relations, they too are choosing negotiation rather than confrontation. In varying degrees, the black community has often favored negotiation. The Urban League has found negotiating to be very useful and effective with corporate leaders, educational officials, and foundation executives.

The respondents unanimously agreed that for negotiations to be successful, they must be backed up by "muscle." A threat, implicit or latent, is therefore extremely useful. The proverbial combination of the "velvet glove" and the "iron hand" has frequently worked best. HEW, for example, has the power to terminate funds to back up the negotiation process. This power is exercised only in extreme situations, and never when there is evidence that the institution or corporation is making a genuine effort to change its policies.

Of course, morality must be on the side of the negotiator who, armed with solid facts, has to establish beyond a reasonable doubt that the problem is not an isolated incident but part of a pattern. The informants also recommended that the desirability of eliminating the unacceptable practice or instituting a new one be related to the subject's own welfare—his business or industry.

The informants suggested that pragmatic considerations are more likely to produce desired results than mere suasion. In the discussions about discrimination against Jews in the corporate world, their emphasis was not so much on the injustice done to the Jewish aspirant but on the effect on the corporation of losing much-needed talent and skills.[6]

The Department of Labor, through its Contract Compliance unit, monitors the employer's compliance with civil rights regulations. In cases of noncompliance, it has the power to terminate contractual arrangements between government and private industry, providing all negotiation has failed.

Most of the negotiations in the Equal Employment Opportunity Commission (EEOC) take place informally and behind the scenes. Nevertheless, the possibility of adverse publicity, which acts as a rectifier and even a deterrent, is ever present. The EEOC prefers to cooperate with the defendant to rectify alleged infringements.

A high official in the EEOC stressed that the conciliation approach employed in the enforcement process does not involve mediation. He contended that in the field of civil rights there is no middle ground between violation and compliance: "You can't be half pregnant." Compliance means total elimination of discrimination, not 90 percent elimination. Hence, there is very little room for mediation. In the view of this official, conciliation means simply that the employer "has the opportunity to obey the edict." "The only matter you are negotiating," he said, "is *how* the employer gets into compliance, not *whether* he gets into compliance." The obligations under the law "are non-negotiable."

The position of this respondent was unique to all the interviewees. However, he did feel that the employer "may *propose* an alternate way of complying in a manner that fits his particular needs better, and still comply with the law." In this way, he made room for "the realities of the industrial relations system."

At the time of our interviews, the International City Management Association sponsored a number of insightful seminars. The seminars were not sensitivity training as such, but they did contain elements of that approach.[7] (The National Training Laboratory collaborated with the International City

Management Association in staffing and programming.) More precisely, the seminars employed a confrontation approach. In the seminars, each city manager from a selected geographical region brought along a minority group representative from the area. The group discussed specific shared problems, and, as a result of this interchange, they learned about new approaches and modified some long-held viewpoints. The participants subsequently reported that the seminars proved helpful in handling disturbances in their communities. The manager of one Midwestern city changed his work schedule, spending much more time with the black community and other minority groups, and delegating many of his administrative functions to top-level staff. Although it was not sensitivity training as such, the NTL collaborated with the ICMA on staffing and programming.

In accordance with Section 809 of the Housing Statute, apart from settling complaints, HUD engages in educational and conciliatory activities. At the time of our interviews, HUD was conferring with the National Realty Board which pledged its support of the statute. Conferences were arranged with fair housing groups concerned at the local level with organizing and disseminating information about fair housing. HUD representatives also conferred with state and local ordinance individuals.

The HUD staff has encouraged local (public) human rights agencies to refer complaints from the state to HUD in order to provide investigative and conciliation efforts on the enforcement side. Another purpose is to create collaborative projects in the state to promote compliance with the local ordinances and HUD's regulations.

Education as an Instrument of Attitude Change

Education for better intergroup relations has long been regarded as an effective alternative to confrontation. In our interviews, we asked the informants what they thought such education can achieve. Most interviewees responded that education as a procedure to affect intergroup relationships needs to be specific: education of a particular group about a particular problem for a particular end. The informants were skeptical about the effectiveness of a general, untargeted approach such as "brotherhood." One black respondent, however, looked upon education as essential to any effort to improve human relations: "I think education is essential; you can't change people's opinions and behavior by brute force or by the invocation of law or its rigid enforcement."

The viewpoint with respect to the role of the mass media in the informal educational approach has changed in recent years. Earlier, passive reception of stimuli through mass channels, without any opportunity for interaction, was thought to have very little impact, especially if permanent change were the goal. With the coming of television, however, and its powerful sensory impact, the role of the mass media on the informal educational process dealing with human relations has been reevaluated. Since television can affect insight both positively and negatively, the content of its programs and its use in terms of educational objectives must be studied very closely.

The impact of television notwithstanding, the informants thought that small-group interaction was much more powerful in modifying attitudes than mass media stimuli. Intragroup interaction has also been found useful in interreligious intercommunication. Dialogue alone has its limitations, however, for frequently "people just talk past one another." In fact, instead of understanding, hostility can sometimes emerge when the issues are especially controversial. When basic hostility between two groups exists, dialogue may sometimes intensify this polarization. Nevertheless, group interaction properly conducted is still considered the most feasible and effective procedure in attitude modification.

According to the interviewees, formal education for better intergroup relations is a rather long process with unpredictable consequences. They expressed dismay over formal public school education for this purpose. Instead, they placed their faith in the small-group discussion in which, face to face, they could "talk it out," revealing personal experiences, laying prejudices out on the table, and working them through.

Those given to the legal approach felt that the "public hearing," properly conducted, had an effective educational potential. Some also felt that the use of mass media "can be effective if related to a specific purpose; such as the interpretation of Israel to the American community, or the plight of Soviet Jewry." They found that a generalized kind of approach did not merit intensive use.

One example of such a generalized approach was the National Conference of Christians and Jews (NCCJ) utilization of a unique procedure of having a priest, a minister, and a rabbi appear together to explain their respective beliefs. The appearance of three representatives of different faiths to explain their beliefs was so unusual that it made "news" and seemed to have had an impact on listeners and viewers. However, when the "news" aspect faded, the NCCJ abandoned this particular approach because "it had lost its potency."

An example of a specifically targeted program was the Urban League's educational program connected with the adoption of black children. The program involves educating adoption agencies to the facts and realities of black family life so that black children can be placed in black foster homes, even when both parents work.

On the other hand, the NCCJ's educational approach remains the promulgation of ideas of brotherhood in the hope of stimulating brotherhood action.

Yet another approach is that used by the League of Cities: "experience reports." The experiences of various cities are discussed in the organizations' conferences and workshops. During 1970, the League of Cities-Conference of Mayors held seventy seminars for mayors centering on issues such as housing, employment, education, community organization, poverty, citizen participation in the poverty program, and the impact of population migration. The mayors concentrated on substantive issues and avoided discussions of methodology. The idea behind the conference was to enable each participant to learn from the successes and failures of colleagues. Hence, this might be considered a nondirective kind of educational experience.

Notes

1. Mrs. Rosa Parks, a black seamstress, was arrested and fined in Montgomery, Alabama, after she refused to give up her seat on the bus to a white man. The boycott that followed lasted 385 days: the number of Negro riders dropped from thirty-four thousand to fourteen per day. See Abie Miller, *The Negro and the Great Society* (New York: Vantage Press, 1965), p. 97.

2. See Bayard Rustin, "From Protest to Politics," *Commentary* (February 1965), pp. 251-53, and Bayard Rustin, "Black Power and Coalition Politics," *Commentary* (September 1966), pp. 35-40.

3. Charles Radford Lawrence, "Negro Organization in Crisis," Ph.D. dissertation, Columbia University, 1952, p. 306.

4. Ibid.

5. "The 'Big Think' Conference Report," *Journal of Intergroup Relations*, Special Issue (Fall 1970), pp. 46-47.

6. Since the effort to place Jews and blacks in executive positions in corporations and academia provides an excellent demonstration of the successful use of negotiation, we have included a more complete account in Appendix A.

7. See Chapter 12 and Appendix B.

9

Some Approaches in
Intergroup Relations

The intergroup relations approaches considered here are by no means exhaustive. Moreover, some have already been mentioned earlier as part of
composite categories of social action or efforts at attitude modification.[1]
Not all of these approaches have equal import, but all have potential utility.
Of course, underpinning these specific techniques are basic macro factors
which should be given consideration. Thus, the informants generally agreed
that improvement in group relations presupposes a modification of our
total value system which should concern itself with such problems as poverty, slums, unemployment, inadequate schools, air pollution, water pollution, and inadequate transportation.

Even if attention is focused on the specific problem of a particular group,
the general welfare and the stability of society should form the context for
pursuing a particular goal. The common or superordinate goal carries with
it a reinforcing leverage. On the whole, the informants concerned with
policy-making supported the position that specific intergroup relations
problems should always be defined in terms of the general welfare.

One policy-maker suggested that defining a problem as an "urban situation" rather than a racial problem might, under certain conditions, be more
helpful. Furthermore, a specific effort by the group involved may frequently be the most effective approach to a particular goal, especially when allies
are available. The universalist aspect is generally best employed in the context of dealing with a particular problem or grievance.

Social justice is an underlying motivation in social action. And while the
individual struggle may be of a specific nature, each person involved in the
particular cause should be concerned with the outcome as a matter of right
for all people. A. Philip Randolph stressed that this was the motivation in
his 1941 conference with President Roosevelt dealing with the blacks'
threatened march on Washington.

During the McCarthy era, various agencies of different religious and
ethnic composition stimulated the formation of anti-McCarthy committees
under various names such as councils, and organized civil liberties unions

and workshops dealing with problems of civil liberties. In general, however, issues which concern one group exclusively are best dealt with by that group alone. For example, an issue that is exclusively Jewish, such as the right to observe Jewish religious holidays in industry, is best handled by the Jewish group.

Generally, polarization is reduced when one group is seen as part of a larger constellation, so that, for example, whites in a given category would not feel deprived when certain resources were made available to blacks of similar economic status. For similar reasons, an interethnic or interminority coalition is often more easily achieved than a simple black-white arrangement. This approach would call for the acceptance of "black" as an ethnic group. However, at this stage in intergroup relations, this objective is still in the realm of fantasy. For some time to come, unfortunately, we will be obliged to live with this restricted image of a "black" and "white" America.

Actually, the least important factor in the quality of personality is skin pigmentation. Differences in skin color only serve to facilitate identification of an outgroup, thus subjecting it to probable discrimination. Hence, the major significance of skin color is its identifying role in facilitating the exploitation of the dominated group by the dominant—in this case—for more than three hundred years in one form or another. This exploitation resulted in the kind of deprivations that made the "black" the victim of the "self-fulfilling prophecy." (By our own doing, we create the undesirable conditions that we supposedly wish to avoid.)[2]

The important differences, in fact, are cultural attributes which to an appreciable extent are determined by social and ethnic factors—a composite of customs, beliefs, and value systems. These attributes have a profound bearing on personality makeup; in comparison, color as such plays little, if any, role. It only tends to distinguish the "dominated" from the "dominant," and much too frequently is accompanied by mistreatment and deprivation, which in turn is usually followed by the victim's reaction of hostility or rage.

In coalitions, a specific ethnic group copes with problems not as a specific group grievance but on more general principles, such as merit, equality of opportunity, social justice, and foreign affairs considerations.

Some informants believed that as blacks begin to feel more secure in their own group identity, superordinate commitments would evolve. Others emphasized the group interest first—what is good for the specific group may be good for the country generally—an idea which, of course, is not always true. The dilemma of working to satisfy one's own group interests or toward a common goal with other groups therefore remains.

Irving Levine, the director of the AJC's Institute on Pluralism and Group Identity, regards the superordinate goal as a "bridge issue," that is, as an issue conducive to the achievement of a common objective basic to effective joint action. According to one informant, a prominent intergroup relations worker (a white), the basic problem is how to achieve thinking based on superordinate goals.

As mentioned earlier, the Community Relations Service of the Department of Justice, in trying to resolve differences between minorities and the majority group, discovered the importance of obtaining the collaboration of the informal leadership of the community. The workers of the Community Relations Service did not seem to place much faith in the commitment of upper-middle-class whites to intergroup relations goals. The agency also found that it was essential that the group with whom they were working have a leader. By encouraging and building inner strengths, the continuance of what had been initiated would be assured. The action of the professional, therefore, took on a catalytic form, without restricting the effort to "educate." A discriminatory practice thought to be the result of ignorance of the facts is different from the practice motivated by prejudice. Similarly, different considerations will determine the nature of the treatment if the problem is related neither to prejudice nor to ignorance but simply to the power factor, i.e., the threatened loss of the exploitative privilege of the "dominant" group over the "dominated."

Universalism and Particularism

Both the universalist and particularistic approaches can be easily discerned in most of our interviews as well as in most of the techniques proposed or actually used in the battle against discrimination and prejudice. The universalists, as we have seen, approach each problem from the direction of the general good. Improve society as a whole, they say, and you benefit your own group. The particularists, on the other hand, try to benefit their own group first. By extension, they may, like Mr. Wilson of General Motors, imply that what's good for their group is good for the nation.

Success with corporate leadership can often best be achieved by appealing directly to economic self-interest (particularism). Corporate leadership needs to be convinced of the economic advantage to their own industrial enterprise, e.g., when minorities are employed and receive adequate incomes, they themselves become consumers of the corporate product. Generally, most of our informants, given the choice of categories, would call themselves universalists.

The general statement voiced by many of our informants was: "We need to enrich the democratic way of life in the total community if we are really to serve our own group." In this respect, however, we should draw a distinction between goal and method. The statement implies that the universalist approach is employed to achieve the particularist goal.

The relationships between blacks and Jews have changed in the past decade. Today it is unlikely that blacks would seek Jewish help or that Jews would offer it. At the time of our interviews, Jews frequently felt rebuffed by the blacks in the civil rights movement. Blacks often prefer to operate on their own power and therefore discourage acts of a "paternalistic" nature: "We do not need you white folks anymore for directing our lives, for from now on we will do it ourselves." Whites now need to prove their sincerity to blacks.[3]

At the time of our interviews, the Jewish group combined with others in superordinate goal action that expressed the interest of all groups. One of the best collaborative efforts in recent memory was the amendment of the McCarran-Walter Immigration Law.[4]

Black organizations, on the other hand, have not always been in a position to make appeals on a universal basis. Instead, they have had to concentrate on specifically black problems. The goals of the black community have ranged from complete integration to complete, even territorial, separatism.

One of our Catholic respondents concerned with the implementation of policy insisted that, although he headed a unit in a Catholic intergroup relations agency, his program was attuned to general welfare legislation, labor relations, and race relations—that is, to problems that affect everybody, not just Catholics. In contrast, his associate on the operational level was convinced that the special interest point of view was of great importance, the dictum "our responsibility to our own" being a motivating factor. As he stated, "The Chicanos are our own. They are Roman Catholics by baptism and upbringing, and therefore we have a special responsibility to them." But it should be noted that white Catholics as such are not generally considered a "minority" group.

Pump-Priming

The term *pump-priming* was made popular during the Great Depression by John Maynard Keynes. In the past, national Jewish agencies such as the American Jewish Committee have done a lot of pump-priming, that is, helping to launch a project and then letting its participants carry on themselves. During 1948 and 1949, for example, the AJC provided funds for a civil rights worker in the educational departments of both the AFL and CIO. Since then, the merged organization has carried on its own civil rights activities. For reasons of discretion and pragmatism, this action was never made public.

Another example is the testimony given by Kenneth Clark in 1954 before the Supreme Court in behalf of the historic *Brown* v. *Board of Education* case. His testimony was based largely on research done under the auspices of the 1950 White House Conference on Children and Youth. The entire Clark project was financed privately by the American Jewish Committee.

Although this support was not confidential, few outside the inner administrative group of the donor organization were aware of it.

Other examples are the Boston Jewish Community Council which helped organize and develop "Fair Housing, Inc." of Boston, a group which was effective in locating housing for large, hard-to-place black families in Roxbury;[5] the Jewish Community Relations Council of Philadelphia which provided seed money to needy groups concerned with black community development, in amounts sufficient to tide them over the initial period; and the Jewish hospitals of Cleveland where the Jewish Welfare Federation in effect has made up the difference between the state subsidy and the higher cost of hospital care, for mostly black welfare recipients.

There are many other examples of collaboration between one group concerned with a problem from its own vantage point and another group motivated by the demands of the overall welfare situation. Assistance given in these actions is of a "seeding" nature—a method that stimulates "self-help."

From a universalist point of view, the outside group rendering help derives an indirect benefit in the long run. One such example was a housing rehabilitation project begun in 1966 under the auspices of the Upper Park Avenue Civic Association (UPACA), in which a section of Harlem was rebuilt for and by local black residents in collaboration with the Commission on Social Action of the Union of American Hebrew Congregations (UAHC). Most of the financing was made available by the government.[6]

As one outstanding black professional leader in the intergroup relations field stated, generally pump-priming is indeed best done behind the scenes, but not for the purpose of relieving an individual or organization from taking a stand on important moral issues.

The Matter of Visibility

The "salting-in" process usually involves furnishing educators, editors, columnists, broadcasters, and speakers with background material pertaining to human equality and civil rights. They, in turn, may use all or any portion of this material in their presentations in whatever form they desire. The original source of the information may or may not be identified; in fact, it is sometimes best that it not be divulged.

This approach avoids the self-serving or exclusively self-interest factor in human relations issues. The "objectification" of the presentation strengthens its impact, for "it is America speaking" in behalf of a minority need in universal terms. This holds not alone for presentations made through mass communication channels but also for such instruments of communication as shop steward manuals, labor history brochures, or corporation personnel publications. The data and general information recently supplied to the media by Jewish intergroup relations agencies on the Arab boycott and the consequences of Petrodollar activity is a case in point.

Retaining "invisibility" by speaking or writing through other, more acceptable channels to avoid the handicap of special pleading was a rather unpopular concept at the time of our interviews. Some informants felt that this approach—"ducking under and having someone else front for one"— may have worked ten, fifteen, or twenty years ago, but not today.

The method of "relative invisibility" was employed in about 1938, when Nazism was being exported to the United States. In March 1938, polls indicated that 49 percent of Americans believed that Jews were partially, and 12 percent that they were wholly, responsible for Hitler's persecution of the Jews.[7] In view of such findings, it would have been dysfunctional to engage in special pleading on behalf of Jews in the United States. Accordingly, a prominent national Jewish intergroup relations agency decided to universalize the appeal, treating Hitlerism not as a Jewish but as an American problem. Americans learned that Hitler's true aim was to divide the American people by promoting intergroup strife in order to more readily conquer the country. The theme of the agency's educational effort was a universal one: "To preserve our country, all Americans must unite to frustrate the Hitlerian design." This message was "salted in" through the mass media—radio, the press, magazines, and public meetings. Thus, Americans were informed of the true aim and the actual meaning of the Nazi philosophy. The destruction of the Jews was to be only a first step toward the destruction of America as a unified sovereign nation. Since Jews were only incidental to Hitler's main aim, they were treated as such; all of America was his target. Hence, self-interest demanded resistance to this destructive goal. From all indications, this strategy was effective.[8]

Today, the Jewish community is visibly in the forefront on matters pertaining to Israel. Nevertheless, Jewish community relations organizations continue to work through communications channels and social change agents such as the mass media and other opinion-molding facilities without the concerned agent necessarily being in the forefront. For example, they provide background materials on Arab intentions and the entire problem of Middle East discord, especially Israel's alleged "intransigence" and/or "inflexibility." These background materials are well-written, factual documents. They are distributed to columnists, editors, broadcasters, and the like who can use them as they see fit. These source materials are used in their names, and not in that of the intergroup relations agency. Thus, it is America speaking out, not the minority group as special pleader.

As illustration, we may cite the positions taken by members of opinion-molding groups with respect to the Arab use of Petrodollars to further their anti-Israel and anti-Semitic designs and the threat posed to Western industrial nations by the newfound wealth of the Organization of Petroleum

Exporting Countries (OPEC). The factual material supplied provides support for the positions taken by the media.

Answering Derogatory Charges and the Matter of "Quarantine"

"Quarantine"—ignoring the allegation or slander—was long considered the best method of dealing with the charges by bigots against a minority group. The rationale behind this method was that it would deprive the bigot of what he wanted most—publicity through the press, magazines, radio, or television to gain public attention and to lend more importance to his anti-minority stance. Answering the charge would advertise it, planting hostile tendencies in the minds of those not so heavily burdened with prejudicial attitudes and perhaps reinforcing them in those already so inclined.

The desire to respond to an attack is natural, and simply ignoring it demands a great deal of control and fortitude. Rather than respond openly, sometimes the best approach is merely to acquaint the media with the disreputable background of the bigot involved and the unreliability of his statements. Care needs to be taken, however, to avoid the appearance of censorship.

Several informants offered qualifications to the quarantine approach. They thought that (1) the status of the individual who made the derogatory statement and (2) the degree of publicity given his allegation must be considered. With regard to the first qualification, if the person who makes a public allegation is well regarded, the accusation should be refuted publicly, but if the allegation is made by a known bigot, the "quarantine" approach can be employed to advantage.

Regarding the second qualification, the informants suggested some modifications of the general approach where desirable. Generally, they thought it best to ignore a bigoted statement which gets extensive publicity especially if the perpetrator is of disreputable character.

These general guidelines notwithstanding, special situations may require individual responses. For example, one of our informants, a public official in New York City, handled a serious charge made by a well-known, irresponsible critic by disregarding the attack. This approach was apparently successful, for the offensive rumor died down and the bigot never again repeated the charge publicly. The official believed that if he had responded to the attack, countercharges would have been made and the undesirable incident would have been kept before the public eye.

In sum, it is futile to answer charges made by demagogues, but in the case of accusations made by responsible persons, a public response is mandatory. However, it is important to avoid a continuing barrage of charge and countercharge.

In the 1940s, "quarantine"[9] was a favorite device used (especially by

Jewish groups) to thwart the attempts of bigots to spread group hostility. Everything possible was done to keep them from achieving their desired end —publicity. By the time of our interviews, however, the popularity of this approach had waned, chiefly because of the mass media's constant search for the sensational event. It had become impossible for "silence" to be maintained in the face of media insistence upon publicizing such incidents. There was, in effect, no way to enforce a quarantine. Bigots had to be answered openly. Attempts to keep the exploits of the hate mongers from the media might backfire, since the press or other media might accuse the agencies of suppressing news and interfering with freedom of speech. Another consideration in assessing the quarantine approach is, of course, the civil-libertarian point of view, namely, that all persons should have the opportunity to air their opinions unless they induce others to break the law—inciting to riot, for example. Thus, intergroup relations workers no longer make extensive use of the quarantine. Nevertheless, it remains important to quarantine unknown and/or notorious bigots.

Some bigots have actually built up their careers through publicity. An example is George Lincoln Rockwell who reached the public eye through the attention of those who should have ignored him, i.e., the Jews at whom his attacks were leveled. By congregating where he spoke and abusing him while he engaged in his vituperations, his Jewish opponents made possible the publicity he so greatly desired.

"Quarantine" can still be used effectively in special situations, providing it is used judiciously and does not play up extremists. Some of our informants believed that if the Black Panthers had been "quarantined" in the news, they would never have become important. The quarantine is a necessary approach to incidents such as vandalism against synagogues and cemeteries, so as (1) not to arouse the concern of the intended victims, and (2) not to bring these events too much into the open and thus create a "halo effect."

One important concern of practically all the informants was that promoters of group hatred and suspicion use sensational methods to reach the media. For example, as a result of his sensationalist approach, Rabbi Kahane's demonstrations[10] with respect to the plight of Russian Jewry focused attention on himself rather than on the problem. His method was counterproductive. The protest actions and public positions of legislators and responsible American leaders, Jewish and non-Jewish, had already brought the problems of the Russian Jews to the attention of the American public.

Mass Communication

Within our formal culture, our mass media are assuming an increasingly important function. Thus, intergroup relations workers have encouraged the removal of negative, invidious group images in the mass media and the introduction of positive inter-group content.[11]

As is well known, of all the mass media television is the most powerful in communicating group relations concepts. As of 1975, 97 percent of U.S. homes had television sets and the average household spent more than six hours a day in front of the tube.[12] Television brings the most monumental events, such as Selma or the Vietnam War, directly into our living rooms, as well as the most thought-provoking discussions of behavior patterns. The program that dealt with homosexuality as an individual behavior devi-ation rather than as a pathological condition is a notable example.[13]

Television has a far greater potential influence than the press or radio. For example, the 1969 National Commission on the Causes and Prevention of Violence (the Eisenhower Commission) concluded that exposure to vio-lence on television tends to stimulate violent behavior rather than divert aggressive impulses to harmless channels.[14] In addition, according to a re-cent article in *Psychology Today*, children who watch violent films on tele-vision are considerably more likely to be apathetic when exposed to real violence than children who have not seen such films.[15] A more recent study (1977) sponsored by the American Medical Association and the National Institute for Health concluded that television violence continues to cultivate feelings of danger, mistrust, and alienation among the public. "Both child and adult heavy viewers were more afraid to walk the streets at night. When junior high school students were asked how often it was all right to hit someone who angered them, heavy viewers were more likely than light viewers to answer 'almost always.'"[16]

In general, our informants reported radical changes in their mass com-munication approach to the modification of behavior. They agreed that it was more effective to influence producers and programmers of public af-fairs programs than to go directly to the public with specific items. While both approaches are important, they found the former to be more produc-tive in the long run. The informants also noted that while the quantity of religious broadcasting had not increased, public discussions of moral and social issues on television and in the other media had expanded.

With specific regard to the presentation of minority problems, however, they felt that there had been insufficient progress. In the early 1970s, at a joint meeting of black and white representatives, it was agreed that the mass media were ignoring the ordinary lives of blacks. News broadcasting was particularly singled out for concentrating on sensational items—violence and general antisocial tendencies. After this meeting, which followed a joint conference held under the auspices of the Columbia School of Journalism on "Race Relations and the Mass Media," steps were taken to present more positive subject matter relating to blacks. Since that time, the number of minority members involved in screen and television productions has increased considerably. One program which has been a leader in presenting wholesome views with respect to minorities is "Sesame Street." In addition, "TV has also quickened the general awareness of the blacks' chronic plight."[17]

The mass media have been widely used to promote positive intergroup relations. For example, just a year before our interview, a television team of three broadcasters in a Midwestern community was persuaded to go to Israel "to see for themselves." The local Jewish community relations agency paid part of the expenses of the trip. On their return, the team presented several half-hour programs and many one-minute spots filmed in Israel; their newly acquired expertise continued to enrich their subsequent news reports about Israel.

Obviously, prejudice that sets off highly emotional reactions cannot be handled as readily through the medium of television as can more minor issues. Nevertheless, television has been effective, some of our informants felt, in reinforcing our moral commitments and in supporting some of our shared values. There has been a gradual increase in the attention given to the positive aspects of human relationships and less to the negative or bizarre.

The current communications explosion is a potential source for intensifying intergroup relations activity. For one thing, television sharpens the rising expectations among the minority groups, for, as mentioned earlier, they are brought face to face with higher standards of living and affluence. As a result, many develop feelings of "relative deprivation," which breeds frustration among the minority poor.

Another negative aspect of television is that it gives instant worldwide publicity to bad news. The Eisenhower Commission report related this problem particularly to children: "Television enters powerfully into the learning process of children and teaches them a set of moral and social values about violence which are inconsistent with the standards of a civilized society."[18]

At the time of our interviews in 1971, some mass communications specialists still felt that the amount of money spent by broadcasting companies on news was "scandalously small,"[19] especially as compared with what newspapers were spending. One of the specialists interviewed previously was again interviewed in 1977, and he repeated the same appraisal. He added that "if broadcasting is indeed owned by the people, then it should be used to allow the people to explore those issues that concern them." Since broadcasting is tied directly to advertising, however, entertainment requirements tend to prevail. To some extent, the increased activity of public broadcasting outlets such as the Public Broadcasting System has begun to ameliorate this problem.

Since television gives priority to entertainment, Elie Abel claims that its usefulness as an in-depth agent is limited.[20] It can, however, engage the emotions to a considerable extent. Alistair Cooke believes that among the influences affecting a child's development, television, though secondary to parents, is far ahead of school and church.[21]

According to some of our informants, cable television (CATV) represents the third revolution within the broadcasting field (the first and second being radio and television, respectively). Much of the enthusiasm for CATV is based on its potential for local broadcasting: it provides "the opportunity to explore in a more intelligent manner some of the local problems that beset the communities."[22]

CATV was created (1) to improve the reach of television communication in mountain areas and (2) to counteract the interference with signals by high buildings in the inner cities. CATV falls under the regulating jurisdiction of the Federal Communications Commission. It has improved reception by stations in mountain and local areas, especially ultra high frequency stations. In all other aspects, CATV is a separate entity, divorced from regular network programming. Some established broadcasting sources are hostile to the extension of and dominance by CATV, since it is competitive with the regular broadcast channels.

Upon re-inquiry in 1977 about CATV progress, one media specialist suggested that the hopes expressed four years earlier regarding the usefulness of CATV as an intergroup relations tool in communicating with people who could not be reached by regular broadcast channels, had not yet materialized. In general our respondents felt that once radio and television station managements are convinced that it is to their advantage to present effective subjects on improving human relations, they would make such time available.

The Use of Social Science in Intergroup Relations

Nearly all of the informants, especially those connected with organizations which themselves use social science in their programs, shared an appreciation of the importance of social science in intergroup relations. Illustrative of this emphasis are the Anti-Defamation League's five-year studies entitled *Patterns of American Prejudice* which were conducted in the 1960s at the Survey Research Center, University of California at Berkeley,[23] and the five-volume *Studies in Prejudice*, including the renowned volume, *The Authoritarian Personality*, which is generally considered a monumental achievement in social science, sponsored in the 1950s by the American Jewish Committee.[24]

The scientific procedure is employed both for analytic purposes and as a tool in social intervention. Social science facilitates program planning by making available documentation and material evidence of the need for specific social changes. The degree of group hostility present in certain situations, and the categories of people involved, can be detected through the scientific approach. As a tool in treatment, the example that comes to mind is in refuting the denials of those guilty of discriminatory practices, whether conscious or unconscious. A more important example is as an aid in convincing officials of the need to do something about existing undesirable practices, such as discrimination in executive hiring, inclusion of anti-Semitic material in religious texts and teaching materials, or the plight of the unemployed blacks.

Social science has helped stabilize expectations and establish realistic goals for action. It is used to test unexamined assumptions, such as whether education or information alone could change attitudes. Social research has the built-in potential of transforming factual findings into action. It can aid in uncovering facts which can then become the basis for action, such as the relation between insecurity and group hostility, and in clarifying the finding that discrimination can exist without prejudice, and vice versa.

The information made available through scientific research to Vatican Council II in Rome in the 1960s greatly strengthened the felt need to cleanse religious teaching materials of prejudicial references. Doubtless, social science findings had a great deal to do with the important pronouncements on Jewish-Christian relations that emanated from this assembly.

The scientific approach has also contributed to transforming general goals into specific tasks. It warns us against confusing shifts in areas of activity with changes in methodology.

Social science has revealed some special characteristics of black anti-Semitism, namely, that there is generally less anti-Semitism among blacks than among whites; that it is more evident in the economic sphere than in other areas; and, strangely, that black youth are more anti-Semitic than white youth.[25] Such findings, of course, help channel efforts to alleviate the problem.

The Authoritarian Personality has had a long-range significance in a number of areas, including that of education. Among other findings, it directed attention to the problems raised by authoritarian traits in the personality of the teacher and the educational administrator. Its great significance for the intergroup relations field lies in its demonstration that bigotry is a product of the bigot and in no sense of the appearance, speech, customs, behavior, or outlook of the victim.

The "do-it-yourself technique" in the use of social science is especially efficacious when an organization or a group guilty of discrimination—for example, executive suite—or distortion—certain religious texts—itself investigates the problem. An example is the matter of hostile references to Jews in Christian religious texts. In 1953, the Divinity School of Yale University agreed to have a study of such references made by one of its former students, a specialist in the field of Christian education. As a result of his findings, one of the denominations studied to undertake the elimination of these harmful references and did so substantially.

Social science has also been useful in diminishing discrimination in executive hiring. The scientific departments of some well-known universities conducted studies on this, and certain industries agreed to implement their results, thereby contributing to the relative success of the executive-suite discrimination program conducted by the American Jewish Committee. Similarly, the findings of the Anti-Defamation League's studies at the Survey Research Center at Berkeley, that nearly half (45 percent) of American anti-Semites have some religious basis for their prejudice, gave considerable impetus to efforts to improve Christian education.[26]

The discovery of the wide gap between actual opposition to anti-Semitism and simply "not favoring it" can become an important factor in social-intervention strategy. Change in economic indices, such as the rate of employment, has been utilized to determine the degree of success of measures employed for amelioration. One informant, a specialist in race relations, noted that after a study he made in New York City on fair contract compliance practice, the mayor issued an executive order which resulted in one thousand new jobs for blacks and Puerto Ricans in one year's time.

More than any other agency, Jewish intergroup relations agencies employ the social science methodology. One such agency has used scientifically designed surveys for more than a quarter of a century to gauge the trends of bigotry (including anti-Semitism) in America. One agency executive told of an unsuccessful attempt to set up indicators or spotters of tension by measuring the differences between majority and minority groups in specific communities in such areas as education, economic status, and health conditions. In addition, new methods are being developed for analyzing attitudes and evaluating the results of efforts to modify these attitudes.

Sociopsychological science has produced sensitivity methods in the training of teachers and intergroup relations workers. *The Authoritarian Personality* became an important factor in this training. Another trend which our informants noted was toward utilization of university personnel and facilities for long-term basic research studies, apparently because of the rising cost of research; short-term applied research studies can still be managed by the agencies themselves.

Without exception, the informants stated that social science has proved effective: it has been valuable in giving direction to programs and it is being put to greater use.

Social science is being used not just to produce change but also to give insights into social problems. Representatives of the U.S. Civil Rights Commission pointed out that their report "Racial Isolation in the Public School" (1965-1967), an important document in its day, relied largely on the findings of social science. James Coleman's study which provided data on six hundred thousand school children proved to be an invaluable scientific tool for the commission's purposes,[27] ultimately yielding information on the relationship of race to scholastic achievement and on children's aspirations and after-school achievement.

The director of a local Jewish community relations council suggested extending the use of social science in the intergroup relations field to include the findings of political science, economics, and social anthropology, as well as sociology and psychology. In the pursuit of major social change, he pointed to the need for developing a science of social engineering.

The consensus of experience in intergroup relations is that practitioners will increasingly find validation in the more controlled observations of the social scientists.[28]

Mass Action

Some private organizations concerned with intergroup relations favor mass action to effect social change. This group places very little reliance on negotiation, discussion ("jawboning"), or persuasion, even in the proverbial "velvet glove-iron hand" approach. These organizations believe that even if the mass action approach does not achieve the immediate goal, certain desirable side-benefits are likely. One side-benefit is that it draws attention to the goal, giving the public a vivid picture of the evil being castigated. Thus, even if no effect is immediately discernible, this approach can have an impact on future remedial action.

The mass action approach generally takes one or more of four forms: the mass demonstration, mass rally, mass boycott, and mass lobbying.

Mass demonstrations are organized mass picketing and marching against an offending party.

Mass rallies refer to mass meetings which are usually held at a distance from the offending group. Such meetings were organized in World War II to protest the Nazi onslaught.

Mass boycott refers to attempts to get large groups of people to desist from economic dealings with the alleged discriminating group. Such an attempt was also made during World War II with Hitler's Germany, but it failed. However, public awareness rather than economic hardship appears to be the more immediate goal. It is believed that public awareness and the annoyance inflicted on the principals will ultimately bring the desired action.

The indirect boycott approach has sometimes had a salutory effect. This procedure can best be illustrated in the area of social discrimination. It consists of (1) persuading an industrial or business establishment, or even a nonprofit organization, to refrain from using the facilities of a social club or other semipublic institution that engages in exclusionary practices based on race, religion, or ethnic origin, or of (2) refusing to meet the expenses incurred by their personnel at such institutions. Such institutions may conclude that it is in their best interests to eliminate the objectionable practice, not only because of the immediate financial loss, but also because of the potential loss of status growing out of a boycott by influential and prestigious groups. Most "actionist" intergroup relations agencies agree that this drastic approach should be used only as a last resort, after all other efforts at negotiation and persuasion have failed.

Mass lobbying refers to mass letterwriting campaigns, organization and agency pronouncements, and newspaper advertisements on behalf of a minority group. The informants generally conceded that this technique accomplishes little unless it is used in conjunction with more direct action, such as litigation, the threat of legislation, and economic boycott.

Although mass action in itself may often fail to achieve the goal sought, a well-planned action within the framework of a rational conflict situation (i.e., used as a process and not as a goal itself) can strengthen a total effort for social change, especially when combined with individualized approaches. A good current illustration is the manner in which the Soviet Union has been induced to consent to the emigration of limited numbers of Soviet Jews—mostly to Israel. Here we have a combination of mass action (demonstrations, rallies, mass boycotts, and mass lobbying) with negotiations at the highest levels (between the governments of the United States and Russia), and including the utilization of legislation bearing upon trade relations between the two countries. On the whole, however, well-structured and skillfully planned mass action has laid the foundation for the effective use of all the other procedures by bringing the dire plight of Russian Jewry to the attention of the American public and its legislators. The mass action persistently pursued has served as a dramatic attention-getting device.

Mass action during the Hitler era (even though it sometimes failed to produce even a fraction of the desired result) did help to arouse our country to the dangers of Hitlerism. In more recent years, mass action by the blacks in the 1960s (marches, rallies, sit-ins, ride-ins, and the like) in all likelihood did lay the foundation for the civil rights legislation of that era, especially the 1964, 1965, and 1968 bills.

Mass action can be dysfunctional if it is merely in the nature of "blowing off steam." When planned, directed, and synchronized with other approaches, and when its goals are clearly defined, it can be the source of constructive social change. First, it gives the wronged group a sense of participation which can serve as a source of inner strength and provide a means of overcoming feelings of frustration. Second, it brings the problem before the public. Third, political officials, policy-makers, and communal leaders are impressed by the total number and quality of the protesting group. Hence, the marshaling of public opinion, coupled with the threat of legislation or litigation, gives the group an effective leverage that can successfully alter unfair and prejudicial treatment.

There is good evidence that mass action in combination with research and individual contacts eventually resulted in the cessation of discriminatory practices in admissions to New York State's medical and dental schools (1948). The New York State System of Higher Education grew out of this achievement. It became evident that the "educational pie" had to be enlarged.[29]

Notes

1. See Chapter 12.
2. See Chapter 1, Notes.
3. Peter L. Kranz, "How Come You Don't Need Me Anymore," *Journal of Intergroup Relations* (Winter 1973): 64.
4. The McCarran-Walter Immigration Law of 1952, amended by the Immigration Act of October 3, 1965, (1) abolished national origins quotas; (2) established numerical ceilings for immigration visas on a "first-come, first-served" basis; (3) abolished restriction on persons of half-Asian parentage; (4) established new preferences in granting visas; and (5) introduced stricter "labor clearance" procedures. (From Sidney Liskofsky, "United States Immigration Policy," *American Jewish Year Book*, 1966, American Jewish Committee, p. 164.)
5. The Fair Housing, Inc., of Boston closed its doors in 1971.
6. In the fall of 1966, at UPACA's invitation, the New York Federation of Reform Synagogues, through the UAHC Joint Committee on Social Action, cosponsored a nonprofit housing corporation in East Harlem, the worst of the Negro ghettos. By spring 1968, Phase I called for plans to rehabilitate twenty-nine buildings; Phases II and III called for construction of a privately financed apartment house, rehabilitation and demolition of deteriorated buildings, as well as vest-pocket housing. (See Anita Miller, "The UPACA Story," *Dimensions* (Spring 1968): 1-4. By 1973, the Ford Foundation was contributing to UPACA. In 1974, the UAHC and Ford Foundation withdrew from the coalition, and the Urban Development Corporation took over the management of the buildings. As an antipoverty program, UPACA is considered an outstanding example of the successful relocation and tenant-orientation process. (Verified by telephone interview with Anita Miller, research associate, Ford Foundation, March 20, 1976.)
7. Charles H. Stember, et al., *Jews in the Mind of America* (New York: Basic Books, 1966), p. 138.
8. Richard C. Rothschild, "Footprints of the Trojan Horse," Citizenship Educational Service, Inc., 1940, and "The American Jewish Committee's Fight Against

Anti-Semitism—1939-1950" (New York: Report to the American Jewish Committee).

9. For further elaboration of these approaches (answering charges and quarantine), see S. Andhil Fineberg, "Deflating the Professional Bigot," American Jewish Committee, February 1967, pp. 1-12; S. Andhil Fineberg, *Overcoming Anti-Semitism* (New York: Harper and Brothers, 1943), pp. 1-225; S. Andhil Fineberg, "Checkmate for Rabble-Rousers," *Commentary* (September 1946): 220-26; Richard C. Rothschild, "Are American Jews Falling into the Nazi Trap?" *Contemporary Jewish Record* 3, no. 1 (January-February 1940): 9-17.

10. Jewish Defense League, Aim and Purpose: "Dedicated to the Six Million with Our Pledge: NEVER AGAIN!" Means of operation through education, physical defense and political power ("The Jewish Defense League: Aims and Purposes," New York, Jewish Defense League, p. 2).

11. John Slawson, "How Funny Can Bigotry Be?," *Educational Broadcasting Review* (April 1972): Columbus, Ohio, 79-82. Also see John Slawson, "Intergroup Relations in Social Work Education," Council on Social Work Education, New York, January 31, 1958, p. 110.

12. "T.V. Notes: Who Watches Even More T.V. Than Americans?," Les Brown, *The New York Times*, June 29, 1975.

13. Slawson, "How Funny Can Bigotry Be?," pp. 79-82

14. Ibid., p. 80.

15. George Gerbner and Larry Gross, "The Scary World of T.V.'s Heavy Viewer," *Psychology Today* (April 1976): 89.

16. *Christian Science Monitor*, April 20, 1978.

17. Alistair Cooke, "What T.V. Is Doing to America," *U.S. News & World Report* (April 15, 1974).

18. Milton S. Eisenhower, chairman, National Commission on Causes and Prevention of Violence, "To Establish Justice, to Insure Domestic Tranquility," 1969, pp. 190-210.

19. Morton Yarmon, director, Public Information and Interpretation, American Jewish Committee.

20. Elie Abel, dean, Columbia University School of Journalism, American Jewish Committee meeting, April 21, 1975.

21. Cooke, "What T.V. Is Doing to America."

22. Interview with Morton Yarmon.

23. Charles Y. Glock and Rodney Stark, *Christian Beliefs and Anti-Semitism* (New York: Harper and Row, 1966). Charles Y. Glock, et al., *The Apathetic Majority: A Study Based on Public Responses to the Eichmann Trial* (New York: Harper and Row, 1966). Charles Y. Glock and Ellen Siegelman, eds., *Prejudice U.S.A.* (New York: F. A. Praeger, 1969).

24. T. W. Adorno, et al., *Studies in Prejudice* (New York: Harper Brothers, 1950–1951). *The Authoritarian Personality* is listed as one of sixty-two social research contributions that have made major advances in the twentieth century. See Karl W. Deutsch, John R. Platt, and Dieter Senghass, "Major Advances in Social Science since 1900: An Analysis of Conditions and Effects of Creativity," Mental Health Research Institute, University of Michigan, May 1970.

25. "Attitudes of the American Public Toward Israel and American Jews: The Yankelovich Findings," American Jewish Committee, December 1974; Supplement, April 1975.

26. Oscar Cohen, "Implications of the Five-Year Studies on Patterns of American Prejudice," Anti-Defamation League of B'nai B'rith, New York, November 1969, p. 5.

27. James S. Coleman, et al., "Report on Equality of Educational Opportunity," Washington, D.C., U.S. Office of Education, July 1966.

28. Slawson, "Intergroup Relations in Social Work Education," p. 112.

29. This subject is treated more fully in Chapter 8.

10

Some Areas of Concern
in Intergroup Relations

From one point of view, the work of intergroup relations agencies can be re-garded as an effort to reduce the social distance between groups—in other words, to enable them to live and to work together, to accept each other without the bitter conflicts which have so long been associated with dif-ferences in race, religion, or ethnicity.

The effectiveness of many of the programs developed over the decades has been evaluated by attitude studies and surveys in which social distance is measured by questions such as:

"Would you live next door to a _____ (Negro? Jew? Catholic?)"

"Would you work alongside a _____?"

The results were used to chart the progress toward greater intergroup ac-ceptance.

The domestic programs of intergroup relations agencies have always been geared to the reduction and elimination of bigotry and discrimination. In one sense, however, they regarded discrimination in the various areas of social living as an extension of prejudice or bigotry. The willingness to live together as neighbors seemed to indicate a greater acceptance of "difference" than the willingness to work together. Social distance was the yardstick by which the degree of prejudice and, by implication, the success of ameliora-tive measures were gauged. The corollary of this orientation was to regard housing, education, employment, and public accommodation as those areas of social life in which prejudice manifested itself. The goal was to reduce prejudice and prejudiced behavior (discrimination) wherever they existed. It was hoped that this goal could be achieved through education or persuasion or, failing that, through sanctions and law.

The last two or three decades have seen a major shift in goals. Essentially, programs designed to change attitudes have been deemphasized, and in-creased attention has been devoted to the social facts of deprivation, the dis-crimination to which disadvantaged minorities in our society were sub-jected. The elimination of discrimination in housing and employment and of segregated education, and free access to public accommodations, have now become targets in and of themselves. The achievement of these goals has become a central aim of intergroup relations agency activity. While attitudes and bigotry continue to form an important element of programs and, most recently, have regained something of their former status, it is the vital areas of social living that concern the disadvantaged minorities. They demand equal opportunities in employment and education, and the right to live where they choose.

With this later emphasis in mind, in the following three sections we present a brief survey of intergroup relations activity in housing, education, and employment, easily the most important "areas of social concern."

Schools and Integration

At the time of our interviews, concepts of school integration varied greatly. Some viewed it as a gradual developmental process (even allowing for temporary separateness as a transitional stage), while others thought we should proceed directly to implement the legal mandate regardless of the degree of resistance, backlash, or evasion. With respect to integration as an ultimate goal, however, there was practically no disagreement among our informants.

One informant made the interesting point that the inclusion of groups has to come about "by design," just as their exclusion was "by design." Two often-heard opposite views were: "Let's have quality education—integration will follow," and "You cannot have quality education until you have initiated the process of integration." One of our most prominent black civil rights leaders asserted that integration has never really been tried in the schools, for the requisite social engineering and long-range planning have been avoided. The informants considered integration in housing central to the entire problem. Especially in the North, it was basic to public education problems (the matter of de facto segregated schools) as well as employment with respect to the need for job-linked housing.

The public agency groups, especially those involved with compliance (civil rights divisions of federal law enforcement organizations), insisted on immediate and vigorous implementation of the law. Black professionals were more optimistic of positive results ultimately than were their white colleagues. The veteran black leader A. Philip Randolph dramatically portrayed the situation as follows: "People don't fight each other because they hate each other, but they hate each other because they fight each other."

The proponents of busing asserted that if busing is found necessary to help achieve integration (desegregation in the first instance), then it may be necessary to look upon integration as a (regional) interschool system matter rather than as an intraschool situation. A representative of a Catholic urban affairs group was convinced that the problem of the 75 percent black and

Puerto Rican student body in many schools of Manhattan could be solved by including the nearby areas of New Jersey in an interschool system, i.e., a regional approach. The 1974 Supreme Court decision reversing a lower court ruling which had permitted Detroit to include its suburbs in an area-wide desegregation plan, and the more recent (December 1976) ruling vacating a finding of illegal discrimination against both blacks and Mexican-Americans in the Austin, Texas, public schools, have jeopardized similar school integration programs in other urban centers.

Nevertheless, the lower courts have so far insisted that desegregation must continue and that cities must find ways to integrate their school systems. Where de jure segregation can be demonstrated, the courts have generally ruled that the responsibility for desegregation falls upon the communities where such segregation exists. Decisions have varied, however, with the special circumstances obtaining in the communities under scrutiny. This has sometimes given rise to varying interpretations of specific rulings. Perhaps more importantly, the problem of adequate enforcement still remains to be solved.

At the time of our interviews we were reminded that in Chicago for some time past three additional blocks have been added to the ghetto every week. A somewhat similar situation prevails in Washington with its 93 percent black school population. Some suggested that this matter has to be handled on an areawide basis, in this instance including Chevy Chase, Bethesda, and other suburbs in the greater Washington area.

Some Catholic educational leaders have taken a courageous stand in preventing their parochial schools from serving as an avenue of escape from the desegregation process. One of these officials asserted that from his viewpoint the bus ride itself is a socializing experience for the children; it is the parents who constitute the problem.

In the educational process in America, the concern is not only with the acquisition of skills but also with attitudes. One foundation executive (white) told us: "Unless he [the youngster] is educated about the ways of the world not alone in arithmetic and reading but about different people in a city like New York, when he is 15 or 16 and even younger he may go off and educate himself in the East Village."[1]

Our hope is ultimately with the child. Diversity of educational experience for our children is essential to a well-ordered society: "Our children must not be excluded from an experience to be educated in an environment representative of diversity—racial, ethnic, and religious—that characterizes American society."

A number of our black informants maintained that upgrading the quality of education for inner-city children in our public schools would not only help solve the busing problem, but would also give the black parent the choice between busing his child or keeping him in his neighborhood school.

In spite of some recent statistics on desegregation in the South made available by the HEW,[2] the full implementation of a desegregation policy, especially as a basis for integration, still represents a formidable task. Thus, a not inconsiderable number of our informants regarded the matter as well-nigh insoluble.

The North poses an even more serious problem than the South. In the South, segregation, being of de jure[3] origin, is simpler and more directly dealt with than in the North. There segregation is in most instances a de facto[4] product, the result of presumably "unavoidable" or "unplanned" factors such as minority residential concentrations.[5] In such cases, the malady is woven into the fabric of the urban condition itself. In the South, as a matter of fact, housing—the core of the North's desegregation problem—is a less important factor because of the traditional proximity of white and black homes. As for busing, the South has had a great deal of experience with this practice because of its form of rigid segregation policies.

We are suffering from the deep-seated, widespread social illness of group prejudice. Again, quoting from an interview with A. Philip Randolph:

Prejudice, whether against race, religion or national origin is a dangerous social phenomenon. To advocate the inferiority of any people is to assume that they are not entitled to live as decent human beings. It is this notorious doctrine of racial inferiority which was the essence of the Third Reich under Adolph Hitler. As a result of this doctrine, Europe was drenched in rivers of blood and tears and became the scene of mountains of corpses and devastated cities.

Built upon these prejudices is the fear of being inundated, of lowering the quality of education, of racial intermarriage, of the decline of property values, of the despoilment of neighborhoods. Our ghettos, our slums, our drug cultures, the devastated regions of our central cities are testimony to the reality of some of these fears and anticipations of danger. But this reality has been and will continue to be the consequence of what Robert Merton has called our self-fulfilling prophecies—we create the conditions that we predict will occur. "He will not learn, therefore it is a waste of time to teach him." "He will pollute the neighborhood, therefore I will not let him into my neighborhood and thus force him to remain in the ghetto, regardless of what the laws say." He does not learn; he is kept out of our neighborhoods; he stays in the ghetto, comparatively uneducated and unskilled. And so his neighborhood suffers from intensified "social pollution."

A large number of our informants, black and white, believed that for the most part, the measures instituted to implement the 1954 U.S. Supreme Court decision—*Brown* v. *Board of Education of Topeka*—and the subsequent civil rights legislation relating to the schools, can achieve at best a degree of ritualistic, legalistic compliance. Only a great deal of sociopsychological input can help bring about the desired change. Such an overall approach should prevent resegregation and gradually transform the achieved desegregation (an administrative phenomenon) into integration—a sociopsychological manifestation incorporating a value system which sustains universal acceptance of differences in race, color, ethnic background, and religion on a plane of human equality. This would be in harmony with the declared and implied commitments embodied in the Declaration of Independence and other American documents of freedom.

Yet, in the South as well as in the North, both at the time of the interviews and subsequently, white children in some areas were transferring to private schools, a move in the direction of resegregation. The resegregation of desegregated areas was and is by no means an unusual occurrence. A district where white children are in the minority must be regarded as an unstable one, for it is a likely candidate for resegregation. One of our informants, an HEW official, stated that if the school board insists that the situation be stabilized, it should shoulder the responsibility for rezoning the area to maximize the continuance of desegregation. Incidentally, this same official, when queried with respect to desegregation, asked—"Is it fair to take away the one thing that black kids in the school have—and that is black teachers with whom they can identify?"

All informants supported the necessity for a legal framework, but, except for the lawyers among them, practically none felt that the law alone and its implementation would accomplish an effective and harmonious transition from separation to union. Translated into social theory, the basic ingredients of a successful "contact" experience were lacking in the usual implementation of legal provisions. Instead, the reaction generally contained the elements of "black rage and white fear" to which Bayard Rustin has alluded.[6] The desegregation procedures reported on almost invariably lacked the requisite components for constructive and satisfying contact. Contact theory, as developed by Gordon Allport and elaborated by Blalock and others,[7] calls for certain conditions as necessary for a successful outcome, and school and housing desegregation efforts involve essentially a "contact" experience.

Successful conflict-free contact, as noted elsewhere,[8] generally presupposes such factors as equality or at least similarity of status, similarity of interests, and common goals sanctioned by institutional supports (e.g., law, custom and/or local mores).[9] Of course, the contact process itself should be carried on within a voluntary framework. Clearly, not all of these criteria can generally be met in any given case of the contact involved in busing. At most, one can hope that as many as possible are taken account of in the social engineering involved in such desegregation procedures.

One essential point which contact theorists tend to overlook is that contact, in addition to the usual criteria set forth, must also be entered into voluntarily—or at the very least not be forced or involuntary. Obviously, this requirement introduces complications into the busing procedures. To begin with, more than one party is involved in a contact experience, and what may be voluntary for one may be involuntary or even forced for the other. The implicit recognition of this factor by community workers and educators led to the demand for "adequate preparation" for the busing experience.

Even so, the failure to recognize the source of some of the objections to busing inevitably led to inadequate preparation and to the imposition of busing before consent or, at the very least, removal of active opposition had been obtained. The legitimate fears of some parents that their children are being subjected to difficult adjustment problems, and possibly even to violence, must of course be dealt with.

These difficulties lie behind the call for adequate preparation; it involves the development of techniques by the community and the educational system to win the consent of the community. That desegregation can be beneficial to both white and black children is supported by the limited evidence bearing upon the question. Some confusion arises in this area because the desiderata are not always made clear. There is no single unified goal: school achievement, after-school achievement, improvement of black-white relationships, and reduction of prejudice or conflict are all different goals. The desegregation experience is itself a complex phenomenon; busing is only one element, a part of a large social transformation. Hence, the cause-and-effect relationship is not simply a one-to-one situation.

The entire busing controversy is essentially a spurious one. Busing has long been an accepted part of the school life of American children. The consolidation of rural schools is a normal procedure for upgrading the education available to country children, even though it entails extensive and sometimes involuntary busing of vast numbers of children. And parents of children in private schools have never been known to object to busing.

The fact is that the controversy over busing is not, nor has it ever been, what it purports to be. It actually is a controversy over the integration of schools with all that this entails, either in reality or in the minds of parents. Much of the opposition to busing, whatever its form (whether expressed in verbal terms, physical violence, or white flight to the suburbs), in fact reflects resistance to integration, or at the very least resistance to court- or government-imposed desegregation.

We must not commit ourselves to any single process of effecting desegregation, whether busing or any other device. What is fundamental is that we be clear as to our goal and then select the method or methods that will best achieve it by determined and persistent effort. That goal is to make people recognize that forced segregation on the basis of race, ethnicity, or religion is an obscenity, an evil, that it is contrary to the democratic commitment, that it is incompatible with human dignity. When we attack a procedure such as busing, we cannot be sure whether we really accept this goal, whether we are not still segregationists at heart, or whether, in pointing to the defects and shortcomings of busing, we are not opposing desegregation in any form or simply are being unconcerned about it.

Once we establish our goal, we can experiment with various approaches, but we cannot permit the evil to continue. The dispute about the virtues and defects of busing should be related to the requirements of each specific situation within the overarching commitment to the eradication of segregation itself.

As noted previously, before busing is instituted adequate planning is essential, all principal groups in the community must be sufficiently represented in the planning process, and a strategy to support the adopted plan must be developed. For example, it should be obvious that high school children are far better candidates for busing than first graders, for whom long-distance travel is more difficult. A desegregation plan which entails busing should include elements contributing to quality education, such as reduction in class size, essential curriculum changes, and addition of specialists. Moreover, before a busing plan is launched, there could be visits to each other's schools, exchanges of teachers, and the like.

Social science cannot help us here. This matter lies in the realm of human values. Social science was not employed in the drafting of one of the greatest documents of all time, the Declaration of Independence in 1776. However, social science can be employed (though with extreme caution) to tell us whether a procedure works or does not work, and perhaps to what degree. The debate among social scientists about the effectiveness or harm of busing is being carried on in an environment of confused values.

If we are really determined to destroy segregation in our schools, then we may have to direct our attention to desegregating our residential centers—the factor underlying school segregation. If our goal is clear and our commitment irrevocable, we will determine what conditions are necessary for busing to work. We should keep in mind that 47 percent of our school children are bused daily and that this busing is not related to color balance; only 3.6 percent are bused for the purpose of desegregation.[10] Busing, therefore, is not really responsible for depriving a child of the benefits of the "neighborhood school." However, there is no doubt that in certain situations and for certain children busing for color balance alone may not prove advisable.

Those who attack busing in general have the responsibility of proposing other methods of desegregation if they are committed to the elimination of segregation. If busing is to be used, care must be taken to avoid the harmful factors that are found to exist. Experimentation, even in a single community, under controlled conditions is imperative if we want to find out what works and what does not.

The courts should not be the agency that determines what is beneficial and what is harmful. This is not a legal matter; it is within the province of the community organizer. Yet, without legal redress, without the courts, our civil rights would indeed be in a pitiful state. When people will not act out of human consideration, the law must step in. And so the courts have become the bulwark of our democratic process; without their determined stand on the matter of school desegregation, very little progress indeed would have been achieved.

Resistance to busing is sometimes based on the incidents of violence between black and white children. But resistance must be overcome if busing is to become an accepted method of achieving school integration. This task, as the Civil Rights Commission never tires of pointing out, is one for community officials, school boards and administrators, teachers, and parents.

About the only element most of the desegregation programs thus far launched share is the sanction of law—federal, though not necessarily local. Social engineering aimed at success has not been much in evidence.

The factor of equality of status is a troublesome one, since it can rarely be met in the absence of a selective mix. In fact, according to the Coleman studies, the quality of the majority peer status in the classroom is probably the single most important factor in the school experience motivating members of the disadvantaged minority group to greater achievement.[11] Recently, this view has been modified somewhat.[12]

There is also the problem of a "forced" or even "induced" versus a "voluntary" desegregation-integration process. Thus far, busing has often been accompanied by a lack of receptivity, or even by hostility, on the part of the "host group" toward the "visitor group." Such negativism is, of course, inimical to a healthy "contact condition"; more frequently than not, it results in feelings of alienation on the part of the visitor group. Furthermore, as noted previously, a positive "contact" experience cannot be achieved without appropriate preparation preceding the initiation of the busing, as in the desegregation program at Berkeley, California, in 1968.[13] There busing was instituted only after months of preparation, involving a cross-section of leadership in the initial planning as well as in the decision-making process.

In general, although "white flight" and flareups of racial violence have induced some communities (Berkeley among them) to suspend busing, studies by the University of Michigan (1976) and the U.S. Commission on Civil Rights point toward more positive results in most communities throughout the nation. The Michigan study of 125 of the largest cities found no significant impact on white residential patterns. The Civil Rights Commission reported in 1976 that 82 percent of desegregation efforts proceeded smoothly; 90 percent of the schools were rated as high or higher in quality after desegregation. Individual success stories such as Denver,[14] where busing has proceeded quite smoothly, can be cited as counterbalancing the Boston experience. They point up the urgent need for further study of the social factors that promise success in a given community, as against difficulties and even failure in another, since it is generally accepted that desegregation is the ultimate goal.

In the Armor-Pettigrew controversy on the effects of busing, an important distinction was made between "induced integration" and "natural integration."[15] The implication of this distinction is obvious. Armor summed up by stating that even though his findings did not generally show a positive achievement, he did not mean to imply that achievement could not be effected. He mentioned some successful outcomes under a program approximating a "voluntary" situation.[16]

Pettigrew, arguing that Armor had misrepresented Allport's position on "contact," contended that "contact" as a basis for successful busing would have to be achieved under the particular conditions specified by Allport and others. Furthermore, he argued, achievement by black and white children in desegregated schools is generally higher when certain conditions, such as equal access to school resources and classroom, not just desegregation, are met.

The earlier part of this chapter mentioned the fears engendered by desegregation programs, especially those involving extensive busing. In this connection, a substantial proportion of our informants expressed an interest in the formerly much-discussed benign quota approach. This approach, as we stated earlier,[17] differs from the more recent discussion of the "quota" as a preferential device to achieve proportional representation of a minority group in the shop, university, or corporation. This issue has been beclouded by much rhetoric and misunderstanding.[18]

Built into this "therapeutic" procedure is the element of "gradualism." This gradualism, however, is not identical to the "quotas" used as a delaying device in years gone by. That time has passed. We now have a framework combining both law and altered mores as a basis for the utilization of the benign quota process in the furtherance of equality. One professional executive (a white) of a national agency stated bluntly, "Without the benign quota approach we will never achieve integration."[19]

And yet, despite all the safeguards and the exercise of the best wisdom available, as well as an undeviating commitment to the goal of integration, one of our most prominent black scholar-activists came up with this odd observation: "It is a snare and a delusion to put all of the educational eggs in one basket [desegregation]."

Many of our professional informants, as well as an increasing number of knowledgeable and well-meaning citizens, shared the view that "forced integration" without the protective devices discussed above, such as conditions created for constructive contact, frequently results in school disruptions (especially in high schools) and even in "resegregation," the very condition we desire to avoid.

If we fail to create an environment of "voluntarism" for the desegregation process, we may not be able to realize the potential inherent in the 1954 *Brown* v. *Kansas* decision. To achieve this potential, much greater study of the powers, opportunities, and responsibilities of the neighborhood will be required.

Is integration still our basic objective, or are we beginning to accept some form of separation? Certainly there no longer is unanimity about integration, and it is probable that most people have become aware of the need to redefine, or to define more precisely, what we mean by integration. The idea of freedom of movement, freedom of association, and freedom of choice within a pluralistic society is much more widely accepted now than the old idea of assimilation of minorities into the majority. The goal of our culture is now seen as interaction on an egalitarian basis among a number of groups, along with the freedom of mobility and choice of the individual within those groups. If the individual wishes to make choices outside his "tribe," so to speak, he should be free to do so.

According to one of our more experienced community relations workers (a white), the head of a privately supported research agency:

The integrated pattern as we have traditionally thought of it has proved so hard to attain; the obstacles to it are so great; a considerable amount of disenchantment has set in. From that viewpoint, we are not talking about anything real—we'd better focus on the real needs which are *quality* education, decent housing. In Washington, D.C., which is predominantly now a black city with a school system 97 percent or 98 percent black, it makes very little sense to expend all your efforts on trying to achieve integration within that pattern. *Quality* education in Washington is indeed what you have to be concerned about—largely within the framework of black schools. Let me say I don't abandon the goal of integration, properly defined. I think given a chance to work, it works. I think integration is a more complex process than was once rather naively thought. We have had this sort of infiltration, one by one, into the mainstream from the minority groups, but they are no longer willing to settle for that kind of conferring of honorary whitehood on individuals. Integration, properly defined, still has got to be what we hope for.

There is, of course, the distinction between integration and desegregation. One of our informants discussed this distinction as follows:

The distinction ought to be made. It isn't often done. Desegregation is really a technical process—a question of *spatial* location of people. This may or may not mean integration in the sense of people relating as equals, on the basis of common interests across racial or other lines. Integration is a matter of *mutual acceptance* and *respect*—all those things that we used to talk about a great deal but don't say much about anymore.

But it doesn't mean that everybody is supposed to be homogenized into the majority culture. I think the styles of dress among blacks, hairstyles, etc., are one way of
saying symbolically that blacks no longer find it necessary to be imitation whites in
order to move freely in the society.

An old-time prominent communal worker stated:

Why shouldn't it become all black, if it wants to be all black? I don't see anything
wrong with that.

I think that the concept of pluralism is a goal, but I think that may take the form of
being mixed in the sense of being integrated in some communities—in housing terms
and in some occupations, employment terms. It may take the form of being parallel—
highly concentrated groupings of people around certain occupations in certain
neighborhoods. As long as there is a civic rapproachment, a system of exchanging
values and making decisions that are compatible with the other interests—I don't
have any problems with that. I haven't had any problems with the Polish neighborhood. They never bothered me. I don't think there is anything wrong with a *black
school*. I do not believe that black children have to have white children around them
to learn.

I don't think it's necessary to bus kids to achieve good performance. I am not optimistic about all those systems.

At the time of the 1954 Supreme Court decision, most intergroup professionals were rather naive about the process of school desegregation. At the
time of our interviews, the view of school integration as a rather simple,
routine process was beginning to be questioned. Integration had turned out
to be a much more complex process than was once thought; the principle
itself was sound enough, but the specifics of its implementation had not
been given sufficient thought.

Since that time, the courts and American public opinion appear to have
been drawing further and further apart—not in terms of the goal but with
respect to its implementation. The courts tend to be faithful to the letter of
the law, yet a Gallup Poll in 1975 showed 72 percent of the public still opposed to busing.[20] The growing opposition to busing and other forms of
mandatory desegregation has taken the form of a backlash, although the
long-range objective of desegregation is supported in principle. The quality
of the educational program, the relevance of its content, and special emphases on nurturing specific talents were the educational objectives stressed
in our interviews.

The then assistant commissioner in charge of HEW's Program for the Disadvantaged (a black) was convinced that the diversification of the schools
(mostly junior and senior high schools) in larger urban centers on the basis
of meeting specific talent needs, such as technology, art, music, or aeronautics, would serve the dual objectives of quality education and school desegregation. This specialist on the needs of the disadvantaged student main-

tained that the parent who knows his child to be art-oriented, for instance, would tend to send him to a school whose curriculum, in addition to general subject matter, emphasized art. Attention to racial composition of the student body might thus be subordinated to the opportunity of meeting talent needs. Such schools might be considered "magnet" schools.

Hence, in addition to quality and relevance, the opportunities afforded for the development of talent might outweigh the interracial and interethnic factors. When a mother discovers that her child loves the violin but she cannot afford to buy one, she may choose a school that will make an instrument available to the youngster and teach him to play over one whose primary concern is with racial, ethnic, and religious differences.

The Bronx High School of Science in New York City is a fairly integrated school. Those with a proclivity for science aspire to go there and do; skin color has ceased to be a factor.[21] Of course, parents must be familiar with their children's abilities and interests, and be motivated by their needs.

Another approach to the utilization of classroom educational experience for harmonious intergroup relations is joint participation in exploratory ventures. A good example of this approach is the transformation of the Woodrow Wilson Vocational High School in New York City from an underutilized "dead-end" facility, with only a 30 percent student attendance, to the dynamic August Martin High School, with excellent attendance record and good relationships between the different groups, both racial and ethnic, in the student body. Woodrow Wilson High School had been called a dumping ground for youngsters whose achievement levels were rather low and whose aspiration was even lower.

Taking advantage of the school's proximity to the John F. Kennedy Airport, in 1971 it was decided to orient the school toward aeronautics, with emphasis on careers in air transport. This was done under the auspices of a knowledgeable Advisory Commission composed of aviation specialists, educators, labor representatives, and community workers. The imagination of the children was captured. Of course, this interest was only one aspect of the curriculum, but much of the subject matter was built around it. Lessons in geography and geology are given over the air. Attendance rose from 30 to 90 percent. The name of the restructured school was changed to August Martin High School, after a black pilot who was killed while on a mercy mission to Nigeria.

In spite of the fact that the black-white ratio is 90-10, the relationship between the two groups is reported as satisfactory. Ninety percent attendance is high for any school in the city. The principal of the school summed up the spirit of the students, both black and white, as well as of the teachers and the community people as "a fantastic kind of dynamism that pervades the entire Jamaica area," the site of the school. Of course, larger school systems would have greater opportunities for developing specialized talent facilities than smaller ones.

Another recommendation by one of our informants was that schools in the ghetto could perform a useful service if they were "lighted schools"—known to be open schools—rendering year-round, day and evening service in educational centers for parents as well as children.

Also highly recommended was the idea of an "educational park" situated on the outskirts of congested areas, even crossing political boundaries. Like all other institutions, ghetto schools are an extension of the culture that surrounds them. The impact of the ghetto on the school is generally negative. The school in the "educational park" can act as a wholesome influence on the ghetto, providing parents participate in the school situation and thereby carry the school influence to the neighborhood. Thus, the school would be influencing the home situation instead of the home situation further damaging the school.

On another level, cognitive growth was emphasized as an essential by the HEW official concerned with the Program for the Disadvantaged. Teachers, he said, should be "thoroughly schooled in some of the new thinking, in terms of cognitive development." The children, of course, do need "love and affection and social acceptance." But they need much more than that; they also need some "in-depth" approaches which tend to develop that life of the mind, the thinking process, and not just to obtain information.

One Mexican-American specialist (a Chicano) in the Department of Justice (Community Relations Service) emphasized the irrelevancy of the contemporary educational system to the needs of Mexican-Americans. At the time of the interview, the Chicano dropout rate was 80 percent nationally and their educational attainment level stood at grade 7.1. Even in a minority-controlled Chicano school system, he pointed out, the entire school board may be Mexican-American, but the superintendent is likely to be "Anglo." In one situation, Chicanos were being tracked into vocational training through testing that was not relevant to their own environment. As a result, many of them were tracked into classes for the mentally retarded. Such a tracking system must inevitably damage students. If they are labeled underachievers, it is usually because of a difference in value system, and not because of inferior mental capacity, according to this Chicano specialist. Another alleged shortcoming of the educational system was that, by and large, teachers were not bicultural—and certainly not bilingual. This lack makes communication between them and their Mexican-American students much more difficult.

One aspect of school desegregation which is often overlooked concerns the benefits accruing to majority group children from their exposure to children from other backgrounds and cultures—in other words from a broadening of their horizons. A study made under the direction of Alice Miel,[22] sponsored by the American Jewish Committee in 1967, glaringly revealed the deprivations suffered by children living in the suburbs. The open spaces, greenery, and modern school buildings cannot compensate for the impairment in personality development, the product of a life spent among people of the same color, life-style, and economic status: "communities like New Village do have a host of advantages...but in one aspect of their education suburban children are disadvantaged...there is little in their education, formal or other wise, to familiarize them with the rich diversity of American life." The basic differences among people are "fenced out." How well are these children prepared for functioning in a multicultural society?[23]

Employment

Employment and employment wages are basic to the social existence of most people, but for many years America's minority groups have suffered severe discrimination in this economic area. Obviously, then, the long struggle for fair employment practices in industry and trade, as well as within government itself, has been given priority in the programs of most intergroup relations agencies. For that matter, the struggle to eliminate discrimination in employment was well established long before the intergroup relations agencies themselves were formed. Consequently, it is natural that the first victories won against discriminatory practices in general included the specific prohibitions against discrimination in employment set forth in the executive orders of the Roosevelt era (Executive Order 8802 and subsequent orders).

Like housing, employment reflects the emphases of various agency programs on fair and/or full employment. By and large, as we noted previously, intergroup agencies have shifted the focus of their activities to governmental policies which would provide full employment. The assumption underlying this change in emphasis was that fair employment would inevitably be associated with a sufficiency of jobs for all.

Of course, this shift does not diminish the continuous concern of intergroup agencies with fair employment and the struggle to eliminate all forms of discrimination in employment. The stark inequality in income between nonwhite and white workers is still with us: "Black income per capita remains less than three-fifths of white income...black unemployment at around 14 percent, twice the rate for whites."[24] Thirty-one percent of the nation's black population remain below the poverty level, more than three times the comparable white proportion of 9 percent.[25]

Similarly, in 1974 the median income of families of Spanish origin was considerably below the U.S. white median income, to the extent of 71.6 percent.[26] The unemployment rates for workers of Spanish origin were also significantly higher than the general rate. In 1975, 13.1 percent of Hispanic male workers were out of work.[27] Moreover, a considerable number of workers have given up the search for jobs altogether. This "discouraged" group, which in 1975 totaled 1.15 million, was made up largely of women, who accounted for two-thirds of the total. Teenagers and elderly men, together with women, made up 85 percent of these discouraged workers.[28]

This discouragement is not a "problem connected solely with economic downturn. For minorities and women in particular, it is a constant problem that simply spreads and intensifies during recessions."[29] Such differential impact puts this development squarely within the area of intergroup relations concern.

A somewhat modified assessment of the effects of prosperity and recession on the position of blacks in American society was made by Reynolds Farley in an article in the *American Sociological Review*. He concludes

that the gains of the 1960s were not solely attributable to the prosperity of that decade, since racial differences in status narrowed in the 1970s as they did in the previous decade.... Racial differences in the occupation of employed workers continue to decline. The income gap separating black and white families has remained constant, but this is largely a consequence of the sharp rise in female-headed families among blacks. Indexes describing the income of specific types of families or the earnings of individuals generally reveal that racial differences moderated during the early years of the 1970s.... However, not all indicators show improvement. Employment opportunities are apparently severely limited for black men. The very high rates of unemployment and non-participation in the labor force suggest that numerous young blacks experience great difficulty in launching careers.[30]

Illustrative of the agencies' shift to a concern with both full and fair employment is the appearance in March 1976 of Rabbi A. James Rudin of the American Jewish Committee before the Equal Opportunities Subcommittee of the Housing Committee on Education and Labor. Drawing on the religious traditions of Judaism and the basic principles of American democracy, he stated

that the mass unemployment we are currently experiencing is fraught with dangers to our society. Unemployment creates intergroup tensions between races, sexes, religious and ethnic groups. Mass unemployment has the potential to foment hostility among various population groups...polarization sets in among our people, those who have jobs vs. those who are without work.[31]

A similar shift of emphasis to *both* fair and full employment was evident among black intergroup professionals. In our recent interview (December 1976) with Ernest Green, then executive director of RTP (Recruitment Training Program, Inc.),[32] he stressed that without economic recovery and full employment there could be no adequate solution of the black unemployment problem, even though, as always, minorities were affected by discrimination as well as by the general state of the economy.

General conditions are that unemployment and the present recession have proved to be harder on minorities in general and blacks in particular.... The problem with this past recession is that it seems to have eroded the gains that were made during the late sixties. . . . I think the basic problem is the state of the economy. . . the inability of the economy to absorb all of the workers that are out there.

More significant from the intergroup relations point of view is the fact that recessions inevitably hit the poor (particularly the black and Hispanic minorities) harder than other groups in the population. The 1974-1975 recession "sharply aggravated the longstanding employment problems of minorities and women and directly undermined the affirmative action efforts of the past decade."[33] Moreover, the technological structure of our economy is such that the unskilled, and more particularly the youth, are the first to be laid off. Thus, while the unemployment rate for white workers in the nation in 1975 stood at about 7.5 percent, the rate for blacks was 13.9 percent, or even higher. At that time the Urban League estimated the unemployment rate for blacks to be even higher—for adults, at three times the white rate, and for black teenagers, at 65 percent or four times the rate of white teenagers.

It is painfully clear that unless remedies are found (e.g., vastly increased training facilities to prepare the youth for skilled jobs), unemployed, unskilled young people, who are predominantly blacks, Hispanics, and other minorities, will continue to clutter the market. And we can look forward with some foreboding to a maladjusted young adult population and the attendant increase in crimes against persons and property. Interracial and intergroup friction generally is also bound to follow in the wake of joblessness and restricted economic opportunities.

Diverse groups seem more willing to work next to each other in shops and factories, but living together in the same apartment house or neighborhood, or having "their" children go to the same school with children of other groups, remain more difficult problems. However, if the present job scarcity continues and training facilities are not measurably increased, we may again have the same low levels of integration in the employment area which now obtain in our homes, neighborhoods, and schools.

As Herrington Bryce, director of research for the Joint Center of Political Studies, a black think tank, has put it: "The greatest challenge which the next Administration will face. . .will be to bring the black unemployment rate to a low and equitable level." Essentially, this involves dealing with

insufficient education that keeps blacks in unskilled occupations most vulnerable to layoffs and technological change; the large numbers of women and teenagers in the black labor force. . .and the fact that 58 percent of blacks as compared to only 26 percent of whites, live in central cities where unemployment is high and chronic.[34]

In the matter of minority employment, four factors stood out in the interviews: (1) manpower training needs, (2) the relationship of housing to employment, (3) the seniority aspect in relation to layoffs, and (4) the general concern about the destructive consequences of unemployment for minorities. All these factors are discussed at some length in the sections below dealing with poverty, affirmative action, and housing.

One serious attempt to meet the training problem is the National Urban League's Manpower Training Program, one of the largest training programs in the country for the past ten years. In 1970, the League received a $10 million government grant for this purpose—25 percent of the total federal on-the-job training program. More recently, the National Urban League was awarded three contracts totaling $7 million for their LEAP (Labor Education Advancement Programs) designed to recruit and train minority workers. Of this sum, $5.7 million was designated for the outreach program.[35] The Urban League does not itself conduct the training program. It assists employers in developing their own on-the-job programs and subcontracts this responsibility. The League follows the trainee through the training process; participating employers are subsidized. In effect, the government contracts with the Urban League and the League subcontracts.

In June 1970, the State Employment Service offices acted as manpower centers all over the United States; at that time, there were four thousand such centers nationwide. Since 1973, with the passage of the Comprehensive Employment and Training Act, grants for manpower programs have been decentralized to state and local levels; e.g., grants have been allocated for job training programs through Opportunities Industrializations Centers, Job Opportunities in the Business Sector, universities and colleges, the National Occupational Information Service, Employment Service offices and other social service agencies, and LEAP.

At the time of our interviews, unemployment was increasing; by April 1977, the unemployment rate was still above 7.5 percent, or more than 7 million unemployed. Moreover, as noted above, the rate for minority groups was nearly double the rate for the nation as a whole. And the problems generated by the seniority systems, namely, that the last hired are the first to be fired, was still very much with us. Because of discrimination, blacks and other minority groups generally speaking are the last hired and, therefore, the first fired. This process results in a continual decrease of minorities, especially blacks, in the work force. On the other hand, affirmative action commitment requires that such employment as is available be shared with the nonwhite labor force. This dilemma makes for a basic conflict between "seniority" and representative minority employment.

With today's emphasis on full employment, the seniority problem has lost some but far from all of its urgency. As Ernest Green informed us: "The problem with the seniority question now is that so many have been laid off...the recession and unemployment have just affected everybody so disastrously. We are coming together, as I see it, over more jobs...I think you find less and less strict seniority being applied."

Some intergroup relations agencies and professionals would disagree with this view. The U.S. Commission on Civil Rights, for example, in its February 1977 report,[36] holds that the strict application of seniority layoffs does indeed jeopardize existing affirmative action programs as well as result in excessive layoffs of minority employees and women. The commission proposes several alternate layoff plans which would reverse this trend. One is the provision of tax-free compensation coupled with reduced work weeks. Another involves the establishment of separate seniority lists for minorities, women, and nonminority males; layoffs would then proceed on a proportionate basis. A third proposal entails temporary layoffs with compensation and the right to return to work for senior employees. A fourth alternative is work-sharing. This proposal has been coupled with suggestions for the use of unemployment insurance to compensate workers whose work week is reduced, and tax relief for employers who maintain full benefits for workers on a work-sharing plan. "In addition to helping protect affirmative action gains, there is some evidence that work-sharing arrangements help to improve employee morale and productivity among the entire work force, white as well as non-white, male and female."[37]

Still other proposals involving the voluntary reduction of fringe benefits or the elimination of other benefits, such as company-subsidized cafeterias, have been offered.

As is stated elsewhere in this book,[38] the most recent Supreme Court ruling appears to give existing seniority systems some added support; this ruling holds that a bona fide seniority system may not be set aside to give some workers special consideration related to observance of other than usual religious holidays. The effect of this decision on some of the remedies suggested above remains to be determined.

In general, as is mentioned earlier, compliance and enforcement in the employment area are dealt with by governmental agencies, e.g., HEW, HUD, the Department of Labor, and their state and municipal counterparts. In effect, this state of affairs allows for some division of labor between public and private agencies. With public agencies concentrating, even if not exclusively, on the enforcement of the laws, the private agencies feel freer to devote some of their resources to "adequate housing," "quality education," and "full employment." This universalist trend toward an overriding concern with economic and social conditions has received added stimulus from the present (1974-1975) recession.

Back in 1970 during our interview with him, a top official of the Equal Employment Opportunity Commission (EEOC) predicted that within a decade there would be a nationwide audit of employment systems with respect to the racial composition of employees. Today, his prediction is coming true; the EEOC has had its powers of enforcement increased. The Equal Employment Act of 1972 broadened coverage of the Civil Rights Act of 1964 by increasing the power of the EEOC to include *all* employers engaged in interstate commerce and labor unions; to bring civil action against any employer named in a charge; to review employer programs of equal employment opportunity; and to require annual review of affirmative programs in each federal department and agency.

The EEOC official we interviewed had indicated that an industry-by-industry audit would be undertaken and would include all major employers and all major labor unions. In other words, as he put it, "we've got to mass-produce the law." It was his somewhat optimistic belief that then discrimination could be totally eliminated from employment.

However, at that time the family income of blacks was about 55 percent of whites, and today it remains slightly less than 60 percent.[39] He called Title VII of the 1964 Civil Rights law "a fantastic statute" because, he said, it prohibited discrimination in the broadest possible fashion in all aspects of employment. This he looked upon as the basis for optimism about the future.

Many of our informants felt that U.S. society had the means, the techniques, and the know-how to virtually eradicate unemployment as well as racial bigotry.

Housing

During the past twenty-five years, the attitudes of intergroup relations workers toward the housing problems of minorities have shifted radically. Formerly, their overriding concern was with instances of exclusion of and discrimination against racial and ethnic groups. Scientific surveys of prejudice invariably included questions about "living next door to a 'Negro' or a Jew" as a measure of social distance. Only rarely did the larger social problem of providing a sufficiency of good homes for lower and lower-middle income groups appear on the intergroup agenda.

For some time now, the emphasis has changed. The change reflects the growing appreciation that the abysmal lack of housing for the poor or near poor throughout America struck principally at minority groups, specifically at blacks and Spanish-speaking peoples. Moreover, the scarcity of decent places to live,[40] an elemental need of all mankind, was often a cardinal factor in the cause and persistence of intergroup tensions.

In more recent years, it became obvious to all concerned that there was also a critical shortage of affordable housing near particular schools which needed to be integrated or near the industrial centers which could provide needed jobs for minority ethnic groups. At the same time, central-city housing for the poor was most often located in predominantly black or Spanish-speaking neighborhoods, far from places of actual or potential employment. The growing movement of industrial and business enterprises to more attractive suburban sites further aggravated the imbalance.

Two of our informants, experienced specialists in the housing area, stressed the need to pressure, and if necessary, compel government agencies to cease putting up massive complexes of housing in the ghettos where no jobs are to be had. Instead, they advocated that vacant land in suburban areas be utilized for developing moderate-income family housing near centers of employment, and that HUD be persuaded to orient its new breakthrough and building programs toward suburbia.

From the point of view of the intergroup relations process and its methodology, two aspects of the housing problem stand out. The first of these has already been noted, i.e., the provision of full and adequate housing for all ethnic groups in itself helps reduce intergroup tensions, on the basis of the generally accepted theory that the removal of major frustrations and the satisfaction of major needs reduce scapegoating and undermine the bases of prejudice and prejudiced behavior. The recognition of this factor contributed to the shift in the agencies' approach to the housing problem. Second, the existence of and the multiplication of open housing in which diverse racial and ethnic groups live together can bring about and help maintain interaction among them. Mutual participation in daily living experiences produces an increasing awareness and a growing appreciation of other points of view and different life-styles; with such heightened awareness comes an increased acceptance of "difference." There are numerous opportunities for wholesome and productive contacts in many areas which can and often do lead to better intergroup attitudes. At the very least, the various groups learn to live and work together with a minimum of friction.

The strategy followed by the "agents" of change can be divided into two successive stages. The first is a complex of steps to remove obstacles to the construction and provision of better housing. This complex may include legislative action, litigation, financing, elimination of restrictive covenants,[41] and rezoning or removal of restrictive zoning codes. The second, equally complex but of a different nature, involves the breaking down of barriers to productive contacts among the occupants of the new or "opened" housing, as well as the encouragement of contacts between the new and older inhabitants of the recently created community.

These and other approaches have long formed part of the arsenal of many intergroup agencies, public as well as private. All approaches have been employed, at different times and with varying success, in the service of the overall goal of providing open housing for minorities. All too often, however, the strategies met with the opposition of governmental housing agencies. It is fair to say that for nearly three decades the federal government itself "either actively or passively promoted racial and ethnic discrimination."[42] Thus, the Federal Housing Authority Underwriting Manual warned prospective builders and banks against the infiltration of "inharmonious racial groups"[43] into established neighborhoods. This warning stood for fifteen years and not until December 1949, after the *Shelley* v. *Kraemer* decision on restrictive covenants, did the Federal Housing Administration and the Veterans Administration reverse their policies of social segregation. The policies of the "four Federal financial regulatory agencies (Board of Governors of the Federal Reserve System, the Federal Home Loan Board, the Federal Deposit Insurance Corporation [FDIC], and the Office of the Comptroller of Currency)...also encouraged overt racial and ethnic discrimination in mortgage lending until the passage of the 1968 Fair Housing Law."[44] Discriminatory lending practices against women have only very recently been rescinded.

Only in public housing, where local authorities were given some leeway—that is, they could build either "separate but equal" or "open" housing—was there any real attempt to provide low-rental housing for minorities.[45]

The 1968 Supreme Court decision in *Jones* v. *Mayer* barred all racial discrimination in all housing, private as well as public. The exceptions were for units occupied by no more than four families, one of which was the owner, and single-family houses sold or rented by an owner residing in the house at the time of sale without public notice—posted, mailed, or written.[46]

Of all the social relationships among groups, housing involves the closest personal contact (in the neighborhood or apartment house)—more so than employment (the shop or factory). Since employment is more public, housing has also been the area of the greatest evasion and infraction.

Our informants expressed two different views regarding the damaging effects of urban renewal on those evicted from premises earmarked for demolition. A leading housing authority in the private sector stated, "I don't know of any redevelopment program that hasn't meant black removal, black displacement, refurbishing the ghetto, but in no way providing other opportunities both in and outside of the ghetto at the same time." However, a prominent public housing official asserted that while his agency was very much concerned with the problem of displacement in urban renewal, the people who are displaced are generally not harmed or taken advantage of:

It would be erroneous to assume that the urban renewal program is discredited. It is not. In fact, if you ask me about the cities, I would say in terms of community groups as to what is the most popular program, it would be the urban renewal.

He added that HUD had been authorized to spend about $2 billion for urban renewal. The U.S. Conference of Mayors (1970) was eager to obtain additional urban renewal funds for the Model Cities Program. An important public official asked his colleagues, "Would the Conference of Mayors meeting in Washington be clamoring for more urban renewal money if urban renewal was as unpopular or as discredited as seemed to be indicated?"

The gap between policy and performance in the effort for human equality is perhaps greatest in the housing area. In spite of the 1968 law, at the time of our interviews both private and public officials pointed out that in the larger cities of this country (particularly in the larger metropolitan sections) minority families were concentrated in severely blighted areas in deplorable, overcrowded housing. Good housing was scarce not only because of economic reasons, but also because of the restricted opportunities to buy housing in suburban areas.

Undeveloped and underdeveloped land still rings the major urban centers of the country. One official in the private sector concerned with open housing reported:

Only within the course of the last couple of months has there been any kind of pronouncement coming out of Washington, out of HUD, that says, in effect, that the principal focus of federal housing programs would be to expand residential opportunities for minority families in suburbia where the jobs are located and where the land is available.

The delay in implementing the provisions of the housing statute of 1968 was caused not only by white failure to accept open housing, but also by "destructive elements and nihilistic groups among the blacks." In the 1970s, according to our informants, progress was stymied by backlash which was not necessarily expressed in overt action; inaction by whites brought the same result.

According to one informant, in the 1970s, discrimination in housing still seemed to be a matter of someone "making up his mind, say an owner of a fifty-unit apartment house, whether or not he wants minority occupants. And having done so, he simply instructed his staff not to take applications from black people or from Mexican-Americans, etc." This situation has changed only slightly in private housing or even in much of public housing, although instructions are not given quite so openly. There is much indirection in keeping "undesirable" minorities out of buildings occupied by whites. As the housing statute was becoming better known, more complaints were filed and more court actions were instituted seeking relief.

At the time of our interviews, the incongruity of industry moving to the suburbs while its employees continued to live in the central cities and its ghettos, and the attendant difficulty of getting to their jobs, was especially striking. The negative consequences of these moves had already made themselves felt in the early 1970s. The federal government also faced the problem as some of its agencies such as HUD, for example, moved out of the inner cities, thus creating problems for their minority employees. When the Government Printing Office (GPO), a mass employer, moved from Washington to a suburb, housing became a problem for its employees. GPO's blue-collar workers are largely minority persons, and they were faced with the choice of either spending more time and money for transportation or moving to the suburbs—if they could find housing at rentals they could afford.

The Department of Labor (Office of Equal Employment Opportunity) was especially concerned with the availability of transportation facilities. Government departments contemplating moves are obliged to take the availability of open housing and transportation facilities into consideration.

Job-linked[47] housing became an increasingly pressing matter as industry moved out of the central cities. Availability of land, reduced costs, and other benefits were counterbalanced by the creation of serious personnel problems. HUD and the Department of Labor attempted to work out solutions to these problems.

By mid-1970, HUD had contracts with about 3,100 grant-in-aid agencies whose local branches obtained annual grants from HUD to pay for public housing loans as well as for urban renewal, water, and sewers. These contracts called for affirmative action in the employment of minorities. Since HUD had the responsibility of administering the 1968 Fair Housing Law, it was obliged to take positive steps with regard to industry moving into the suburbs. Using enforcement mechanisms available to it and government incentives, HUD endeavored to guarantee optional housing opportunities throughout the metropolitan area[48] for all persons, regardless of income level or racial or ethnic background.

HUD's assistant secretary of equal opportunity felt that one could not comply with the fair employment provisions of Executive Order 11063 unless one were concerned with housing.[49] He pointed out that when an industry moves twenty-five miles from a central city, it is unlikely to find any new black employees. Their old black employees are obliged to leave shortly after the move because, as a rule, people do not drive more than twenty-five miles to work. Consequently, the new labor force generally will include fewer and fewer minority group employees.

In the early 1970s, HUD recognized that affirmative action programs could not be carried out by asking industrial firms in remote suburban areas to hire blacks when there was no place for them to live. Some industrial concerns bus workers to and from work, and mass transportation for workers has been made available in some central locations. However, for the most part the problem of transportation remains. The cities blame the suburbs for the problem, and some have devised solutions for it such as transporting residents of "model" neighborhoods to their jobs by special bus services. Other local solutions have been emerging.

Zoning

As far back as 1917 (*Buchanan* v. *Worley*, 245 U.S. 60, 1917), the Supreme Court declared racial zoning ordinances to be unconstitutional.

Similar subsequent rulings by federal and state courts led real estate interests to devise other means of perpetuating discriminatory patterns. Realtors, property-owners, and mortgage-lending institutions developed a host of measures, all of them well known to intergroup professionals: racial covenants, discriminatory mortgage and exclusionary land-sales practices, specific land-use decisions, minimum zoning ordinances, and many others. Though not explicitly racial or ethnic in character, the minimum zoning ordinances were just as effective in barring minority groups from access to the interdicted land or housing.

It was not until the 1960s that exclusionary land-use zoning became a "major focus of the overall legal attack on housing discrimination and segregation."[50] This change was largely the result of the universal recognition that there could be no fair housing without full housing, and that full housing often meant the construction of public housing for lower-income families on land outside the central cities—land which in many cases was covered by exclusionary land-use ordinances.

At the time of our interviews, the challenge to discriminatory zoning had already been underway for nearly a decade. According to reports from the Civil Rights Division of the Department of Justice, law suits were then being conducted against the City of Lansing, Michigan,[51] Lackawanna in New York,[52] Union City in California, Lawton in Oklahoma,[53] and a number of cities in New Jersey.

The year 1970 was seen as the high point for discriminatory zoning litigation. Since that time, some reverses have taken place, and the law on the subject has remained in a state of flux.

By 1974, housing specialists were giving particular attention to exclusionary land-use litigation as an instrument for achieving fair housing goals. Federal courts, the principal forum for this litigation, had at first seemed receptive to exclusionary land-use challenges. They had consistently struck down, as racially discriminatory, municipal zoning and other land-use powers designed to block federally subsidized housing. However, these same courts have begun to show signs of retrenchment. Thus, in a fairly recent decision (*Mahaley* v. *Cuyahoga Metropolitan Housing Authority*, July 9, 1974),[54] the U.S. Court of Appeals flatly rejected the claim that statistics alone were adequate proof of discrimination. In a more recent decision,

The [Supreme] Court held, in a case involving the nearly all-white Chicago suburb of Arlington Heights, that the refusal of a suburb to rezone is not unconstitutional just because it has a "racially disproportionate impact." To be unconstitutional, the Court said there must also be an "intent" or "purpose" to discriminate.[55]

The ruling effectively blocked the construction of a proposed public housing project in the area and, unless modified by subsequent cases, may well hinder or prevent similar projects elsewhere. Some considered the decision to be a "major setback" which "severely restricts use of the Federal courts in suburban zoning challenges."[56] Other officials, however, thought that "state courts would not necessarily be affected" and that the ruling would not necessarily have an adverse effect upon such projects as those involved in New York City's "current fight against so-called exclusionary zoning in this area's suburbs because local efforts are based on state constitutional guarantees and state laws, and are being waged in state rather than Federal courts."[57]

In the early 1970s, state courts were beginning to be receptive to judicial forums for the challenges aimed at protecting the rights of the minority poor. Perhaps more importantly, in both New Jersey and Pennsylvania, the courts included in their consideration not only the particular municipal housing projects at issue, but the housing needs of the entire region.

The Housing and Community Development Act of 1974 changed many of the ground rules under which federally aided housing and community development programs had operated. Under the new law, a community's request for federal development assistance is linked to its willingness to provide lower-income housing. In order to receive development funds, a community must produce a housing assistance program not only for lower-income families already living there, but also for those who may wish to move there to take advantage of job opportunities. This provision not only furthers the movement of lower-income families from the central region to the suburbs, but also provides the communities themselves with an incentive for discarding exclusionary zoning practices.

In 1976 this section of the law was successfully used in a Hartford, Connecticut, action to compel a suburb (Windsor), which had applied for HUD community development funds, to include provisions for lower-income housing in its plans. The federal court held that without such a plan HUD could not approve the request for the funds; thus, in the words of the city officials, the suburbs were compelled to share in the problems of the central city.

In a recent decision, the Supreme Court ruled unanimously that federal courts can order the construction of low-cost minority housing in a city's white suburbs if such housing is needed to relieve racial segregation within the center city.[58] While there is still some question regarding the applicability of the ruling to similar situations, the decision gives HUD a mandate to encourage suburbs to include minorities in their housing plans. At the same time, recent court decisions have brought increased doubt regarding the efficacy of case-by-case, project-by-project litigation in breaking down exclusionary land-use barriers. There also was increased uncertainty[59] as to the efficacy of exclusionary land-use litigation as a technique for achieving equal housing goals. There was even a difference of opinion among fair housing advocates as to what those goals should be.[60]

A major part of the National Committee Against Discrimination in Housing (NCDH) litigation program in 1975 was intended to restore vitality to discriminatory zoning litigation. The use of law remains the most potent approach to advancing fair housing, primarily because whites continue to resist sharing housing with blacks. Increasingly, litigation by citizens' fair housing groups has challenged municipal exclusionary zoning laws which traditionally have kept low-income housing out of the suburbs.

The HUD official whom we interviewed emphasized that as long as there is a shortage of low-income housing, inequality in housing will persist. In order to enforce the fair housing law, or at least take advantage of the legal tools we now have with respect to fair housing, the housing available to low-income people must be increased. He stated that some land-use controls are even more damaging and debilitating than overt discrimination in housing. The minimum cost of new housing in many areas is way beyond the economic capacity of the average worker.

A fair housing law is inoperable if the cost of an available dwelling unit runs to $50,000. In such circumstances, a fair housing ordinance can do very little for minority groups. When a community's minimum zoning laws call for half-acre lots, the typical minority group member cannot even afford the land itself, let alone build something on it. The legal tools for dealing with land-use controls are indeed very limited. Since zoning and land-use controls usually fall under the jurisdiction of local governments, not of the state, there can be as many zoning ordinances as there are local communities.

Generally, the methods employed by intergroup professionals to stimulate or support the setting up of federal or local housing programs do not differ in their essentials from those used to reduce or eliminate discrimination. And, of course, these various goals do not conflict with each other. Legislative measures and litigation lend themselves readily to the furtherance of either of the goals. Negotiation, confrontation, and the marshaling of community resources can be employed in the cause of *more* housing for the poor as easily as in the cause of the abolition of racial covenants. And perhaps they can be used even more easily, since the very existence of a vast reservoir of demand for full as distinct from fair housing makes the mobilization of community action that much simpler.

The broadening of intergroup objectives to embrace the goal of full housing led naturally to a concern with financing, urban renewal, rezoning and exclusionary land use, and many more related problems. The goal itself remains a long way off. In 1968, the minimum need for housing units for low- and lower-middle-income families was estimated to be in the neighborhood of six million, to be built by 1978.[61]

At the time of our interviews, only about 700,000 federally subsidized housing units had been erected. At the end of 1974, the total had reached

2,315,000—still far short of the required number. (By 1978, this figure reached 2,886,723 federally subsidized units.)

In general, then, the housing scene as viewed by the intergroup relations practitioner takes on a dual aspect. The actual creation of housing for minorities—whether through new construction, rehabilitation, rezoning, or other means—becomes, in and of itself, an operational priority. In addition, the housing plant itself, once it is built and occupied, becomes a means to many ends. The use of housing for the improvement of intergroup relations takes on new significance. Not only does it serve as a natural center for the development of beneficial contacts among various racial and ethnic groups, but it also furnishes the indispensable physical base for desegregated schools. And it provides the necessary living quarters for minority group job seekers.

The "Planned Interracial Community" (Benign Quotas)[62]

Long before the current controversy with respect to "quotas" in relation to affirmative action programs set in, the matter of the "benign quota" for housing was debated with varying force at different periods. This approach had been recommended on occasion to help with the problem of desegregation and possible integration. By avoiding the "tilting point," the stage at which members of the majority begin to withdraw, the fear of being "inundated" by members of the minority is reduced, as is the likelihood of the resulting resegregation—the very condition the new effort aimed to abolish. In the past, setting a percentage limit on minority representation so as to avoid reaching the tilting point was usually practiced in a sub rosa manner. Then and now, it was employed largely in the area of housing. In so intimate a situation as housing, it is not likely that resistance to and evasion of civil rights provisions and/or executive order stipulations will be readily detected and dealt with effectively. The question therefore arises as to whether the benign quota approach,[63] with appropriate safeguards to prevent its deterioration into a "malignant" exclusionary quota, may not in fact expedite integration, or at least weaken the tendency toward segregation. This plan must of course be instituted by mutual agreement between participants of both the white and black groups.

This matter was put before some of our informants in the form of a query about their views on the use of the benign quota. The representatives of the public sector generally opposed this approach, largely for legal reasons: "All quotas are against the law," a number of them stated. Incidentally, it should be pointed out that occasionally the manner in which a federal agency, HEW, for instance, implements the executive order for affirmative action calling for the use of goals, stated guidelines of procedures, and "patterns" of actual results, might be interpreted as an illegal use of quotas.

There also was considerable opposition among our informants to the use of benign quotas in housing in the private sector. Their rationale was that it was difficult to prevent "benign" from turning into "malignant." They also insisted that antidiscrimination laws and executive order stipulations for affirmative action should be implemented directly and with all deliberate speed.

The benign quota concept had appreciable support among top-echelon policy-makers in the private sector, especially, strangely enough, among black informants. Their positive reactions were based primarily on pragmatic considerations. Of course, they thought the necessary safeguards should be kept in mind; as one black leader in the private sector stated: "I am in favor of the judicious use of the benign quota, not as a policy but as a technique." Another one said: "When there is really a tipping point, the approach is o.k. The test to be used should be 'Will it really achieve integration?' It is solely a pragmatic matter." "Use it as an entering wedge" was the reaction of another black policy-maker.

A leading black scholar-activist in the intergroup relations field expressed a positive attitude toward the use of the benign quota, providing it is used as an approach "toward a systematic social engineering effort in the direction of social change, and that it does not partake of tokenism, sentimentalism, and, of course, is not used as an evasive device."

The head of a national community relations service indicated that his support of the benign quota would involve examining each specific problem in its broader aspects. He asked what happens to those who are not admitted and indicated that the approach must not be considered in isolation: "My support of the benign quota concept would be very much contingent upon a much broader consideration of the overall community's problem."

One top national agency executive (a white) with many years' experience in communal work stated forthrightly: "Benign quota is usable. Without it we are not going to achieve integration in any respect." (He meant this process to take place on a purely voluntary and experimental basis.)

An executive of a local Jewish community relations agency stressed that in the midst of all the discussion of quotas the central issue, i.e., the enormous scarcity of housing, must not be overlooked: "Expansion of housing opportunities should be our concentration." As a substitute for concern with the tilting point in the educational area, he recommended the introduction of innovative programs in the schools and the creation of superior housing facilities in minority neighborhoods rather than benign quotas in housing. He concluded that: "we have deliberately avoided putting on the agenda of our agency specifics with respect to benign quota for formal discussion because I think if we were to formally discuss it we would reject it out of hand as a principle."

Other Jewish community relations workers were even more forceful: "I am against benign quota. It scares me." Or, "There can be no good quotas."

Two respondents, one a Catholic professional executive, the other a Jewish lay community leader, emphasized the desirability and importance of leaving the decision on the use of the benign quota to the minority group and to the "people involved, both black and white"—and not to introduce outside pressures.

An executive of the Equal Employment Opportunity Commission pointed to the obvious fact that "if the housing laws were really enforced, the benign quota issue would never come up." He followed this observation by saying:

However, I would favor a system whereby the apartment owner who was obeying the open housing law but, because most everybody else was disobeying it, suddenly finds his apartment house getting 50 per cent, 60 per cent, 70 per cent black, could go to an appropriate government agency and say, "Look, there are ten apartment houses over there that are discriminating and the reason I am 70 per cent black in tenants is because their percentage is zero. I want you to enforce the law against them."

In such an instance, he asserted, it should be mandatory for the government to take action.

Others in the public field insisted that people should have choices, even the choice of segregation. Such an observation came from a white local community relations head:

I still believe in the right to resegregate. I believe there are many people in the country who have no desire to move into suburbia—who have no desire to live with white people. I'm just as staunchly in favor of their right to resegregate among themselves as I am for those blacks who do want to move out to be enabled to do so.

Several informants connected with a national housing organization considered the benign quota a discriminatory approach devised by "liberals" to maintain the "integrity" of their neighborhoods. One Jewish community relations director, although opposed to both "positive and negative" quotas, nevertheless accepted benign quotas, but only as an expedient—as a step to achieve integration.

A high official in the Civil Rights Division of the Justice Department, opposed to benign quotas on legal grounds, had this to say:

The secret of success in the tilting area is to keep the whites in the schools by demonstrating that the educational program in the tilting school is better than the one in the all-white school that may be out on the outskirts of town. . . . The vast majority of white parents concern themselves mainly with educational quality.

As is evident from some of the comments quoted above, those who approve the use of the benign quota do so with some reservations. Some are worried by the moral and legal aspects, and others by the difficulties of its implementation in relation to the desired goal of integration and by the problem of its misuse for purposes of exclusion and perpetuating segregation. Those opposed to the benign quota, however, do so with no reservations.

Similar findings were published in 1964 by L. K. Northwood and Louis H. Klein in one of the rare systematic empirical studies of this controversial subject:

This study was part of a larger survey in which two samples were specified: a "quota of experts in fifteen large cities scattered throughout the nation, except the South" and one or two interviews in each of thirty-seven other cities, including several in the South.[64]

Three sectors of social welfare organizations were represented in the study samples: housing, traditional social work, and intergroup relations. A total of 134 out of 138 persons responded to questions on the benign quota. One-third rejected the practice and two-thirds accepted it with one or more goals in mind, such as preventing a housing project from remaining all white; helping blacks find housing in predominantly white neighborhoods; and allowing old established residents in a neighborhood the right to control the kind of new neighbors who move in. Four percent thought the quota should be applied to Negroes only.[65]

Although two-thirds favored the benign quota, there was "a marked division regarding the ethics and practicality of this technique for the control of neighborhood desegregation...factual ambiguity among practitioners, and contradictions in their ideologies.[66]

The responses to our questions on this issue were obtained before the controversy over the use of quotas relating to the affirmative action program erupted. With some notable exceptions, black informants were more favorable to the benign quota approach—with, of course, the appropriate safeguards—than were whites. Jewish professionals were most opposed to its use, even as a pragmatic device unrelated to principle (voluntary by both groups and on an experimental basis). These group differences among our informants are merely generalizations based on a review of the interviews; they do not constitute statistical evidence.

The meaning of these differences between black and white professionals, because of the tentative nature of the findings, can only be a subject for speculation. Nevertheless, qualitatively, these observations may be relevant to the use of benign quotas to achieve integration.

The benign quota can only be viewed as an affirmative act. It can be legitimatized only as a process, not as a goal, to help achieve integration and to reduce or possibly prevent backlash.

Integration should perhaps be considered as a progressive, step-by-step process. If so considered, its ultimate success may actually depend upon the benign quota approach because one needs to get *accustomed* to new thinking, new feeling, and new performance. This approach reduces the likelihood of an antagonistic reaction built on the fears of inundation, loss of property values, detrimental effects on children, and the like. It is most useful in areas such as housing rather than employment, where its use may no longer be essential. Since housing is closely related to the school, the job, and the social situation, it is the core of the segregation problem. The benign quota should not be confused with gradualism, which before the enactment of civil rights legislation in the late 1950s and 1960s had frequently been utilized as a stalling device. To be effective, the benign quota must operate within the context of law and a federal policy of affirmative action. Until desegregation actually comes to pass, those who sincerely want to promote an integrated society are still often forced, especially in the housing area, to resort to the benign quota on a sub rosa basis in order to avoid the whites' mass abandonment of residences, schools, and entire neighborhoods.

Even the most optimistic exponents of the progress made by nonwhite and other minority groups during the past decades are not fully satisfied with the advances in housing desegregation—particularly in the private sector. Indeed, the results in housing have been most discouraging. The benign quota is, of course, subject to abuse and evasion and may perhaps even be used to defeat the implementation of the civil rights laws. Safeguards have to be devised. Now that we are evolving affirmative action guidelines and achievement patterns, these safeguards can more readily be formulated and put into practice.

To put it bluntly, we are getting practically nowhere in the housing area—witness the fights over scatter-site housing.[67] We are bound to make some headway with this additional approach within the framework of legal enactments and operational policy thus far developed. We must have laws, for they constitute the framework and set the norm. But without the aid of procedures required in the implementation of these laws, they alone cannot change individual behavior. Certainly they alone cannot change attitudes.

The late Saul Alinsky, who was not given to pussyfooting on any occasion, made this rather surprising statement in his testimony before the Hearing of the Commission on Civil Rights on May 5, 1959:

For those who are shocked by the idea of opening up white communities to Negroes on a quota basis aiming toward the diffusion of the Negro population throughout the city scene, I can only ask what solution do they propose? The price of responsible criticism is a constructive alternative.[68]

Notes

1. The East Village comprises an area roughly between 14th and 7th Streets, and Third Avenue to about Avenue A. It acquired its new character when rentals in Greenwich Village proper skyrocketed. Artists and intellectuals who wanted to live

in the neighborhood found cheaper quarters among the ethnic residents east of the Village. East Village has a "negative" character because of its proximity to the Bowery and its deteriorated housing. In recent years, some rehabilitation of this old housing and general improvement of the neighborhoods has taken place. Some new residential construction has also been undertaken.

2. Figures on ethnic enrollment published by the Office of Civil Rights of the Department of Health, Education and Welfare for Fall 1970 to the 1974-1975 school years included 31,800 schools with an enrollment of 90 percent of the nation's black students. In his analysis of these reports, Gary Orfield of the Brookings Institution concluded that (1) there has been little change in the high levels of school segregation of black children in the 1970s, (2) pupils from Spanish-speaking backgrounds have become increasingly segregated, and (3) 67 percent of black children are in schools with predominantly minority enrollment, down from 71 percent in 1970.

Before the passage of the 1964 Civil Rights Act, about 98 percent of black children in the South were in all-black schools. By 1970, Southern schools had become more desegregated than schools in the North and West. By 1974, more than 44 percent of Southern black children were in schools with minority enrollments of less than 50 percent. By the 1974-1975 school year, the Northeast and the Middle West were the most segregated, with about 81 percent of black pupils in schools with predominantly minority enrollments. Examples of extreme segregation were found in the North; 45 percent of all black students in the Midwest were attending schools with 99 percent or more minority enrollments. Such schools serve about one-third of black children in the Northeast, 25 percent in the West, but only about one-seventh in the South (*The New York Times*, June 20, 1976).

3. De jure segregation is segregation sanctioned by law.

4. De facto segregation is segregation in fact; it is not legally sanctioned.

5. In 1974, almost half of the Northern cities had schools which were almost as segregated as six years earlier. "In such Northern cities as Chicago, Cincinnati, Cleveland, New York, Newark, Philadelphia, and St. Louis, schools were actually more highly segregated in 1974 than in 1968...by 1974, schools were much less segregated within Southern Central cities than in cities in other regions." Reynolds Farley, "Can Government Policies Integrate Public Schools?," Population Studies Center, University of Michigan, September 1976, based on data from tape files, *Directory of Public Elementary and Secondary Schools in Selected Districts, Enrollment and Staff by Racial/Ethnic Group*, Fall 1968 through 1974.

6. Bayard Rustin, "Black Rage/White Fear," an Address before a Bricklayers Convention in Washington, D.C., September 30, 1970.

7. Gordon Allport, *The Nature of Prejudice* (Reading, Mass., Addison-Wesley, 1954), pp. 261–81; Hubert M. Blalock, Jr., *Toward A Theory of Minority-Group Relations* (New York: John Wiley and Sons, 1967).

8. See Chapter 12.

9. Allport, *The Nature of Prejudice*, p. 281.

10. "Fullfilling the Letter and Spirit of the Law: Desegregation of the Nation's Public Schools," a report of the U.S. Commission on Civil Rights, August 1976, p. 159.

11. James S. Coleman, "Equality of Educational Opportunity," Washington, D. C., U.S. Government Printing Office, 1966.

12. In his 1966 report, Dr. James S. Coleman, supervisor of the survey mandated by the commissioner of education, had supported the position that children from disadvantaged backgrounds performed better when they attended schools with children from more affluent homes. In 1975, as a result of new research, Dr. Coleman announced that court-induced school desegregation had contributed to white exodus from the big cities. At the same time, he stated that his public comments in 1966 went beyond the scientific data which had been gathered (Nancy Hicks, *The New York Times*, October 29, 1975).

13. Jack Rothman, ed., *Promoting Social Justice in the Multigroup Society* (New York: Association Press, 1971), pp. 58–67.

14. James P. Sterba, "Denver School Busing Succeeds; Social Mixture Called a Factor," *The New York Times*, October 26, 1976, p. 34.

15. David J. Armor, "The Evidence on Busing," *The Public Interest* 28 (Summer 1972): 90-126. Thomas F. Pettigrew, et al., "Busing: A Review of the 'The Evidence,'" *The Public Interest* 30 (Winter 1973): 8-118. David J. Armor, "The Double Double Standard," The *Public Interest* 30 (Winter 1973): 119-31. James Q. Wilson, "On Pettigrew and Armor: An Afterword," *The Public Interest* 30 (Winter 1973): 132-34.

16. Armor, "The Evidence on Busing," p. 116.

17. See our discussion of benign quota in Chapter 9.

18. John Slawson, "Affirmative Action and Quotas," Letters, *Commentary* (December 1972): 26–28.

19. John Slawson, "The 'Planned Interracial Community' Approach," *Journal of Intergroup Relations* 4, no. 3 (July 1975): 3-15.

20. The Gallup Opinion Index, Princeton, N.J. (May 1975): 23.

21. As of 1975–1976, student composition was 14.8 percent black, 7.2 percent Oriental, 7.6 percent Puerto Rican, and 68.7 percent other (New York City Board of Education, July 5, 1977).

22. Alice Miel with Edwin Kiester, Jr., "The Shortchanged Children of Suburbia," Institute of Human Relations Press, Pamphlet Series No. 8, 1967.

23. Ibid., p. 14.

24. *The New York Times*, December 29, 1976, Editorial, "A New Beginning; The Social Crisis."

25. "The Social & Economic Status of the Black Population of the United States, 1974," U.S. Department of Commerce, 1975, p. 41.

26. "Last Hired, First Fired: Layoffs and Civil Rights," U.S. Commission on Civil Rights, February 1977, p. 82.

27. Ibid., p. 80.

28. Ibid., p. 11.

29. Ibid., p. 14.

30. Reynolds Farley, "Trends in Racial Inequalities," *American Sociological Review* 42, no. 2 (1977): 206.

31. "Statement on 'Full Employment' Before the Equal Opportunities Subcommittee of the House Committee on Education and Labor." (See Appendix A, Statement by Rabbi A. James Rudin.)

32. A federally aided private agency which assists in the training and placement of black and Hispanic workers.

33. "Last Hired, First Fired," p. 10.

34. Tom Wicker, *The New York Times*, November 23, 1976.

35.

The LEAP contract for $5.7 million continues the apprenticeship and journeymen outreach program for its tenth year. Under the new contract, LEAP will prepare more than 3,500 disadvantaged minority youth and semi-skilled construction workers for apprenticeship jobs, primarily in the building and construction industry . . . . Five new cities will be added to the 15 cities currently conducting projects for the recruitment and placement of women in non-traditional jobs including apprenticeship. In addition, Tallahassee, Florida will be added to the 42 other LEAP project cities. A new feature of the program will be two mobile units which will enable two LEAP projects to service minorities located outside large urban centers . . . . During the past nine years, LEAP placements have earned more than $470 million and have paid an estimated $113 million in taxes. Thus, the government has received almost $4.25 for every dollar invested in the program.

News release, National Urban League, December 15, 1976.

36. "Last Hired, First Fired," p. 61.

37. Ibid., p. 55.

38. See Chapter 3.

39. According to the "Social and Economic Statutes of the Black Population in the U.S., 1970," the median income for nonwhite families was 61 percent of white families. In 1974, it declined to 58 percent.

40. The 1968 Housing Act set a goal of 26 million new and rehabilitated housing units to be built by 1978, a goal which will not be attained ("Twenty Years After Brown: Equal Opportunity in Housing," U.S. Commission on Civil Rights, December 1975, p. 23).

41. Restrictive covenants were declared unenforceable in the courts by the Supreme Court in 1948 (*Shelley* v. *Kraemer*). The Fair Housing Act of 1968 declared such covenants illegal.

42. "Twenty Years After Brown," pp. 29, 40.

43. Ibid.

44. Ibid., p. 41.

45. By 1961, thirty-two states were operating on an open housing basis, and 492 out of a total of 886 public housing projects had mixed occupancy patterns. See "Twenty Years After Brown," pp. 46, 47.

46. See Title VIII, Civil Rights Act of 1968, p. 36—LW 92.

47. Housing within easy access of industrial or other employment. Such housing may sometimes already be available; if not, it may have to be constructed.

48. The Bureau of the Census defines "metropolitan area" as including a central city, the county containing that central city, and any surrounding counties which are economically integrated with the county containing the central city. See Reynolds Farley, "Can Governmental Policies Integrate Public Schools?," address presented before the American Sociological Association, September 1, 1976.

49. Since 1970, HUD's budgets have included appropriations for assisted housing, community development and planning, housing production and mortgage credit, housing management, policy, development, and research—all in the interest of furthering equal opportunity in housing. The Housing and Community Development

Act of 1974, which became effective on January 1, 1975, provides for greater local discretion and specified citizen participation in the assistance plans administered by HUD to meet the needs of lower income families. The report of the U.S. Commission on Civil Rights, December 1974, "The Federal Civil Rights Enforcement Effort to Provide for Fair Housing," criticizes HUD for failing to carry out the objectives of equal opportunity housing legislation (pp. 1–2). According to the Housing and Community Development Act of 1974, HUD continues as the agency committed to "administrative and enforcement responsibility" of racial and economic housing patterns. See "Trends in Housing," National Committee Against Discrimination in Housing (NCDH), November-December 1974, p. 1.

50. "Fair Housing and Exclusionary Land Use," NCDH, 1974, p. 1.

51. *Ranjel* v. *City of Lansing* (1970), in which the court refused to entertain the charge that a referendum on zoning, which would have permitted construction of a housing project for lower-income blacks and Mexican Americans, was racially motivated.

52. *Kennedy Park Homes Association* v. *City of Lackawanna, N.Y.* and *Daily* v. *City of Lawton, Okla.* (1970) involved requests for rezoning and applications to permit construction of subsidized housing to be occupied largely by black families. In both cases, the court found that the denial of building application was racially discriminatory. Particularly significant was the court's ruling in the Lackawanna case that all that was necessary for an ordinance to be held to be discriminatory was to prove that the *effect* of the ordinance was discriminatory. In earlier cases, courts had required proof of discriminatory motives on the part of municipal officials.

53. In *Sasso* v. *City of Union City, California* (1970), the court went even further; it supported the principle that proof of discrimination against the poor would be sufficient for a finding of unlawful racial discrimination. *James* v. *Valtierra* (402, U.S. 137, 1971), involving a challenge of a California state constitutional provision, reversed the Sasso decision. Proof that governmental conduct or ordinances discriminated against the poor was no longer to be accepted as sufficient unless it was also shown that such conduct was "aimed at a racial minority."

54. "Fair Housing and Exclusionary Land Use," NCDH and Urban Land Institute, 1974, pp. 16–17.

55. *The New York Times*, January 12, 1977, p. 1.

56. Ibid., p. B6.

57. Ibid.

58. *Hills* v. *Gautreaux*, U.S. Supreme Court, April 20, 1976.

59. In his Overview to "Exclusionary Land Use Litigation: Policy and Strategy for the Future," Martin E. Sloane, general counsel, NCDH, states:

Exclusionary land use litigation is currently at a cross-roads and its future as an effective instrument for achieving equal housing opportunity is uncertain. Federal court challenges are relatively recent—barely six years old. They have achieved some outstanding successes, at least measured by the establishment of legal precedents, if not practical results, and have added a new and vigorous dimension to the fair housing movement. But, efforts to achieve major break-throughs in federal litigation, as in Valtierra and Mahaley, have thus far failed and the case law is in a state of flux.

60. Sloane, "Exclusionary Land Use," pp. 1–2.

61. "Twenty Years After Brown," p. 23.

62. There has been considerable change in sentiment on the issue of quotas on any level, including benign, voluntary, or experimental. The verdict of "one of the most anxiously awaited lawsuits of the century," *Regents of the University of California v. Bakke*, was rendered on June 28, 1978. The U.S. Supreme Court declared that racial quotas are unacceptable but an applicant's race can be considered in a university's admission policy. Generally, the role of diversity and educational pluralism seemed to be factors in admission policy.

63. Slawson, "The 'Planned Interracial Community' Approach," pp. 3–15.

64. "The Benign Quota. An Unresolved Issue: Attitudes of Personnel," *Phylon* 25, no. 2 (Second Quarter, Summer 1964): 109–23.

65. Ibid., p. 114, Table 1.

66. Ibid., p. 110.

67. Scatter-site housing is low-income subsidized housing in middle-income enclaves.

68. Oscar Cohen, "The Case for Benign Quotas in Housing," *Phylon* (First Quarter, Spring 1960).

11

Assistance to Become Qualified

Affirmative Action

Affirmative action tends to directly benefit disadvantaged groups in society, but through the consequent equalization of opportunity and inevitable reduction in intergroup tensions, the benefits indirectly accrue to *all* groups. The affirmative action concept in its extended form was formalized in 1965 by Executive Order 11246, issued by President Johnson. Earlier, it was practiced informally and enjoyed fairly wide support. From the very beginning, affirmative action has been a source of conflict both in theory and in practice, and a good deal of confusion exists as to its implementation. Although it applies to all groups subjected to exclusionary and discriminatory treatment, it has mostly been considered in relation to blacks. Its aim is clear enough—to compensate for the inequality produced by two hundred years of abject slavery and more than one hundred years of postslavery discrimination.

Affirmative action, which can express itself in many forms, is designed to compensate for the fact that whites generally start from a much more advantaged position than blacks. The same disparity exists with respect to work skills, formal education, and experience in the application of individual initiative to work problems. While there are abundant exceptions, they are just that—exceptions that prove the rule. It is therefore obvious that in the vast majority of cases the black person who is handicapped because he is black does not have the same opportunity in all areas of life as his white rival. Prohibition of consciously practiced discrimination alone, while essential, cannot by itself achieve the desired effect. Hence, as a matter of social justice, the encumbrances of the "shackle on the leg of the shackled one" must be removed.

Wohlstetter and Coleman report that even though nonwhite family income has grown relatively faster than white income since World War II, "nonetheless (even at these rates) convergence would take place only in a distant future—even for median income to persons, at some time near the end of the century."[1] Edmund K. Faltermayer (1968), as cited by Wohlstetter and Coleman, states: "The reality seems to be that some Negroes, especially those in the middle and upper income brackets, are gaining rapidly on whites, while others, particularly those in the slums, are losing ground in relative terms."[2] The greatest disparity between blacks and whites can be found among the black residents in poorer neighborhoods, including the slums and ghetto areas.

Statistics on black versus white income are discouraging indeed. According to the Potomac Institute group:

While the number of workers of "Negro and other races" employed in the better-paying white-collar, craftsmen and operators' occupations increased by 69 per cent and the number of whites in these occupations rose only 23 per cent, such dramatic increase in fact only brought the proportion of blacks up from 6 to 8 per cent of the total.

Even within each occupational group, earnings for full-time male workers are substantially and consistently lower for blacks than for whites. Earnings in the professional and craftsmen classes show the greatest differentials: in 1969, $3,500 less for black professionals and $2,200 less for black craftsmen than their white counterparts...earnings differentials have been maintained with very little change between 1959 and 1969. Towards the end of the 'sixties, within each job category blacks were earning almost the same amount less than whites as in 1959.[3]

In 1969, black males 25 to 34 years old with four years of college had median earnings of $2,400 less than their white counterparts. However, black males 35 to 54 years old with four years of college did not fare even that well, their median earnings in 1969 being $5,300 less than for whites...increased education beyond high school generally improves the relative earning levels of blacks to whites for younger men... At an educational level above high school, the earnings of black and white female workers are about equal regardless of age.[4]

The Potomac Institute's group statistics for younger black men and black female workers quoted above seem to indicate a pattern of progress. However, the institute points out that while this development is encouraging, since the fastest growing employment fields are in the professional and technical areas, "blacks with their poorer educational opportunities, will be most heavily disadvantaged in competition with whites unless widespread and effective affirmative action can neutralize their disadvantage."[5]

Another discouraging aspect of the employment situation for blacks is the layoff problem; those most recently hired are usually the first to be laid off. Because of the relative newness of civil-rights laws, these layoffs frequently involve minorities. Ideally, layoffs should be carried out in ways that do not destroy job opportunity gains for minorities and women.

Blumrosen and Blumrosen suggest some alternative procedures, such as reduction in hours and rotating layoffs:

This means that reductions in hours worked by all employees are preferable to any layoffs.... Both the shorter work week and rotating layoff options mean that senior whites and/or males share in the lesser amount of work.... We conclude that the sharing of this burden by senior whites and/or males is appropriate under the law, while subordinating them to minorities and women would be unlawful.[6]

The May 31, 1977, ruling of the Supreme Court has complicated the problem of ameliorative action in this area. "As long as there is no intent to discriminate," the Court said, "employers and unions may continue to use the seniority systems," even though "such seniority systems perpetuate the effects of past racial discrimination." The ruling, in the opinion of dissenting Justices Marshall and Brennan, locks many blacks into inferior positions. "Thus equal opportunity will remain a dream for all incumbent employees."[7] But, "equalizing opportunity alone will not bring about equality with respect to the way our society distributes its resources."[8]

The facts cited above bear out the need for affirmative action of a compensatory nature.[9] Adopting this approach means a search for employees in the minority group areas and on campuses where minority groups constitute a large proportion of the student population. It means eliminating the practice of recruiting predominantly persons referred by current white employees of the institution. Further, it entails the need for providing special training—an obligation on both employer and union. Federal funds are still available for training in skills required in specific industries. Compensatory services in education should also be maintained for disadvantaged individuals through concentrated and innovative educational programs.

In 1968, the Council on Legal Education Opportunity (CLEO) was established by the American Bar Association, the National Bar Association (black), the American Association of Law Schools, and the Law Schools Admission Council. CLEO's declared purpose is to provide summer institutes taught by regular law faculty members "to expand and enhance the opportunities to study and practice for members of minority and disadvantaged groups—chiefly Negroes...and thus to help to remedy the present imbalance of [these] and other disadvantaged groups."[10] A number of Appalachian whites have also participated in this program. CLEO is considered a success; by the end of 1976, it had assisted 2,188 students, of whom 929 had been graduated from law schools.

In other words, affirmative action places the obligation upon the employer, the union, and the educator to increase the competitive position of minority group members and women by turning not fully qualified, but potentially capable, individuals into qualified workers and students. This especially holds true in situations with inadequate representation of minority group members and women.

This is not to say that admission requirements should be lowered. All of our interviewees (black and white) were opposed to the lowering of standards, but they were enthusiastic about "assistance to become qualified." They supported compensatory service, primarily training, but unqualifiedly opposed preferential treatment on any basis other than merit.

In December 1974, the Office for Civil Rights of HEW published a memorandum clarifying the Higher Education Guidelines issued in October 1972. The memorandum states clearly that

the affirmative action process must not operate to restrict consideration to minorities and women only . . . . But it must be emphasized that nothing in an affirmative action plan requires the employment of any specific number of women or minorities. [Nor is it intended] that affirmative action should result in a dilution of standards . . . . The executive order does not require that job requirements be waived or lowered in order to attract women and minority candidates   once valid job requirements are established, they must apply equally to all candidates.[11]

Affirmative action means the provision of compensatory services for meeting the standards set; it does not mean preferential treatment based on color or race or sex.[12] It precludes, and even prohibits, the use of tests for job placements that include built-in, discriminatory elements of little or no value in predicting quality of performance. In fact, in *Griggs* v. *Duke Power Co.* (401 US424 [1971]), the U.S. Supreme Court ruled that job tests which screen out black workers are illegal under Title VII of the Civil Rights Act of 1964.

Affirmative action through compensatory aids definitely does *not* involve the lowering of standards. It is not based on quotas, nor does it set them up on the basis of the ratio of the minority group to the total population.

The basic query in determining whether affirmative action is being pursued is whether the employer or other responsible official *in good faith* is doing everything possible to seek, train, attract, and deal equitably with the minorities and women in his employ. The only quantitative factor (which is erroneously confused with the concept of quota by those who do not comprehend the essence of affirmative action) is that an effort be made to have the minority representation in the work force approximate the percentage of the qualified members of that minority in the available labor pool of that particular minority group in that particular region.[13]

Goals and time-tables are supposed to be adopted by mutual agreement of the appropriate public agency representative (federal) and the head of the institution (industrial establishment, university, and the like), after adequate deliberation and appraisal of the total situation by both. This means: how many, over how long a period of time, and presumes that the effort is made *in good faith*. And *good faith* is the crux of the matter. It is very much a qualitative criterion which may frequently be interpreted differently by the subject and the appraiser. The U.S. Commission on Civil Rights describes the difference as follows:

The essential difference is that under a quota system a fixed number or percentage of minorities or females is imposed upon the employer, who has an absolute obligation to meet that fixed number. Goals and timetables, by contrast, are result-oriented procedures by which the employer—subject only to the requirement that the targeted results are as much as reasonably can be expected—determines goals and a time schedule for correcting minority underutilization, and then makes every goodfaith effort to achieve the self-imposed goals. Contrary to what would be true in the case of quotas, failure to meet goals and timetables is excused if the employer can show that goodfaith efforts have really been made. However, an employer must be prepared to demonstrate in detail why goodfaith efforts failed to produce desired results.[14]

According to Squires, "Rather than creating a system of preferential treatment, affirmative action laws attempt to undo a system which has provided preferential treatment for white males."[15]

Judicial interpretation of Title VII of the Civil Rights Act of 1964 has by and large supported a strong enforcement posture on the part of federal and state agencies concerned with employment discrimination: "Title VII has emerged as a major legal instrument for combating discrimination in employment."[16]

Court rulings have spurred employers to institute affirmative action programs. According to Herbert Hill, this development is the result of several factors:

Private parties are guaranteed the right to go to court free of administrative restraints. A class action may be maintained by an incumbent employee, by a discharged employee or by an applicant refused hire when it is *claimed* that the discharge or refusal to hire was based in whole or in part on discriminatory grounds.[17]

"There are four reasons," Hill continues, "why Title VII creates serious exposure for a defendant."

First, the plaintiff can be almost anyone who has any connection with the employment practices of the employers. Second, the range of complaints can be as broad as the employer's total enterprise. Third, the proof may be accomplished on the basis of statistical data. Fourth, the relief given by courts may involve substantial amounts of money and serious alteration of established business practices.[18]

Clearly, the risk entailed in noncompliance is greater than is consistent with sound business policy.

The government official, because of work pressure, rigid administrative procedures, or ignorance, may at times in good faith interpret goals and time-tables as quotas, and the head of the institution, factory, or university concerned may well yell "quota" in order to befog the issue. The affirmative action approach, when followed meticulously, by no means even approximates reverse discrimination. Racism in reverse is a complete misreading of the intent of the law.

Racism means a systematic, total domination of minority groups by the majority. Organizations which have implemented affirmative action programs are trying to end a situation where one group dominates others. They are not trying to reverse the situation by making the formerly oppressed group the new oppressors.[19]

Of course, ending discrimination will not automatically end all inequality in society. As earnings statistics show, the income range of American workers, white or black, is far greater than the 50 percent difference between the median incomes of black and white workers. Nonetheless, the elimination of discrimination must be regarded as an essential step in correcting a major social injustice. From this point of view, the following often-quoted statement of Christopher Jencks and his colleagues does a disservice to the struggle for economic equality of blacks and whites:

It seems quite shocking, for example that white workers earn 50 percent more than black workers. But we are even more disturbed by the fact that the best-paid fifth of all white workers earn 600 percent more than the worst-paid fifth. From this viewpoint, racial inequality looks almost insignificant.[20]

It improperly contrasts an inequality stemming from a particular social evil—prejudice and discrimination—with an economic injustice in society as a whole (if a large disparity may be considered an injustice).

At the same time, it may be safely asserted, as Gregory Squires does, that "the institutionalization of the concept of affirmative action was a major step in combating discrimination."[21]

Courts have ordered minority quotas, but only in cases where they have found discrimination and resistance to eliminating it. However, quotas as opposed to goals, imposed without a court order as a remedial measure, may well be ruled illegal. "Court decisions on employment practices have been aimed at discriminatory systems, rather than at giving or condoning preferential treatment as such."[22]

In general, all Title VII suits are viewed as class actions, whether specifically designated as such or not. Where the court finds discrimination, the entire class of which the individual complainant is a member is affected by the ruling. But we must pursue affirmative action in the hope that over a period of time the required corrective will evolve, thus avoiding the perpetuation of an America consisting of "two societies, living side-by-side, separate but unequal,"[23] and hence necessarily hostile.

A large number of our informants both fully supported affirmative action programs and stressed the need for economic expansion and recovery as a major factor in the improvement of minority status and wholesome intergroup relations. They were, they said, concerned with *full* resources and not merely with making available resources on a *fair* basis. That is, the magnitude of the pie that is to be divided is a basic factor in intergroup relations. An excellent example of the essential components of an affirmative action program is given in the appended 1977 Statement on Affirmative Action of the American Jewish Committee.[24]

Earlier, in testimony before the Congressional Special Subcommittee on Education in September 1974, Bayard Rustin and Norman Hill of the A. Philip Randolph Institute expressed their concerns over the complexity of this issue:

While both men approve of the affirmative action principle and its implementation, they argue with other black leaders about making it the prime mover of black progress: "We do not believe, however, that affirmative action can or should occupy the pivotal role in a strategy for racial progress. Affirmative action, we are convinced, can only succeed when combined with programs which have as their objective a much more fundamental economic transformation than affirmative action could bring about. We are, furthermore, unalterably opposed to the imposition of quotas or any other form of ratio hiring."[25]

The assistant secretary for equal opportunity at HUD suggested that working with contractors associations would result in an increase in the proportion of black contractors in the building industry:

I said last year that we had about 3½ billion dollars worth of construction. We estimate that less than 2 per cent of this amount went to minority group individuals. We want to see that tripled or quadrupled, and the only way that we are going to achieve this is by working directly with the contractor associations.

He and others believed that the Federal Housing Administration insuring office had an affirmative responsibility to see to it that residents of the area, i.e., minority group individuals, would share the economic benefits resulting from the mortgage it guarantees. It was held especially important that the impact of the contributions of HUD was as important in the economic as in the social area. The economic area means new economic opportunity for minority groups as consultants and planners of the housing they are going to live in. It means economic opportunity in building the housing and managing it. It means economic opportunities in maintaining the housing and rehabilitating it. It was felt that some of the billions of dollars that were being spent by HUD should go directly into the hands of minority group entrepreneurs and that minority group individuals should be employed on the job.

None of our informants, black or white, confused "compensatory" with "preferential"; unfortunately, the distinction is not always maintained today. There is a vast difference between the two terms. As indicated previously, "compensatory" implies assistance for the disadvantaged person through special services or through educational training as required, so that he or she might become qualified. "Preferential" signifies favoritism because of race, color, religion, ethnic origin, or sex, with little or no regard for qualifications. In the former, merit is a basic factor; in the latter, merit plays an insignificant role, if any.

The SEEK program in the colleges of New York City was an attempt to provide such "compensatory" treatment. The term SEEK stands for Search for Education, Elevation and Knowledge. At present, the fate of SEEK is uncertain for two reasons: (1) shortage of funds for New York City departments, and (2) abuse of the plan through retention of students for longer periods than originally contemplated.[26]

Compensatory service is an *obligation that the majority has incurred* and must fulfill if the members of the discriminated minority are to be brought into the mainstream of American society within a reasonable period.

With respect to compensatory services for the disadvantaged members of minority groups as "assistance to become qualified," a number of views were expressed in the interviews and several illustrations noted. Underlying the consideration of compensation for past deprivations is the implied assumption that persons with equal credentials but different ethnic or racial backgrounds do not have equal opportunities. The college quota system of old, designed to exclude applicants for reasons of race, color, ethnic identity, or religious affiliation, has practically disappeared. However, one of our informants reported that among the recent graduates of a large medical school in New York City not a single Italian student was to be found.

This is a strange phenomenon in a pluralistic society which places a premium on upward mobility. It is conceded that group membership as such should not be a criterion for selecting students for professional training. Nonetheless, if we are not to abandon the merit system basic to the democratic process, some questions still must be asked: Has sufficient effort been made to attract representatives from the various ethnic groups through instituting the procedure of *search*, if necessary? Once found, are they given the assistance needed "to become qualified for admission," which constitutes the basic requirement for an affirmative action approach in which "compensatory treatment" plays a significant role? A periodic reevaluation of student ethnic representation by educational institutions, professional and general, is in order. This also holds for employment in industry.

Most of our informants favored open enrollment in college as a right of all who had completed their high school training, provided that tutorial educational facilities were also made available to those disadvantaged educationally for whatever reason. Such facilities should consist of both remedial and counseling services. Unless this is done, the dropout rate will continue to be enormous. The executive of the New York City Human Rights Commission asserted that a quota system, even if utilized to increase the admission of members of disadvantaged groups to educational institutions, is undesirable and in all probability illegal: "An affirmative effort is the duty of any democracy which contains within it many different kinds of populations."

At the time of our interview, the National Urban League found its Street Academy program effective in their compensatory activities.[27] Another informant reported on an intensive senior-year program for black students in Maryland high schools to prepare them for admission to the University of Maryland. Brandeis University at one time rendered special assistance to certain black students after admission. In Israel, the Pre-Academic programs of the Hebrew University offer compensatory services for educationally disadvantaged immigrant students from North African and Asian countries. These programs have proved successful, and a research project is now being conducted by the university to evaluate the special education methods employed.

All of our informants shared the view that a "larger pie" was essential to avoid discriminatory practices in our educational institutions which insufficient resources tend to promote. The urge for "preferential" treatment arises most readily under conditions of scarcity.

The conscientious application of affirmative action goals has at times led to charges of "reverse discrimination," charges which have resulted in litigation in various states. Thus, in 1971, *DeFunis* v. *Odegaard* challenged the admission policy of the University of Washington Law School. DeFunis, a white, had been rejected by the school, even though his test scores were higher than those of thirty-eight of forty-four minority students accepted. The university admitted that it used two different, parallel sets of scales to evaluate minority and white applicants:

It reserves the right to use subjective criteria and claims it should not be compelled to adhere solely to test scores in its admission policy. The crucial issue is the university's assertion that it is constitutionally permissible to give the preference to minority students.[28]

The case went to the U.S. Supreme Court, where it was declared moot since DeFunis had by that time graduated, and under the Constitution the federal courts "are without power to decide questions that cannot affect the rights of the litigants before them."[29] In New York, the Federal District Court (1976) held that the City College of New York had discriminated against whites and Asians in the selection of students for a special training program for the medical profession.

More recently, the University of California Medical School at Davis set aside a specific number of places for minorities (blacks, Chicanos, Asian-Americans, and so forth) in their admissions programs, primarily in order to increase the number of minority physicians in the community. In so doing, the school had to reject better qualified white applicants, one of whom was Allan Bakke. He filed suit in the California courts claiming that the equal protection clause of the Fourteenth Amendment was violated in his case. The lower courts upheld his contention. The Regents of the University appealed to the U.S. Supreme Court, where a decision was recently rendered.[30]

In some quarters, this situation has been referred to as "the case of the century," or as the most important civil rights case since the 1954 *Brown* v. *Board of Education* decision. The decision raises some important questions that may still have to be dealt with. (See Chapter 10, note 62.) Our own belief, and that of some informants, is clearly in favor of "compensatory" as opposed to "preferential" treatment. Unfortunately, opponents of affirmative action continue to confuse it with preferential treatment and to oppose legitimate efforts to compensate for inequalities. In the course of our interview, A. Philip Randolph spoke out against preferential treatment: "In other words, I'm opposed to letting down the qualification bars for Negro applicants to enter college." His clear position is in stark contrast to the many confusing statements still being made about the valid and much-needed affirmative action programs.

The Matter of Training

One phase of the affirmative action program at least evokes little or no controversy: the worker training program. Frankly compensatory, the programs of the various federal and state agencies concerned with the provision of training facilities for workers have been in operation for more than a dozen years.[31] The administrator of the Bureau of Apprenticeship and Training of the Department of Labor pointed out that the training facilities that have been made available since the regulations went into effect in January 1964 were designed to facilitate the preparation of members of minority groups, especially blacks, to function in vocations requiring special skills. According to this administrator, members of minority groups generally score fairly low in qualifying examinations. This holds true not only for blacks, but also for Spanish-speaking individuals (including Mexican-Americans), American Indians, and, to a limited extent, Orientals.

At the time of our interviews, the regulations for training had been revised and were based on minimum, basic qualifications. One training program is Outreach, which is the responsibility of the Labor Department's Manpower Administration (1970). Its aim is to develop contacts in the minority communities in order to inform them about opportunities available for training in trades.

The State Employment Services throughout the United States disseminate information with respect to apprenticeship training, including the utilization of mass communications. Minority participation in the apprenticeship program, which is primarily an on-the-job training program, has been stepped up. Generally, the training facilities are limited to those between the ages of seventeen and twenty-five or twenty-six.

Representatives of the Bureau of Apprenticeship and Training located in 175 field offices act as contacts with industry. The wage of the apprentice is approximately 40 to 50 percent of a journeyman's wage. The term of apprenticeship is from two to five years, or possibly six; on the average it is four years. (Many trades require four-year apprenticeships.) However, a person who has worked in a given trade is given credit for his experience. At the time of our interviews, 280,000 young people were registered in this federal training program. Three hundred and fifty occupations were represented.

Manpower programs are products of the Manpower Act of 1962. As automation displaced employed workers, the manpower programs, which also comprised retraining, took on great importance. They were designed to prepare persons for the "world of work" in a variety of ways and under a variety of umbrellas. The programs were all administered by the Department of Labor as the overall supervising agency. At the time of our interviews, training grants were being made by the Department of Labor, and HEW compliance review was administered by the training program itself to determine the extent to which minority groups were represented.

The training of disadvantaged individuals is a prime objective of manpower programs. Hence, a large number of blacks, Puerto Ricans and other Spanish-speaking individuals, Indians, and others are found in them. Part of the contract with the employer (especially when grants are made) provides that the employer agrees to engage those who have met training requirements. The employer guarantees a job to the person who finally qualifies.

One complaint registered by one of our informants was that even when industry is obliged by compliance regulations to train black people, it expects the government to pay for this training.

The Manpower Administration attempts to (1) retrain individuals displaced as a result of automation, cybernation, and technical change generally; (2) prepare for employment the young person who has never been employed, the school dropout, and the young person who needs assistance in order to stay in high school; and (3) develop a program for those who have been displaced as a result of age and other factors. HEW is also concerned with the training of teachers to work with disadvantaged youth. Nonetheless, inequalities in the administration of this program still exist. The assistant secretary of HEW administering the Program for the Disadvantaged at the time of our interviews pointed out that in New England federal funds were used to train one teacher for every two hundred and fifty disadvantaged children; in Louisiana, with a much larger impoverished population, one teacher was being trained for every ten thousand children.

A high official in the Department of Labor was very critical of American business's practice of "importing manpower from overseas that couldn't speak English, that couldn't read English, that weren't even citizens, instead of training blacks from our urban and rural ghettos." He indicated that this practice continued through the 1960s, when a recommendation was made— he did not know by whom—that this practice should be pursued to meet manpower shortages. Yet, at the same time, employers were saying that they could not employ nonwhites. Had effective training programs leading to meaningful employment been instituted, it would not have been necessary to encourage immigrants to fill manpower needs.

The same official also pointed out that in certain industries such as ship-building, in which billions of federal dollars were being spent, aliens were being employed while at the same time, practically adjacent to the shipyards, were unemployed nonwhites. He stated, "We certainly should not adopt a policy of bringing in people from other countries rather than training nonwhites who are unemployed."

The current (1976-1977) competition for jobs does not reflect active industry recruitment of aliens. National concern has been expressed, however, that thousands of aliens in the South are being employed as farmworkers.

One problem was revealed in relation to the Davis-Bacon Service Contract Act, passed in 1931 and amended in 1935 and 1964, which provides that in construction contracts involving amounts of $2,000 or more in federal funds, the prevailing rates shall be paid to laborers and mechanics. "Prevailing rates" are frequently union rates, and that means the rate to be paid would have to equal that of a journeyman. The employer does not wish to, nor can he, train a person and pay him a journeyman's rate, both because he cannot afford it and because the already-trained journeyman would object to a trainee receiving the same pay he does. Therefore, if the Davis-Bacon rule is not waived in such instances, it becomes a barrier in apprenticeship training programs. If not handled properly, the Wage Determination Division could become an instrument for perpetuating discrimination.

Philadelphia Plan

One of the most successful training plans in operation during the 1970s was the Philadelphia Plan instituted in 1969. This plan was set up to increase the proportion of minority employees engaged in construction work as well as to provide a craft training facility for minorities. Enforcement of the plan is the responsibility of the Office of Federal Contract Compliance.

It was anticipated that at the end of the calendar year 1973, 23 to 25 percent of minorities—primarily black—would be available for construction jobs in the six higher-paying trades in the Philadelphia area. During the plan's second year of operation, the minimum hiring goals were exceeded.

Under this plan, standards were set in advance in the construction industry, and the action taken was of a specific affirmative nature without negotiation on any general issues. It was anticipated that there would be some discussion with respect to the proportions of minority group workers taken into the construction industry in the Philadelphia area each year.

In July 1975, the Labor Department proposed a new plan for increasing minority employment in the federally involved construction work in the Philadelphia area. The proposed plan applied to twenty-three of the Philadelphia area trades rather than only to the six presently covered. It would cover all contracts and subcontracts in excess of $10,000, instead of the $500,000 figure now used as the basis.[32] Since this new plan has not yet been put into effect, for the time being the old plan with its $500,000 lower limit on contracts remains in force.

The training aspect of affirmative action, including specific education and remediation, cannot be too strongly emphasized. Assistance to *become* qualified is essential in the prehiring stage for employment as well as in the preadmission stage for colleges and specialized professional schools. Such assistance to disadvantaged minority groups is the principal avenue to the equality of opportunity envisaged in President Johnson's Executive Order 11246. Without it, the existing gap between black and white education, employment status, and income may well continue for decades.

Notes

1. Albert Wohlstetter and Sinclair Coleman, "Race Differences in Income," in Anthony H. Pascal, ed., *Racial Discrimination in Economic Life* (Part of the RAND Corporation's studies on the connection between racial discrimination and economic opportunity), (Lexington, Mass.: Lexington Books, D. C. Heath and Co., 1972), p. 66.

2. Ibid., p. 4.

3. "Affirmative Action: The Unrealized Goal," The Potomac Institute, Inc. (Washington, D. C., 1973), pp. 25, 26.

4. Ibid.

5. Ibid., pg. 27.

6. Alfred W. Blumrosen and Ruth G. Blumrosen, "Layoff or Worksharing: The Civil Rights Act of 1964 in the Recession of 1975," *Civil Rights Digest*, U.S. Commission on Civil Rights, Washington, D.C., Spring 1975, p. 36.

7. *The New York Times*, June 1, 1977.

8. Gregory D. Squires, "Affirmative Action, Quotas and Inequality," *Journal of Intergroup Relations* 3, no. 4, 1974, p. 36.

9. In contrast to preferential action which is not essentially motivated by merit.

10. Council on Legal Education Opportunity By-Laws, 1968.

11. A joint memorandum, issued on March 23, 1973, by EEOC, the U.S. Civil Service Commission, the Department of Labor's Office of Federal Contract Compliance,

and the Department of Justice, affirms that "all agencies agree that the use of such goals does not and should not require an employer to select on the basis of race, national origin or sex, a less qualified person over a person who is better qualified by objective and valid procedures."

12. "Memorandum to College and University Presidents," U.S. Department of Health, Education and Welfare, December 1974, pp. 2, 7.

13. Revised Order No. 4, Affirmative Action Programs, December 4, 1971, Office of Federal Contract Compliance, Department of Labor (Section 60–2.11). Nondiscrimination in Employment, the Conference Board, 1974.

14. U.S. Commission on Civil Rights, "Statement on Affirmative Action for Equal Employment Opportunities," February 1973, p. 20.

15. Squires, "Affirmative Action," p. 28.

16. Herbert Hill, "The New Judicial Perception of Employment Discrimination: Litigation under Title VII of the Civil Rights Act of 1964," *University of Colorado Law Review* 43, no. 3 (March 1972): 253.

17. Ibid.

18. Ibid., p. 255.

19. Squires, "Affirmative Action," p. 31.

20. Christopher Jencks, et al., *Inequality: A Reassessment of the Effect of Family and Schooling in America* (New York: Harper and Row, 1972), p. 14.

21. Squires, "Affirmative Action," p. 34.

22. Ibid., p. 18.

23. "Report of the National Advisory Commission on Civil Disorders," U.S. Government Printing Office, March 1, 1968, p. 1.

24. See Appendix A (Statement on Affirmative Action).

25. Daniel Elazar and Murray Friedman, *Moving Up: Ethnic Succession in America* (New York: Institute on Pluralism and Group Identity, 1976), p. 51.

26. Recently, the state comptroller charged that overpayments of $1 million were made to CUNY's SEEK program participants during the 1973-1974 academic year (*The New York Times*, September 26, 1976).

27. The Street Academy program was developed to aid black students who did not benefit from the regular public high school program. Subject matter and teaching methods are adapted to the requirements and abilities of the students. The schools emphasize self-image, cognition, and the skills needed to ensure survival ("Rethinking Alternative," National Urban League, 1976).

28. Squires, "Affirmative Action," p. 26.

29. *The Washington Post*, April 26, 1974.

30. The Bakke decision was rendered on June 28, 1978. See Chapter 10, note 62.

31. On March 30, 1977, the House of Representatives approved a one-year extension of the Comprehensive Employment and Training Act to allow time to study President Carter's plans to change the federal role in the program (*The New York Times*, March 30, 1977).

32. *Black News Digest*, U.S. Department of Labor, July 14, 1975.

12

Attitude Modification

As previously indicated, the early 1960s saw a gradual decline in reliance on attitude modification as a method of improving intergroup relations. The method began to lose favor because of (1) the difficulty of gauging the effectiveness of past efforts; (2) the pressure to achieve results expeditiously and the need to influence the mass, rather than just the individual or even the small-group effects inherent in attitude change procedures; and (3) a growing conviction that behavior change, externally induced, could produce the desired result and also perhaps some modification of attitude either in the future or presently. Hence, during the 1960s, there was a marked diminution in the attention given to attitude change in programs of intergroup relations, including human relations education in our school systems.

During this period, the emphasis was largely on the change of social and external conditions generally. Economic improvement, enactment and implementation of civil rights legislation, improvement of housing conditions, and better desegregated educational facilities became the focal points of intergroup relations practice. However, the past few years have witnessed some revival of concern with the reduction of prejudice as a basic adjunct to programs of change in the environmental situation. For example, it is now generally recognized that resegregation is usually the result of faulty attitudes. On the other hand, success at achieving attitude change, as reflected in genuine integration in schools, housing, and jobs, can act as stimulants to further change.

The creation of effective contact and communication between different ethnic groups and individual members of those groups is basic to the achievement of changes in attitude. This is no simple matter. Contact alone is far from being the cure-all it is sometimes taken to be: "At most, it merely serves to facilitate or insure the *possibility* of some kind, indeed of any kind, of interaction or communication among groups or their individual members."[1] Properly handled, however, such contact between peoples remains one of the most potent methods of developing harmonious intergroup relations, since isolation and separation are known to foster negative stereotyping. We must broaden the opportunities for persons of different ethnic, racial, and religious groups to get to know each other better, to meet across group lines, and to do so on a peer basis. However, contact requires certain conditions for success; otherwise it can be dysfunctional.[2]

Opportunities for contact need to be multiple. To assure productive contact, it is important that, if possible, the groups involved be of relatively equal status. Differences in status between individuals can mar constructive contact relationships. Gaps in income, cultural levels, education, housing, and other areas need to be narrowed before useful contact can occur. Coalition[3] is one method of achieving contact on an impersonal basis. The real problem for intergroup agencies is to be fully aware of the conditions under which group contacts can promote harmonious relations and to overcome the obstacles in the way of better intergroup communication.

Let us turn to some views on the role of attitude change expressed by a number of our informants, all of whom were professionals engaged in policy formulation, program planning, and practice in special areas.

The late Whitney Young was acutely sensitive to the role of attitudes:

I think more than ever today we are dealing with attitudes. I think it has become a serious problem because the backlash of the so-called silent majority, those attitudes are being exploded and feared by the present administration....the legal framework is not enough. Legislation can be sabotaged by failure to implement the resources to carry it out...[by] simply not supporting the necessary bond issues or taxes necessary.

One outstanding policy analyst (a black) stated that while he formerly paid scant attention to attitude change, in recent years he had become convinced of its importance, primarily because white backlash had become a reality and black militants were then heading toward separatism. He emphasized the need to tackle attitude change at the school level; in the labor area, he asserted that a direct assault on blue-collar white anti-black attitudes was long overdue. Generally, attitude modification can best be achieved through those institutions that mean most to the persons involved; they are the ones to reach them most effectively.

On the other hand, several informants stated that attitude education has to be an adjunct to external change of conditions. One informant put it even more strongly: "I think when we began making the switch in our field from emphasis on changing attitudes to the emphasis on changing conditions, we made an important leap of progress forward."

Today there is less faith in the premise that changes in conditions produce changes in attitudes. There have been too many evasions of the law, too much backsliding and backlash, to justify the belief that legislation alone or other forms of external change will ultimately produce the desired change in attitude.

A prominent black informant expressed this view: "The Negro minority, being only one-tenth in number in this country, could never have even survived if it had not given some attention to the attitudes of the white majority."

Interviews with two executives of an important national organization (one black, one white) gave somewhat different responses to the query, "What do we do about attitudes?" The answer of the black executive was: "It is a problem for the white people," and his white colleague said: "Don't bother with attitudes."

A. Philip Randolph spoke at length on the importance of changing attitudes to improve social and intergroup relationships:

We need to work on both [change of social conditions and change of attitudes] because social conditions create attitudes and attitudes in turn reflect on social conditions. Now there is a backlash among white people in various areas of the country. That's a natural thing. Blacks should have known that was going to happen, but you can't stop fighting for your rights because it makes some people mad. And the Blacks fortunately are realizing how some of them employ tactics and strategies that are self-defeating and this must be eliminated. Time will do that and the difficulties of the struggle will build strength. I have no fear or worry about the future of the young black boy. Conditions will make him move.

Two opposing views on the importance of attitude change in modifying relationships between groups are well illustrated by the following responses to our queries. The more negative viewpoint was expressed by a program specialist in a local Jewish intergroup relations agency:

I had always felt that the first thing to do was to try to end discrimination—worry about attitudes later. I was in that school of thought that did not subscribe to the idea that discriminatory practice was always rooted in attitudes. We had the term "the nonprejudiced discriminator"—a guy who was a manager, who had to accept the boss's prejudices. In order to cotton to the boss, he had to carry it out. I remember shortly after our FEPC bill was passed, 25 years ago, when going out to speak to an organization, a fellow from a corporation got up and said, "I am so happy that you got FEPC passed because it holds up my arm. I have always wanted to be fair but now that I have got a law, I know that I have to be fair. That makes a lot of difference to me." So far as attitudes are concerned, your field is psychology. I don't know how much you really change attitudes over a long period.

The proponent of attitude change, a program specialist in a local urban affairs agency under Catholic auspices, stated:

I am still an "attitude" man. I still feel for any kind of meaningful change to occur in society it has to be backed up with changed attitudes. Otherwise you will have the kinds of repressive backlashes that I think we are experiencing now. We simply don't have the foundation; we've built much of our human relations effort on sand and I think we've got to support our human relations effort with real meaningful attitude changes.

Affirmative views on the role of attitude change were stronger among black than among white professional leaders. This finding is conducive to a certain amount of speculation on the importance of the attitudinal factor. Nonetheless, awareness among blacks of the persistence of white negative attitudes toward them is not as powerful as the feeling of blacks that they are the victims of social injustice. The hostility of blacks to whites appears to be of a *reactive* nature.

White informants (particularly Jewish ones) generally agreed, and strongly so, that changing existing conditions was the important consideration and that "we can leave attitudes in the background." On the other hand, a program director of a prominent national Jewish agency said: "I think that I would be somewhat of a phony if I pretended that we will effect environmental change in any meaningful way." He maintained that all aspects of the diversified American society had to be made part of the school curriculums of America.

Perhaps we now have enough of a power base to become concerned with attitudes. It may be that in years past this approach was premature.

Several of our informants believed that black antagonism toward whites in the last few years was primarily hostility toward the establishment, that it was of a sophisticated variety rather than being a person-to-person response. One black executive suggested that the antipathy of the black community was directed against the system rather than against the white individual: "Such animosity is as severe against a black police force as a white one."

There is, of course, the important matter of changing the attitude of the favored majority group with respect to the need for social change, i.e., the improvement of the general living conditions of the minority.[4] Generally three persuasive reasons may be given to gain majority support for the requisite action: (1) Poverty and crime are more expensive than prevention and rehabilitation; (2) the older generation will lose the respect of the younger if it continues to tolerate inequality and racial injustice; and (3) crime, including mugging, would decrease if group discrimination and poverty were alleviated.

In the five- to six-year period preceding our interviews, polarization of racial attitudes on both sides had become more overt; white resistance had increased, perhaps because of increased fear, as had black bitterness and disillusion, in all likelihood because of the persistence of racial rejection. Therefore, the policy analyst (a black), referred to previously, felt that we must attempt to modify the attitudes that should accompany overt support basic to social change; however, he cautioned that such efforts must not replace social action. Above all, there was strong support for the view that social change is achieved largely through change in the institutions of society themselves—in the school, the factory, the labor union, the business organization, the church, and the neighborhood center. It is assumed that this kind of change ultimately helps bring about change in the behavior of the members of a particular group. In this regard, too, our respondents expressed much more faith in achieving changes of behavior than of attitudes.

One respondent, an urban specialist with broad research experience, held the rather extreme view that, "to the extent that one works on attitudes, one neglects the sociopolitical structure." He attributed the revival of concern with attitudes on the part of certain black professional leaders in the intergroup relations field to their view of backlash as "white racism," which they believe must be fought. However, he continued, "how does one fight white racism?" Just what is gained, in pragmatic terms, from this label? The essential societal changes can be achieved primarily by changes in the outside factors of power structure, economics, and social conditions generally, he contended. In his view, these same forces will eventually transform attitudes.

Until now, we have concerned ourselves with the role of attitude modification in producing desirable social change. We must now turn to how attitude change itself may be achieved.

The "how" of attitude change may be considered in relation to both the individual and the small group. Our interviewees indicated some interest in various forms of sensitivity training, especially for workers in intergroup relations—particularly religious workers. For example, professionals with competence in sensitivity training and related skills who have met with nuns and Catholic religious educators in the Midwest area have reported considerable success.

In any modification of attitudes, the small-group interaction process was held preferable to the direct educational approach. The reaction to skin color in and of itself was found to be a powerful, irrational factor in the negative group attitude. The small-group process, in which the laboratory (or small group) is used to facilitate interaction among the members of the group, aims at giving its members insight into their own prejudicial attitudes and emotional reactions to difference in color, ethnic origin, and religious commitment.

Attitude Modification Techniques—A Survey

It is now widely accepted that prejudiced attitudes toward other groups are formed at a very early age. Mary Ellen Goodman demonstrated conclusively that prejudiced attitudes were found in children below the age of five.[5] As children grow older, their attitudes become more firmly fixed, for better or for worse.

Differences of opinion over the causes of intergroup prejudice have centered on whether such prejudices are primarily the result of environmental factors or whether they are inherent personality traits. Are the major influences affecting attitudes derived from forces within the individual or from society at large? Or are they a combination of both?

Social scientists and practitioners have discussed the origins of prejudice for many years without arriving at definitive conclusions. However, even though theories vary, some useful insights and methodologies for the practitioner have emerged.

Human Relations Training

It is probably valid to consider the basic premises of human relations training as the foundation of most techniques employed in attitude modification. In turn, such modification may influence the process of social change itself. The three premises of human relations training most relevant to intergroup relations (attitude modification) are:

(a)...learning is achieved best when thinking and feeling are combined with experience and practice. (b)...attitudinal and behavior changes occur more readily when the participants are involved in making decisions which affect them. (c)...a feedback control system; behavior changes as persons learn how they behave in response to others and vice versa.[6]

Human relations training is largely an outgrowth of the research in group dynamics by Kurt Lewin, who, more than anyone else, conceived the basic theory for the development of group dynamics concepts.[7] He believed that the individual, in order to alter long-cherished attitudes, must understand the relationships between personality, ideas, prejudices, *and* the manner in which society is viewed. Those links might be established through the small-group process, where the probing of the group brings the innermost feelings of the individual to the surface and leads to an understanding of relationships between individuals and the larger community. The "feedback" in the group is an especially important consideration.

The laboratory approach which underlies practically all of the group dynamics methods employed was initiated at a workshop in intergroup relations in 1946 at State Teachers College in New Britain, Connecticut. In 1947, this workshop was followed by a more sophisticated residential laboratory at Bethel, Maine. Since that time, the technique of laboratory training has experienced remarkable growth and its meaning has expanded. A variety of alternative techniques comprise the principal factors of the laboratory method.

While the laboratory approach is variously interpreted, in the main it provides for the involvement of participants in intimate face-to-face situations. Sessions vary in length and take place in a setting offering privacy and relaxation. Initially, the laboratory method was designed to provide a base for individual and personal growth. It was assumed, and evidence supported the assumption, that a better understanding of one's self and one's ability to relate to others would help one's understanding of the relation of self to society and to various groups, and thus improve intergroup attitudes. Later, the Laboratory Method was applied to effecting a change in systems of institutions through modifying the attitudes of individuals in the laboratory situation.

The aim of the Laboratory Method, which quickly evolved into the T-group process, was not only to enhance self-understanding but also to evaluate how members of a group regard each other. In the course of this process, personal attitudes as well as personal value systems are explored.

As the Laboratory Method broadened to include social as well as individual attitudes, creative compromises on differences were encouraged. In some instances, this involved a process of team-building. It became apparent that an approach that provided personal insights and learning experience as well as effecting social or institutional change through the individual could serve a dual purpose. It could affect the individual in terms of both the inner and outer dimensions of attitude causation. Another aspect of the laboratory approach was the utilization of social science research, of subjecting the results of laboratory procedures to additional scientific investigation. The laboratory approach requires highly trained and skilled leaders or facilitators, a situation that does not always obtain.

The term Laboratory Method is now applied to a wide variety of techniques, but, whatever its application, it has had a profound influence on attitude modification programs. The small-group process, which involves full participation, interaction, and feedback among the members of the group, resulting in individual insights, is utilized in practically all current attitude modification programs.

One major assumption about the benefits of sensitivity training is that improved self-insight will reduce prejudicial attitudes toward minority groups. Insofar as attitudes are affected by internal individual needs, the greater security which an individual may acquire from his new understanding of the causes of his irrational attitudes may bring changes in attitude.

T (Training) Group

The T-group techniques of attitude modification originated in the early work of Kurt Lewin, who in collaboration with Kenneth Benne, Leland P. Bradford, Jack R. Gibb, and Ronald Lippit,[8] undertook to resolve an abrasive racial situation in Connecticut. Out of their observations grew the concept of a formal sensitivity training program, the first of which was held at Bethel, Maine, in 1947. This marked the establishment of the National Training Laboratory (NTL), which in 1950 was taken over by the National

Education Association (NEA) and later became an independent division of the NEA. Today, the NTL conducts extensive T-group programs in a number of cities and deals not only with problems of intergroup relations but also with such specialized areas as management, career development, managerial skills, and organization development.

The NTL is associated with a number of institutions in organizing regional training and engages in research and publishing. Since 1947, T-group programs have expanded enormously. Just as the T-group has developed quantitatively, the process itself has developed variations. Initially, the T-group was conducted in an isolated atmosphere—in a retreat such as Bethel—and was largely unstructured. Members as individuals and as part of the group were encouraged to develop their own agenda. In the process, individuals would examine their feelings and would feel free to express opinions, at times highly critical, about the beliefs and behavior of other members of the group.

This process led to the development of intensive interpersonal relationships and to the capacity to function as a group. The drawing up of an agenda necessitated a tentative, yet intense, examination of each other and a focus on the dynamics of the group. The group focused on its own problems and very decidedly on the present, disregarding both the past and future. Interaction was entirely verbal, and the leader or trainer intervened only minimally. External goals of the group were not discussed to any significant degree.

One of the important functions of the trainer was to analyze the interaction and to clarify what was happening. He also would intervene to prevent abrasiveness, since emotions tended to rise when individuals would make personal comments about others in the group.

The group often floundered considerably in setting its own rules and agenda. Once the group decided on its course, the trainer tried to assure adherence to the elected program.

T-group sessions lasted from three days to two weeks. Groups were small—ten to fourteen was considered ideal—but a number of groups might be meeting at the same time and could come together for plenary sessions.

Since the pioneer days of the T-group, considerable changes have been made. Research and experience stimulated experimentation. Still the original model has held up very well, although new techniques with new names offering variations of the original process have proliferated. Among the changes that have taken place is the greater participation of trainers in the T-group process. There is no norm for the ideal extent of leader participation; extent varies with the nature of the group, the leader, and the agenda of the specific T-group. In addition, T-groups today may deal with problems of the past and of the future, even though trainers may try to steer the group toward the here and now. T-groups have become much more structured and can be problem-oriented. The NTL's list of programs now includes problem-oriented sessions ranging from "Women's Development Programs and Leadership Training for Teenagers" to "Back-packing for Young Hikers." Moreover, since specific problems are dealt with, the early preference for heterogeneous groups has given way to greater homogeneity.

Techniques which have proved valuable in attitude modification programs, such as role-playing and decision-making, have been introduced. There has been an attempt to divert T-groups from involvement with themselves and their own group to real-life situations. Thus, a variety of different training programs have developed from the original T-group concept, such as the Clarification Group, the Tavistock Model of Laboratory Training, and the Laboratory Confrontation or Communications Laboratory.[9] One pioneer of group dynamics, Max Birnbaum, writes, "The T-group emerged as a new social invention that bears some rough resemblance to a combination of seminar and therapy group, but it actually is neither."[10]

Another important change has been the trend toward utilizing T-groups for institutional as well as individual change. While differences of opinion as to the effectiveness of the T-group technique remain, the fact that participation now numbers in the millions reflects a widespread belief in the effectiveness of the program. Even those who are unsure about the benefits they have gained seem enthusiastic. One graduate T-group conferee remarked at lunch one day, "My boss said he got something out of it. He said he knew he's not so stupid that he can stay anywhere two weeks without getting something out of it—but damned if he knew what it was!"[11]

The competence of the T-group trainer is crucial. Sensitivity, ability to gain the confidence of participants, and skill in participation and feedback can spell the success or failure of the T-group process. Moreover, with the increasing role trainers play, an important distinction needs to be made between "participating" and "persuading" leadership. The latter can distort the purpose of appropriate training.

The T-group process is still evolving and has spawned many developments. Indeed, nearly every training program involving group process and attitude modification to a greater and lesser degree utilizes the research findings, experiences, and techniques developed by the T-group process.[12]

Clarification (C) Group

The prime mover of the C-group concept is Max Birnbaum, who has conducted C-groups at the Boston University Human Relations Laboratory for a number of years.[13] The C-group, a small-group process, focuses on intergroup relations training and deals with problems inherent in differences in race, ethnicity, and religion. Dissatisfaction with the effectiveness of T-group training in this area was reflected in a statement by Donald Klein, former program director of the National Training Laboratory Center for Community Affairs. In a letter to a colleague, he wrote:

The application of sensitivity training without modification to the field of intergroup training does not appear to work. In fact, as the blacks suggested in your project, sensitivity training may have the effect of by-passing the intergroup hostilities and tensions just because the individuality of people is emphasized. In usual sensitivity efforts it rarely becomes necessary to open up and deal with group stereotypes.[14]

Birnbaum and his associates have long been convinced that traditional T-group techniques cannot effect any lasting changes in intergroup attitudes. Accordingly, they developed a process which offers a promising variant, although the research studies of its effectiveness are not yet definitive. The process may be roughly divided into three phases. The first is devoted to the exposition of the life histories of the participants. The trainer may initiate a program by relating his personal history in some detail. However, the emphasis in accounts of personal histories is on the ethnic, racial, or religious group of the individual. Events and background related to group identity are stressed.

In the second phase, participants are encouraged to offer their reaction to the world about them, and to analyze how they view members of other groups and how they feel they are viewed by others. Individuals are asked to give their candid reactions to membership in their own group and to the manner in which others refer to their own group. They question whether or not they are typical of their own group. Other questions arise. What is a valid generalization of one's group? What are stereotypical notions of these groups? They are asked to examine whether they play the role expected of them by society or act as independent thinkers.

In the third phase, individuals analyze their thinking about other groups. Do they tend to generalize about various groups? Do they think in stereotypes? They look at their actions in the light of their own group interests, and they may find that they are motivated not by group interest but by personal prejudice. While change in the individual is extremely important, the discussions reveal that the resolution of historical group differences requires more than individual change.

The C-group technique, unlike any other group dynamic technique, attaches no great significance to the possibility that the program may not end in group cohesion. Disagreements may remain at the conclusion of the process. Participants usually have the courage to stand up for themselves and their opinions, and they are able to argue against the opinions of others.

The C-group also differs from the T-group in the cognitive input from direct discussions between group members and the analysis of community experience. The C-group must be heterogeneous and consist of members of various subgroups who can bring individual experiences and problems to it. Another unusual attribute of the program is its concentration upon back-home problems and real-life situations. Consequently, it is important that the trainer have practical experience with intergroup relations problems; academic acquaintance alone is not enough.

The C-group does not emphasize the therapy aspect of the T-group. It aims at individual acceptance of one's own group and modification of irrational attitudes toward others. It also embodies some teaching attributes of the classroom since factual information dealing with problems of intergroup relations is introduced and reading may be assigned.

C-group programs at the Boston University Human Relations Laboratory have extended over various periods of time—some have been six weekly offerings with three-hour sessions, or three hours a week for fifteen weeks. The C-group program has been received with some enthusiasm. It appears to offer the advantages of learning, problem-solving, self-acceptance, and clarification of inner-group viewpoints, while avoiding the abrasive and possibly harmful conflicts between participants in the T-group.

The Structured Group Interview

The structured group interview is designed to involve large groups of up to fifty persons and to effect institutional and attitudinal change. Although the process centers on the group rather than on the individual, the attitudes of the individual will inevitably be affected. The purpose of the structured group interview is to achieve change by evaluating the situations faced by participants and to agree upon changes desired by the system or institution under examination. The process calls for involvement of the influential members of institutions concerned and for the achievement of open communication, and in the final analysis, preparation and consent of the group for change. Above all, a climate in which open communication can take place is crucial. The process usually requires two days of sessions.

Initially, each individual is asked to describe personal attitudes toward relevant groups, but therapy is not an objective and feelings are not individualized. Rather, the individual's statements are examined as they have meaning for the group; second, problems which could arise in the event of possible changes within the institution are analyzed.[15]

The large group is seated in a hollow square, a form which has been found useful in group dynamics processes. The large group may be divided into subgroups for more closely focused discussions. Interviews are held with individuals, and their frank opinions are encouraged by the interviewer. These open up issues for analysis by the group. This first step will often result in the exposure of hostilities and differences. Once these differences are exposed, the group sets about exploring them and their meaning for themselves personally, but mainly for the institution. Finally, the group focuses on what can be done.

The process calls for the active intervention of the leader or interviewer, who is not necessarily one and the same person. The leader's own attitudes and experiences are freely expressed and a feeling of trust in him is fostered. Above all, the leader and the interviewer constantly raise questions based on what is being said by the participants. The interviewer must be skillful enough to expose hidden feelings and opinions and to break through deeply felt attitudes. The final phases of the process comprise pragmatic discussion. At the end of the sessions, each participant is asked to express an opinion on what has been achieved both on a personal and a group level.[16]

Clinics and Workshops

A large number of institutions concerned with intergroup problems, including school systems, conduct clinics and workshops in an effort to modify individual attitudes and institutional practices. A clinic will usually consist of one or more small-group sessions. Workshops may utilize a similar model but are frequently one-day events with as many as a thousand participants; after listening to lectures, they are assigned to small groups for discussions, followed by plenary report sessions.

A variety of group dynamics techniques are utilized in small-group sessions in clinics and workshops. There is also frequent reliance on "experts"—consultants who deliver generalized lectures—although there is increasing discussion of back-home problems.

Sessions may begin with a problem census, and the problems may be discussed in a sequence determined by the group. Role-playing, sociodrama, and psychodrama are employed in more sophisticated programs.[17] Extensive use is made of relevant audiovisual materials for informational and discussion purposes.[18] The participants may play problem-oriented games. For example, a school may be concerned with the lack of academic success of disadvantaged students. An appropriate game might be based on the hypothesis that the school has a limited amount of money to spend on this situation. Participants would be asked what they would do. Role-playing or sociodrama might be employed, and oral or written answers to the question might be asked for, followed by discussion. Participants could then compare their answers with the group decision.

Sociodrama, Psychodrama, and Role-Playing

Sociodrama dates back at least to the Middle Ages, when audiences were often brought to the stage and involved as actors.[19] The present practice of sociodrama and psychodrama was largely originated by a Viennese social scientist, Jakob Levy Moreno, who believed social and psychological therapy goals could be attained by acting out personal and group problems. He introduced these concepts to the United States in 1925 and later founded an institute bearing his name in New York City. His techniques were quickly adopted as valuable instruments for use not only in laboratories but also as effective therapy tools and methods of attitude modification. Pioneers in the field of sensitivity training such as Lippit, Bradford, Benne, and others incorporated the Moreno techniques in their programs.[20]

While sociodrama and psychodrama are related by origin, sociodrama is used largely to deal with groups or social problems. It may take place in a laboratory situation or in a workshop discussing practical back-home problems; one or more problems may be presented in sociodrama form. Those most concerned with the problems in their day-to-day activities are usually involved as actors. A scenario is agreed upon and a "warm-up" process is permitted. The play then begins in earnest.

Psychodrama is more of a personal therapeutic experience than sociodrama. While an important element of group therapy may be involved, depending upon the ability and skill of the leader, the process is essentially centered on the individual. The sequence of events is closely related to sociodrama, though the latter is usually of much shorter duration and does not focus on psychotherapy. The central character is asked to portray private feelings and to express freely matters which come to mind during the play. The therapist may play an important interventionist role in prodding the subject. Other participants in the play may act as *auxiliary equals or assisting therapists* in the development of the psychodrama. In this they are assisted by the leader, who is a trained therapist. There is an important sharing of emotions during the process, which may continue for a number of sessions.

A widely used technique related to sociodrama and psychodrama is that of role-playing which is a much simpler technique of short duration, but there is hardly a workshop, clinic, or other training program that does not utilize role-playing. Simply stated, role-playing is the acting out of a problem under discussion by a group. A problem in a workshop situation, for example, one in which teachers are involved, may be examined. A small group is selected by the leader, or individuals may volunteer. Participants usually include those who have actual experience with the problem under discussion. The actors are given a few minutes to prepare their play, and they then appear before the entire group and act out the problem situation.

The group leader or facilitator usually calls a halt to the role-playing session after about ten minutes. The group then offers observations on the way in which the problem was handled by the various "actors." Role-playing is almost always used in human relations training and in essence is related to sensitivity training.

An innovative device originated by Moreno, role reversal, may also be combined with role-playing. The leader will suddenly stop the play at any point and reassign roles. He may do this a number of times. When he deems it advisable, he will end the play, and discussion ensues. The objective is a critical analysis of the solutions to the problems enacted in the sociodrama, of the group process that was revealed during the play, and of the attitudes of the individuals involved.

Sociodrama serves not only as a problem-solving device but also as a group-learning process. Frequently, inaccurate information will be introduced into the play by misinformed individuals. It is essential that such information be corrected. Consensus of the group is the goal.

Such participation by individuals with a commonality of purpose in peer-group situations, examining everyday problems in an atmosphere conducive to wholesome human relations, cannot fail to have some salutary effect. However, while attitude modification may occur, such discussions do not assure institutional change. Such change may take place in a clinic, where a small group is assigned a specific task and where the institutional leaders are determined to effect change. As a rule, however, this action commitment is not built into a clinic or workshop. When it is not, and when practices continue as heretofore, the effects either on the individual or on the institution may not be lasting. Nonetheless, individuals who have experienced a change in attitudes may have some impact on functions under their jurisdiction.

Human relations clinics and workshops are frequently held on an annual basis, although some seem to be organized for cosmetic purposes only. Nevertheless, given the spread of group dynamics techniques, the resultant reduction of bias and development of personal growth are, to some degree at least, of consequence.

In-service training frequently utilizes some variants of clinic or workshop techniques and may take place on a system-wide basis in which groups of employees are brought together to discuss intergroup problems. Participants learn from each other and from senior staff and/or consultants. One drawback of in-service training is that it frequently does not encompass supervisory personnel.

Simulation Games and Training

For our purposes, a sharp distinction needs to be made between simulation games[21] and simulation training. Simulation training is a process involving real-life situations with which participants are already familiar. Its purpose is to enhance skills in dealing with on-the-job intergroup problems and to increase sensitivity to human differences as well as to modify prejudiced attitudes. While the components of simulation training may be called games, in fact they are not. Rather, they are scripted simulated incidents ideally based on conditions in the institution in which the participants function. This, however, may not always be possible since development of a separate simulation training program for each institution concerned would be required. It is possible, however, to develop programs which can be used by similar types of institutions.

Simulation Training

Simulation training can include the most desirable features of many attitude modification techniques—group dynamics, in general, T-group and C-group techniques, role-playing, and so forth.[22] In the main, however, the simulation training here described consists of a well-designed series of situations closely related to the human relations problems that may confront participants in their professional or community activities.

Simulation training attempts to achieve institutional as well as individual change. Its optimum impact can be achieved only if the activity is intimately related to the specific problems encountered by individuals in their own experience. Ideally, training should extend over a prolonged period of time and should include techniques which proved successful in individual and social change.

A skilled social diagnostician, who is familiar with the human relations field, able to gain the confidence of respondents, and sensitive to the attitudes of individuals and the mechanisms activating institutions, should be assigned to undertake a problem census of a specific institution.

Assuming that management has decided to solve problems, the diagnostician should then interview various levels of management, particularly first-line supervisors who are in direct contact with entry-level workers. An effort should be made to ascertain who are the "leaders" among minority groups, and they should be interviewed. It will be necessary to secure their confidence, and if possible, leaders inside the plant or in the community should vouch for the integrity of the diagnostician. At this stage, it is best not to take notes or to record interviews. After one or two days of interviewing, problem patterns will emerge; problem areas in an institution may number anywhere from a few to thirty or more. These problems should then be written up as hypothetical situations and disguised so that no individual feels threatened.

The simulation module describes a problem but does not provide an answer. It is open-ended. It leaves the group with the question: "What do you do now?"

The problem now is to determine in what form the simulation module should be presented to participants. There are a number of alternatives, depending upon available funds.

(1) The sequences can be mimeographed and be presented to participants who will read them for the first time at training sessions. This is the least expensive but least effective of all techniques.

(2) A more effective method is to record the sequences on a tape or cassette recorder. The recording should be made by personnel of the institution concerned.

(3) The third and most effective method of presenting the simulation game is by means of videotape.

At this point, training resources should consist of an involved training group of the institution and a series of written, audio, or audiovisual case histories, ready for presentation to the simulation training groups.

Leaders and Facilitators. The next step is the careful selection of discussion leaders or facilitators.

The Participants. Participants in training groups should also be selected carefully. Participants should have work responsibilities that are as similar as possible. Within this limitation, there should be heterogeneity, with an ethnic and racial mix, if possible.

The Presentation. The next step involves the presentation of the key incident or case history. It is extremely important that the group understand that they have a responsibility to make recommendations and that these will be carefully reviewed.

The discussion itself, as has been stated, must be open and candid. In the process, there is opportunity for the utilization of various group dynamics techniques that have been helpful in attitude modification.

Time, resources, and other factors may require curtailment of the process there.

Much of the success of simulation training will depend on the time available for the training, inasmuch as behavior and attitude modifications are complicated and difficult matters.

Another step which has been found effective is to call groups back periodically to review what has happened since the training sessions were held.

During the course of simulation training, members of the group bring in problems. It is important to offer information on how similar problems have been dealt with successfully by others. Followup sessions will show whether the training process has been successful. The most common faults of simulation training are the failure to allow enough time for the process, the inability or lack of will to put important recommendations into practice, and the failure to follow up so that the process can be evaluated.

The Cognitive Approach

At one time, in the effort to affect intergroup attitudes it was felt that "the truth would set people free." All that was needed, it was thought, was a series of informative techniques which through radio, television, films, and the lecture platform, would acquaint students, adults, and special interest groups with the facts about prejudice, race, integration, and other problems. Enlightenment and understanding would automatically follow. In the past two decades, these various methods have been supplemented by the institutionalization of information, so that now it forms a part of the school curriculum. Appropriate units are built into courses in sociology, psychology, political science, and intergroup and/or race relations. Adults are exposed to vast amounts of informational material through television and film sharply opposed to prejudice. But mass communication does not permit discussion or personal exploration. In addition, the entire character of the problem has changed since the passage of civil rights laws. Moreover, there is some question about the lasting effect of information which conflicts with environmental and peer group influences. It can hardly be doubted, however, that the vast increase of information through the communications media and formal education has had considerable impact. However, the more sophisticated methodologies grouped under the rubric of group dynamics have revolutionized attitude modification techniques.

It is difficult to evaluate the various factors that have modified attitudes on group relations in America. Polls and surveys indicate vast improvement in intergroup understanding over the past twenty years. One important influence may be deduced from the research findings that increased years of schooling bring increased understanding and tolerance.[23] The college explosion of the last decade may, therefore, be presumed to have had a considerable effect. At the same time, environment and societal influences outside the institutions of learning must be taken into account. For example, in a three-city study it was found that prejudice against Jews and blacks increased from grades 8 through 12. A possible explanation for this increase may be that the attitudes of teenagers at this age level reflect their dating patterns and the related increased clannishness of their parents.[24]

A number of other techniques designed to help resolve personal psychological difficulties are listed below. Detailed descriptions of these techniques can be found in the works listed in the notes.

Esalen Institute at Big Sur, California, giving rise to the encounter-group approach[25]

Transcendental Meditation (Science of Creative Intelligence), for relief of internal stress[26]

Transactional Analysis, for the enhanced understanding of one's own personality[27]

EST, for the resolution of personal problems.[28]

In considering the "how" of attitude change as a factor in the ultimate production of social change, we have examined the various group processes (group dynamics approaches) employed. Basic to all is the aim to achieve insight into matters pertaining to social relationships that frequently also require the acquisition of self-understanding. While sensitivity training can at times be helpful, its use in intergroup relations requires a considerable degree of problem-orientation.

The degree of direct leader participation will depend largely on whether the goal is self-understanding or problem-handling. In time, the leader's role in the group dynamics process appears to become increasingly active. Feedback, the reactions of group members to expressions and actions by the subject, can play a powerful role. Through this means, irrational attitudes toward others can be brought to the surface and their true nature perceived. If the matter under consideration is primarily intergroup relations, a certain amount of group heterogeneity is, of course, required. The degree to which problem-orientation is stressed, especially the "back-home" problem, will determine whether the group experience is guided along "seminar" or "therapy group" lines.

Notes

1. Marc Vosk, "Contact," *Adult Leadership*, journal of the Adult Education Association, 1954, pp. 1–4.

2. Gordon Allport, *The Nature of Prejudice* (Reading, Mass.: Addison-Wesley, 1954), pp. 261–81 ("The Effect of Contact").

3. See Chapter 7.

4. We learn from the Hebrew Prayer Book that on Yom Kippur, the Day of Atonement, when asking for forgiveness of one's sins, one asks for forgiveness for acquiescence in conditions conducive to the creation of crime and violence.

5. Mary E. Goodman, *Race Awareness in Young Children* (Reading, Mass.: Addison-Wesley, 1952), rev. ed. (New York: Collier, 1964).

6. Alan F. Klein, *Effective Groupwork* (New York: Association Press, 1972), p. 365.

7. Kurt Lewin, "Frontiers in Group Dynamics," *Human Relations* 1 (1947): 5–41; 2 (1947): 143–53.

8. Kenneth D. Benne, Leland P. Bradford, Jack R. Gibb, and Ronald O. Lippit, *The Laboratory Method of Changing and Learning* (Palo Alto, Calif.: Science Behavior Books, 1975).

9. See Appendix A.

10. Max Birnbaum, *Saturday Review* (November 15, 1969): 83.

11. Spencer Klaw, *Fortune* (August 1961): 160.

12. George Henderson, *Human Relations* (Norman, Okla.: University of Oklahoma Press, 1974), Chapter 10.

13. Benne, et al., *The Laboratory Method*, Chapter 12.

14. Letter from Donald Klein to Richard Wagner, Bucknell, October 29, 1968.

15. B. Cottle Thomas, "Strategy for Change," *Saturday Review* (September 30, 1969).

16. James F. Small and Max Birnbaum, "The Structured Group Interview," *American Training and Development Journal* (September 1971): 26–32.

17. See "Sociodrama, Psychodrama, and Role-Playing," pp. 190-92 below.

18. In recent years, audiovisual materials which focus on intergroup matters, particularly school problems, have become more widely available. Such materials have limitations since many are too general in scope to be relevant to localized problem-solving.

19. Benne, et al., *The Laboratory Method*, pp. 365–67.

20. Jakob L. Moreno, *Group Psychotherapy* (New York: Beacon House, 1945).

21. See Appendix A.

22. Examples of Simulation Training Programs: Oscar Cohen, *Human Relations in the Office* (New York: Friendly House, 1972); Frederick P. Venditti, *Solving Multi-Ethnic Problems* (New York: Friendly House, 1970).

23. Gertrude J. Selznick and Stephen Steinberg, *The Tenacity of Prejudice* (New York: Harper and Row, 1969).

24. Charles Y. Glock, Robert Wuthnow, Jane A. Pilivin, and Metta Spencer, *Adolescent Prejudice* (New York: Harper and Row, 1975), p. 115.

25. Henderson, *Human Relations*, Chapter 11.

26. Harold M. Blomfield, Michael Peter Cain, Dennis T. Jaffe, and Robert Kory, *TM* (New York: Dell Publishing Co., 1975).

27. Eric Berne, "Transactional Analysis: A New and Effective Method of Group Therapy," *American Journal of Psychotherapy* 12 (1958): 735-46.

28. Adelaide Bry, *60 Hours That Transform Your Life* (New York: Harper and Row, 1976).

13

Concluding Thoughts

This study analyzes methods of dealing with malfunctioning relationships among racial and religio-ethnic groups in our society both on the ameliorative and preventive levels. The materials for this study derive principally from experiences of representative, well-qualified practitioners in the field of intergroup relations in various categories. In addition, some consideration is given to available findings from the related social sciences and the findings of well-known theoreticians in the field. Comparative analyses are made on the basis of historical perspectives.

In view of the progress achieved thus far in the intergroup relations area, our emphasis should henceforth be shifted from a concern with *whether* a particular action should be taken to *how* a specific problem should be approached. Certain general formulations have naturally evolved as a result of our analyses to which we now direct our attention in summary form.

It is difficult to deal effectively with the "unequal" (minority) group problem in isolation. The problem is integral to the total situation, including the economic conditions and the social values prevalent at any given time. The restructuring of relationships among groups requires as a basis the reduction of the absolute level of inequality among them, especially economically.

Group power (including "black power"), properly interpreted, is an essential for collaborative effort. The strong, the "surefooted," are the ones capable of certain required statesmanlike compromises; they are also the ones who can contribute to progress in human rights. The weak, the unsure, can contribute little or nothing to such aims. However, the inculcation of superordinate goals (the common good) in the American population is essential to preventing an ethnocentrism that could destroy our chances for realizing our goals and even be detrimental to the general welfare.

Compensatory systems designed to render assistance (training, remediation, and education) to those disadvantaged because of former racial, religious, ethnic, or sexual discrimination should be encouraged. "Preference" practices should not only be avoided but forbidden. Decisions should be made solely on the basis of merit. This applies to the majority as well as the minority.

Pluralism in the United States is on the upswing, but the distinctiveness of the group identities should be solely in the nature of boundaries, never barriers, for barriers would prevent the establishment of productive and fruitful relationships—the opposite of what is intended.

Our continuous and rapid technological development should be accompanied by a deep concern for its social consequences. The latter receive scant attention today.

Economics is the basic ingredient in the quality of group relations. The poor are most affected by economic adversity. "Minority" groups are largely found among the poor.

Citizen participation is essential in urban development, including "redevelopment" operations and all matters vital to the functioning of society.

The cities are central to our intergroup problems and require concentrated attention. Urbanism needs to assume front rank as a serious study and research endeavor, as a basis for far-sighted planning and innovative programming. The creation of urban colleges paralleling our agricultural schools is definitely in order.

The rise of some of our "unequals" (minorities) in the last two decades to middle-class status[1] should help reduce the problem of the class factor in the achievement of integration. The narrowing of the gap in class status between the minority and majority groups should ease the integration process. In addition, the present tendency toward greater tolerance for "individual deviation" in behavior and ideology, according to recent research findings, should facilitate the acceptance of the intergroup "difference" factor as a natural manifestation in a pluralist social order.[2] However, this manifestation by certain minority groups should not reduce our concern for the plight of the populations living in slum areas, including the ghettos. The "hard-core" in the ghettos has not even been touched, and the conditions there are now even worse than in the past because of their cumulative effect.

Housing today appears to be the area least amenable to the elimination of exlcusionary practices. The problem of discrimination is much greater where we live than where we work. This was as true of the days when Gunnar Myrdal made his study (the early 1940s) as twenty years later (the early 1960s), when Arnold Rose wrote his postscript on Myrdal's study.[3] Genuine movement in this area will not take place until some controlled experiments are undertaken in an attempt to eliminate the factors responsible for the fear of "inundation." This could serve as an exemplary influence, as described in the text.[4]

The use of confrontation as a means of discarding undesirable intergroup relations practices is both useful and harmful. Under any circumstances, however, confrontation should be employed as a *process* and never as a goal; this approach should be carefully planned with the objective clearly formulated, and not as a means of letting off steam.

The religious institutions of the United States have a moral obligation to contribute interreligious and intergroup understanding. While some progress has been made in recent years in ridding religious texts of prejudicial material, much more needs to be done. The religious institutions have a great opportunity to render a positive valuable service by assuming an "affirmative" role in their educational activities. Through these educational programs, they can help inculcate a commitment to the sanctity of the person regardless of ethnic ancestry, religious belief, or color.

The various racial, ethnic, and religious groups are expected to give top priority to those matters in the intergroup situation that directly concern their respective groups. However, it would indeed be shortsighted for them to limit their efforts to this particularistic objective. Each group should have an eye on the total situation of which it is a part. A "sick" society is a threat to all groups, regardless of racial, ethnic, religious, or sexual identity.

The increasing complexity of society calls for more rather than less social science in the field of human relations, but with a change in direction. The sociopsychological approach of the 1950s and 1960s, with *The Authoritarian Personality* as an outstanding example, should be reduced in behalf of studies in the politicoeconomic area. Since we are now concerned primarily with this area and need data for guidance purposes on the operational level, research in the latter direction is urgently needed. Why do some "busing" programs work and many do not? What are the essentials in practice for a busing effort to be successful? What happens initially with a well-prepared busing program and what are the changes that take place after a period of time?

What has happened to the progress made some years ago in eliminating discriminatory practices in the "executive suite"? What guidelines are needed for success in this area? Where do we stand today in the matter of "social discrimination," which is tied up closely with the "executive suite"? What is needed to strengthen the basis for its obliteration? Research in the area of affirmative action would help to destroy the misleading attacks on these efforts that consciously confuse "preferential" with "compensatory" and thus befog the issue by the overgenerous use of the term *reverse discrimination*. And finally, what is needed is the gradual evolution on the basis of long-range social research of methods and ingredients required for avoiding the recurrence of the social pathology of group discord, suspicion, and frustration.

In the early 1960s, in his postscript to Myrdal's *American Dilemma*, Arnold Rose predicted "the end of all formal segregation and discrimination within a decade and the decline of informal segregation and discrimination so that it would be a mere shadow in two decades."[5] His predictions are on the way to fullfillment. He reminds us that twenty years earlier, Myrdal had already predicted the early destruction of the popular theory behind racism (the Negro as a different species, and the like). When he started his study, however, Myrdal reported: "I was shocked and scared to the bones by all the evils I saw, and by the serious political implications of the problem which I could not fail to appreciate from the beginning."[6]

In our own time, we can note with satisfaction that the hundred-odd professional anti-Semitic organizations that existed in the United States in 1948 were practically all gone in the 1970s. Only thirty years earlier we experienced the Holocaust; to be sure it occurred abroad, but in the United States around that time, anti-Semitic attitudes and anti-Semitic organizations were in abundance.

In spite of regressions, it can be stated that America is well on the way to becoming a truly civil rights-conscious nation. We must continue to be vigilant, however, to curb the regressions we continue to experience today.

While the group conflicts of the future will more likely be in the area of economics—the "haves" and the "have nots"—than between religio-ethnic and racial groups as such, we must keep in mind that prejudice lingers on very much longer than discrimination. We have no evidence that prejudice is ever really completely eliminated. Hence, in our rightful emphasis on dealing directly with discrimination, we should be concerned with its reactivation under circumstances conducive to the revival of hostile intergroup action. Frustration stemming from economic want and hardships incident to depleted energy resources or increasing atmospheric pollution could well reactivate prejudice with its resultant discriminatory practices.

In times of unaccustomed relative calm, there is danger of complacency. While we have gradually been making bigotry unfashionable, we have to make "scapegoating" as taboo even as incest.

Notes

1. For extensive presentation of data which reinforce this observation, see Ben J. Wattenberg, "In Search of the Real America," WGBH-TV, first transmission on PBS, May 17, 1977.

2. J. Allen Williams, Jr., Clyde Z. Nunn, and Louis St. Peter, "Origins of Tolerance; Findings from a Replication of Stouffer's 'Communism, Conformity, and Civil Liberties,'" *Social Forces* (December 1976): 394–408.

3. Gunnar Myrdal, *An American Dilemma* (New York: Harper, 1944).

4. See Chapter 10.

5. Myrdal, *An American Dilemma*, Postscript.

6. Ibid., Preface to Twentieth Anniversary Edition, p. xxv.

Appendix A

General

Informant and Respondent

The term informant is utilized in our study instead of *respondent* in accordance with the usage employed by Herbert Hyman, et al.:"...the informants generally are selected by judgement, are few in number, and are questioned through intensive, unstructured interviewing."[1] (Some structuring was done in our own study when placing the questions initially.) A further differentiation between informant and respondent is implied in the Hyman paper. Informants are said to be "informed by their knowledgeability and not distorted by their psychological characteristics."[2]

The Interviews

Three approaches were utilized to obtain information for the study: (1) taped interviews; (2) review of documents from interview agencies; and (3) library research.

Most of the interviews took place in 1970; however, the information at those interviews has been updated wherever possible. For the most part, the interview questions dealt with approaches, methods, and guiding principles which interviewers use in coping with intergroup problems and issues. One major objective of the interviews was to determine the impact of historical events on changes in agency policies and programs. (The list of informants and their agency association, selected on the basis of criteria specified in the Introduction, appears later in this appendix.)

Although guided by specific questions, the interviews were conducted in a conversational manner and the questions directed to interviewees were open-ended. They related as much as possible to the particular experience of the interviewee and to his or her agency's objectives and program. Hence, not all questions were duplicated in each of the interviews. The questions from which the selections were made in the interviews are listed in three groups, as follows:

I.

1. What is the scope of your agency's activities?

2. In which areas, i.e., education, housing, employment, poverty, etc., does your agency carry on its intergroup relations work?

3. How does your agency carry on its work generally in intergroup relations? (Discuss your methods, techniques, and approaches.)

4. Have the activities of the federal government in intergroup relations had an impact on your agency's program? How? (Question for the private agency only.)

5. Have recent black-white confrontations made an impact on the work of your agency? How?

6. In the decade of the 1970s, what do you think will be the basic problems in the intergroup relations area?

7. Are there any specific strategies, methods, or techniques that you employ in your program?

8. How well do black and white agencies work together in your experience?

9. How shall we pursue the goal of integration?

10. How do we prevent white backlash?

11. Have you evolved some effective approaches in dealing with Jewish-black relationships? (Question generally for workers in the Jewish agencies.)

12. Do you believe the method of confrontation works? On what occasions?

II.

1. Do you see a shift in emphasis in the directions of group identification? Has this affected the work of your agency?

2. In the recent past, have there been any major historic events causing your agency to modify its approaches and methods in carrying out the objectives of your program?

3. Do you have any illustrations that reflect the results of our programs in the intergroup relations field?

4. Can intergroup relations agencies have any criteria for measuring results?

5. Should we concern ourselves with attitudes? External conditions? Both? To what extent?

6. What is the role of the religious institution in intergroup relations?

III.

1. How would you identify the conditions that have an impact today on our group relations?

2. What, in your opinion, should be the relationship between the private and public agency? Between government and the private (communal) intergroup relations agency?

3. What is the relative importance of the economic, political, sociological, and psychological factors in intergroup relations programming?

4. Do you believe that a prevailing social theory (melting-pot theory, cultural pluralism, differential racial or ethnic capacities, etc.) has an influence on the nature of your program?

5. Has your agency's goals and methodologies changed during the different periods of American history? e.g., during the 1920s (the Red Scare); the 1930s (importation of Nazism; the Depression; the New Deal; World War II; the growth of social research; the Cold War); the 1950s (McCarthyism; entry into American affluence; the Warren Court); the 1960s (the period of the protest movements and widespread confrontation).

6. Do you believe we are actually separating into two societies? (black and white)

7. Is the use of violence ever permissible?

8. When is the use of coalitions (allies) indicated?

9. Should the use of quotas ever be permitted? Benign quota? How about compensatory and/or preferential services? (At that time goals and time-tables were not yet in appreciable use.)

10. What qualifications do you look for in appointments to your professional staff? Have your standards for selection of your staff changed in the last decade or two?

The Interviewees

(Agency association designation as of time of interview)

ALLEN, Alexander J.
Regional Director
National Urban League
New York City

BARONI, Msgr. Geno
Director
Center for Urban Ethnic Affairs
U.S. Catholic Conference
Washington, D.C.

BIRNBAUM, Max
Director
Center for Applied Social Science
New York City

BLOOMGARDEN, Lawrence
Director
Public Education and Interpretation
American Jewish Committee
New York City

BROWN, Dr. Sterling
President
National Conference of Christians
    and Jews
New York City

CHAPIN, Arthur
Director
Office of Equal Employment
    Opportunity
Department of Labor
Washington, D.C.

CHERNIN, Albert D.
Executive Director
Jewish Community Relations Council
Philadelphia, Pa.

CHISHOLM, Terry
Regional Representative
Model Cities
Housing and Urban Development
Washington, D.C.

CLARK, Kenneth B.
President
Metropolitan Applied Research Center
New York City

COHEN, Oscar
Program Director
Anti-Defamation League
New York City

CULBERSON, George W.
Deputy Director
Community Relations Service
Justice Department
Washington, D.C.

DAVID, Preston
Assistant Director
City Commission on Human Rights
New York City

DAVIS, Lloyd
Director
Office of Assisted Programs
Housing and Urban Development
Washington, D.C.

DODSON, Dan
Director
Center for Human Relations
New York City

DUNBAR, Leslie
Director
Field Foundation
New York City

EPSTEIN, Benjamin R.
National Director
Anti-Defamation League
New York City

FEILD, John
Director
League of Cities/Conference of Mayors
Washington, D.C.

FINKS, Father David
Co-Director
Urban Task Force
U.S. Catholic Conference
Washington, D.C.

FLEISCHMAN, Harry
Director
Labor and Race Relations
American Jewish Committee
New York City

FLEMING, Harold
President
Potomac Institute
Washington, D.C.

FLETCHER, Arthur A.
Assistant Secretary
Wage and Labor Standards
Department of Labor
Washington, D.C.

FRANCK, Isaac
Executive Vice-President
Jewish Community Council of
    Greater Washington
Washington, D.C.

GLICKSTEIN, Howard A.
Staff Director
U.S. Commission on Civil Rights
Washington, D.C.

GOFF, Regina
Assistant Commissioner
Program for the Disadvantaged
Health, Education and Welfare
Washington, D.C.

GOLAR, Simeon
Executive Director
New York City Commission on
    Human Rights
New York City

GOLD, Bertram H.
Executive Vice-President
American Jewish Committee
New York City

GREEN, Ernest
Executive Director
Recruitment and Training Program
New York City

HIGGINS, Msgr. George
Director
Division of Urban Life
U.S. Catholic Conference
Washington, D.C.

HOLBERT, Kenneth F.
Director
Housing Opportunity Division
Office of Equal Opportunity
Housing and Urban Development
Washington, D.C.

HOLMAN, Ben
Director
Community Relations Service
Department of Justice
Washington, D.C.

HOWDEN, Edward
Regional Coordinator
Community Relations Service
Department of Justice
San Francisco, Calif.

HUNTER, Rev. David R.
Deputy General Secretary
National Council of Churches
New York City

HUNTON, Harold
Director
Training and Staff Development
Health, Education and Welfare
Washington, D.C.

HYDE, Floyd
Assistant Secretary
Model Cities
Housing and Urban Development
Washington, D.C.

INNIS, Roy
National Director
Congress of Racial Equality
New York City

KEANE, Mark E.
Administrator
International City Management
     Association
Washington, D.C.

KLAVAN, Rabbi Israel
Executive Vice-President
Rabbinical Council of America
New York City

LEONARD, Jerris
Assistant Attorney General
Civil Rights Division
Department of Justice
Washington, D.C.

LEVINE, Bertram
Assistant Attorney General
Civil Rights Division
Department of Justice
Washington, D.C.

LEVINE, Irving
Director
Urban Projects Division
American Jewish Committee
New York City

MARSHALL, James
Board of Governors
American Jewish Committee
New York City

MASLOW, Will
Executive Director
American Jewish Congress
New York City

MIDDLETON, Jack
Executive Director
Urban Affairs
Archdiocese of Hartford
Hartford, Conn.

MINKOFF, Isaiah M.
Executive Vice-Chairman
National Community Relations
   Advisory Council
New York City

MORSELL, John
Assistant Executive Director
National Association for the
   Advancement of Colored People
New York City

MURPHY, Hugh
Administrator
Bureau of Apprenticeship and
   Training
Department of Labor
Washington, D.C.

NORTON, Eleanor H.
Chairman
New York City Commission
   on Human Rights
New York City

NUNEZ, Louis
National Executive Director
Aspira
New York City

OLSEN, Dr. C. Arild
Vice-President
Program Development
National Conference of Christians
   and Jews
New York City

PARKER, Dr. Everett
Director
Communications
United Churches of Christ
New York City

POMPA, Gilbert
Associate Director
Division of National Services
Community Relations Service
Department of Justice
Washington, D.C.

RANDOLPH, A. Philip
President Emeritus
Brotherhood of Sleeping Car Porters
New York City

ROBERTSON, Peter
Director
State and Community Affairs
Equal Employment Opportunity
   Commission
Washington, D.C.

ROSE, David
Chief
Employment Section, Civil Rights
   Division
Justice Department
Washington, D.C.

RUSTIN, Bayard
Executive Director
A. Philip Randolph Institute
New York City

RUTLEDGE, Edward
Co-Director
National Committee Against
   Discrimination in Housing
New York City

SABLE, Jack
Commissioner
State of New York
Division of Human Rights
New York City

SAMET, Seymour
Director
Intergroup Relations and Social
  Action Department
American Jewish Committee
New York City

SASSO, John
Executive Secretary
National Model Cities Directors
  Association
Washington, D.C.

SCHERMER, George
Director
Schermer Associates
Washington, D.C.

SCHWELB, Frank
Chief
Housing Section
Civil Rights Division
Justice Department
Washington, D.C.

SCULT, Allen
Assistant Area Director
Community Services
New York Chapter,
American Jewish Committee
New York City

SEGAL, Robert E.
Executive Director
Jewish Community Council of Boston
Boston, Mass.

SIMMONS, Samuel J.
Assistant Secretary
Equal Opportunity Division
Housing and Urban Development
Washington, D.C.

SLOANE, Martin E.
Assistant Staff Director
U.S. Commission on Civil Rights
Washington, D.C.

SMITH, Robert
Acting Director
Training and Staff Development
Health, Education and Welfare
Washington, D.C.

TANENBAUM, Rabbi Marc
National Director
Interreligious Affairs
American Jewish Committee
New York City

VINCENT, Sidney
Executive Director
Jewish Community Federation of
  Cleveland
Cleveland, Ohio

VORSPAN, Albert
Director
Commission on Social Action
Union of American Hebrew
  Congregations
New York City

WHALEY, Betti
Program Director
National Urban League
New York City

WILKINS, Roy
Executive Director
National Association for the
  Advancement of Colored People
New York City

WILKS, John
Director
Contract Compliance Division
Labor Department
Washington, D.C.

WOOD, Jack E., Jr.
Co-Director
National Committee Against
  Discrimination in Housing
New York City

WRIGHT, Arthur   YOUNG, Whitney M., Jr.
Executive Director   Executive Director
Catholic Interracial Council   National Urban League
New York City   New York City

YARMON, Morton
Director
Public Education and Interpretation
American Jewish Committee
New York City

Official Summary of the Statement on the Jews in the Vatican Council's Declaration on Non-Christian Religions
(Voted October 14–15, 1965)

The Council searches into the mystery of the Church and remembers the bond that spiritually ties the people of the New Testament to Abraham's stock.

The Church acknowledges that according to God's saving design, the beginnings of her faith and her election are already found among the Patriarchs, Moses and the Prophets. She professes that all who believe in Christ—Abraham's sons, according to the faith—are included in Abraham's call. The Church cannot forget that she received the Revelation of the Old Testament through the people with whom God in His ineffable mercy concluded the ancient Covenant.

Indeed, the Church believes that by His Cross, Christ our Peace reconciled Jews and Gentiles, making both one in Himself.

The Church recalls that Christ, the Virgin Mary, the Apostles, as well as most of the early Disciples sprang from the Jewish people.

Jerusalem did not recognize the time of her visitation, nor did the Jews, for the most part, accept the Gospel; indeed, many opposed its spreading.

Nevertheless, God holds the Jews most dear for the sake of the Fathers; His gift and call are irrevocable. In company with the Prophets and Paul the Apostle, the Church awaits that day, known to God alone, on which all peoples will address the Lord in a single voice and "serve Him shoulder to shoulder."

Since the spiritual patrimony common to Christians and Jews is so great, the Council wants to foster and recommend a mutual knowledge and respect which is the fruit, above all, of Biblical and theological studies as well as of fraternal dialogues.

Although the Jewish authorities and those who followed their lead pressed for the death of Christ, nevertheless what happened to Christ in His Passion cannot be attributed to all Jews, without distinction, then alive, nor to the Jews of today.

Although the Church is the new people of God, the Jews should not be presented as rejected by God or accursed, as if this follows from Holy Scriptures.

May all see to it, then, that in catechetical work or in preaching the Word of God, they do not teach anything that is inconsistent with the truth of the Gospel and with the spirit of Christ.

Moreover the Church, which rejects every persecution against any man, mindful of the common patrimony with the Jews and moves not by political reasons but by the Gospel's spiritual love, deplores hatred, persecutions, displays of anti-Semitism directed against Jews at any time and by anyone.

As the Church has always held and holds now, Christ underwent His Passion and death freely, because of the sins of men and out of infinite love, in order that all may reach salvation. It is, therefore, the burden of the Church's preaching to proclaim the Cross of Christ as the sign of God's all embracing love and as the fountain from which every grace flows.

Resolution Adopted by the Third Assembly of the World Council of Churches at New Delhi, India, December 1961

The Third Assembly recalls the following words which were addressed to the churches by the First Assembly of the World Council of Churches in 1948:

> We call upon all the churches we represent to denounce anti-semitism, no matter what its origin, as absolutely irreconcilable with the profession and practice of the Christian faith. Anti-semitism is sin against God and man.
>
> Only as we give convincing evidence to our Jewish neighbours that we seek for them the common rights and dignities which God wills for His children, can we come to such a meeting with them as would make it possible to share with them the best which God has given us in Christ.

The Assembly renews this plea in view of the fact that situations continue to exist in which Jews are subject to discrimination and even persecution. The Assembly urges its member churches to do all in their power to resist every form of anti-semitism. In Christian teaching the historic events which led to the Crucifixion should not be so presented as to fasten upon the Jewish people of today responsibilities which belong to our corporate humanity and not to one race or community. Jews were the first to accept Jesus and Jews are not the only ones who do not yet recognize him.

Executive Suite

The position of the Jews in the United States has changed markedly in the last few years. In 1960, when the AJC launched its executive suite program, there were only four or five junior college presidents. In 1966, approximately ninety of the presidents, chancellors, or provosts of the nation's two thousand universities and colleges, of which eleven hundred are accredited, were identified as of Jewish birth.[3] Jews and, to a considerable extent, blacks have since made great gains in the executive suite area. Having a Jew in a visible and important line position is no longer thought a handicap.

In the AJC study, the major approach to the problem of executive suite[4] discrimination involved the use of social research techniques which gave the chief corporation executive, generally the first person contacted, a clear view of the nature of the discrimination and its prevalence. The excuses given for the meager representation of Jews in the executive category were various: "Jews don't want to work for us," "Jews are not attracted by this industry," "Jews are unreliable," and even "Jews don't come to us."

Almost every company executive approached was willing to listen. In the past, the initial contact with the chief executive was a difficult one. As a rule, it was set up by a lay person, possibly a lawyer or a businessman, interested and concerned with matters of this kind. There has been a marked change in the attitude toward Jews in elite positions.

At certain stages of the AJC project in executive suite discrimination at banks, even the question of the business ethics of Jews was brought up. One of the queries posed to the AJC lay representative was: "Because of centuries of oppression, are not Jews overly aggressive and excessively scheming, often dishonorable, influence-wheelers and responsibility-avoiders?" Whenever such queries were made, interviews were terminated, for experience had shown that where such bigotry existed very little could be accomplished.

Today we rarely hear such sentiments, although we still hear that "Jews don't come to us," or "They don't stay long enough," or similar remarks. In such instances, the reason for why Jews fail to apply or remain has to be determined and recognized as a problem amenable to a solution.

Eventually it became possible to deal with the issue of executive discrimination, not just from the point of view of the discrimination Jews faced, but also with respect to depriving the entire economy of an important pool of talent.

The ratio of Jews among college graduates—the group from which most business executives are drawn—is many times higher than the ratio in the executive suite, roughly 8 percent versus less than 1 percent. One steel executive asked an AJC official in genuine astonishment: "Why would a creative people like the Jews want to go into a dull business like steel?"

The AJC studies revealed that executive suite discrimination begins with the recruitment of college graduates, continues in corporate personnel and promotion practices, and extends into social clubs and social activities where executives mingle with potential executive recruits.

Strange though it may seem, executive suite discrimination is a relatively new practice. Even as recently as the Civil War, it hardly existed. Jews figured in the commerce of Colonial America; they founded many of the mercantile empires; they were among the first cotton brokers and investment bankers. In the latter half of the nineteenth century, bankers felt that their investments would be protected best by "people like us who spoke our language," "safe" people who had come from the "right" families and had gone to the "right" schools, belonged to the "right" clubs, and attended the "right" churches. Thus, the Anglo-Saxon attitude toward the newcomer and others who were "different" manifested itself. Jews, seeing little or no opportunity in the corporation, sought their careers elsewhere, frequently in the professions. Thereupon the legend grew that Jews were too impatient for the long grind of corporate advancement. The proof lay in the fact that there was a dearth of applications.

The social club as a segregated sanctuary did not help matters. The situation in the executive suite in public utilities was similar to that in the banks; in this area in the executive suite, they were represented in about the same ratio as in banks, namely, one out of a hundred. In insurance companies and other businesses requiring actuarial skills, however, Jews were well represented in staff positions. As a matter of fact, the distinction between staff and line positions became sharp, the line position involving visibility before the public, and the staff member working inside the organization. Of course, most Jews who worked for corporations were staff members. Some time ago, the head of one of the Federal Reserve Banks, when faced with this duality, replied, "Jews have a proclivity for research."

In 1967 the Pennsylvania Railroad Company had one Jew on its management staff, and he was an accountant. A study at Cornell sponsored by the American Jewish Committee in the early 1960s, found that the attitudes of young Jews planning to enter business were scarcely distinguishable from those of Protestants and Catholics holding like aspirations.

The extent of representation of Jews and other minorities in the executive suites of top corporations lies primarily in the hands of the recruiters. The Ward Studies (1959-1963) at Harvard sponsored by the American Jewish Committee[5] reveal that "it is relatively easy to see that anyone perceived as clearly different from the current members of management would tend to be rated down." What is needed is a change in values.

The 1968 University of Michigan study,[6] which was also sponsored by the AJC, proved that supervisors in sales departments considered social background and religion to be highly important factors, especially for top executives, for they would be meeting people as representatives of the company. Recently, the chief executive of one of the largest U.S. corporations was a Jew. The University of Michigan study also revealed that there was frequently a "third party" who allegedly objected to a deviation from the criterion ("Does he look like us?"). This hypothetical third party could be the customer, the top officer, or a colleague who would be offended by the appointment of "someone different" to an executive post.

A case in point: The AJC chapter of Philadelphia conducted studies in the late 1960s on the degree of discrimination in the executive suites of local industries and asked the presidents of banks in that city for appointments to discuss the studies' findings. In one case, the largest bank in Philadelphia, it was found that there was "an extremely low proportion of Jewish officers and no Jewish officers of senior rank," even though the bank had a policy of nondiscrimination. The bank's executive vice-president reported: "Few, if any, of our people thought of themselves as prejudiced about Jews as a group. All said they would reward with promotion and raises people with ability, no matter what their ethnic background. The fact remained that this aggressive, talented group had *not one* representative among the top 15 positions in the bank."

How had this situation come about? A thorough investigation by the executive vice president disclosed that Jewish executive trainees, aware of the lack of Jewish bank executives, felt that even in the absence of overt hostility, they had little chance of reaching the top. To do so would demand superhuman gifts.

In spite of the bank administration's effort to attract Jewish recruits, after ten years the figures showed that only two out of ten Jewish recruits had stayed with the bank as long as five years, as compared to seven out of ten recruits from other religious groups. As an explanation, it was suggested that Jews found banking too dull.

The bank took the following ameliorative steps: first, it continued to recruit Jewish college graduates; second, it reevaluated the Jewish officers in its employ, promoted or raised some of them, and informed its Jewish employees that they were not relegated to "nonvisible" functions but were considered to be in the executive "pipeline"; and third, each time an executive position opened up, the bank made a search for Jewish candidates.

Here we have an illustration of affirmative action. As a result, several Jews have been placed in top executive positions and one is on his way to becoming a senior vice-president. As an important corollary, sensitivity with respect to other minorities has increased. That same bank was the first to name a black vice-president.

These changes took place not only "because it was the right thing to do," but also because these changes were seen as good, sound business practice: many of the bank's corporate customers were Jewish and a number of the accounts handled by the bank were Jewish family trusts.

Improvements in other banks and industries followed. The Mutual Savings Banks of New York City, aided by the AJC, arranged seminars on "fair personnel practices" for bank presidents and their trade associations; and the Savings Bank Association of New York distributed a recruiting brochure throughout the state's high schools in an attempt to attract minority group members. A number of large utilities and life insurance companies, after meeting with AJC representatives, took a new look at the effectiveness of their "nondiscrimination policies." Eventually, these companies set up procedures for actively reaching out to potential employees of Jewish and other minority backgrounds. One paper company in Pennsylvania discovered that it had been hiring Jews for research, laboratory work, and other "staff" positions, but few, if any, for "line" jobs to assist the departments in their sales production, jobs likely to lead to executive positions. The company subsequently concluded that it not only should change its image, but also that it was missing out on potential new talent. With the aid of AJC, orientation sessions were arranged for the company's personnel department, which was advised on how to contact promising Jewish students and how to change the company's image. For instance, although the company had had only one feeler from Brandeis University, it was counseled to send a recruiter there to demonstrate its serious interest in Jewish employees. This is another example of affirmative action.

A fact-finding program on corporation executives commenced in the mid-1950s at the AJC. Fundamental research was conducted, and data were presented to top officials of the corporations involved. It was sometimes found desirable to feed information to the press—not necessarily naming the corporation, though perhaps the industry. The program demonstrated that recruitment could be expanded by including such sources as City College and Brooklyn College, as well as its former contacts.

By 1972, Jewish leadership in communities had met with two hundred major U.S. corporations. In addition, at this time a consultative service was established in Philadelphia, financed by private foundations in that city. As a result, the percentage of Jews in the top management of large corporations nationwide began to rise gradually. In an attempt to attract larger proportions of Jews to banking, the Chairman of the Board of the Chase Manhattan Bank brought the American Bankers Association and the American Jewish Committee together in early 1972 to discuss the situation in the nation's fourteen thousand banks. The American Bankers Association urged chapters of the Hillel Foundation (the nationwide Jewish organization of college students) on 250 campuses to encourage Jewish students to enter banking and drew up a special brochure on banking opportunities for them.

Earlier, during 1967, at its annual convention in New York, the American Bankers Association held an Equal Employment Opportunity workshop with AJC assistance. More than one thousand bankers at the session were advised on how to establish equitable personnel and promotion policies.

In the 1960s and 1970s, the American Jewish Committee and other private groups struggling to overcome executive suite discrimination have gained a powerful ally—

the U.S. government. Since 1961, government contractors—which means anyone doing business with the government, no matter how small—have been required to refrain from practicing discrimination in hiring and promotion and to take "affirmative action" to eradicate it.

In 1965, it was made clear to President Lyndon Johnson that equal-employment programs had to deal with religion as well as race and that executive positions should be included in the problem of nondiscrimination in employment. In 1966, President Johnson declared banks handling federal funds to be government contractors. Hence they had to be concerned with affirmative equal-employment programs, including both routine and executive jobs. At that time, the federal Medicare program for the aged was launched and was accompanied by an "equal opportunity" program that reached specifically and systematically into the executive suite. In the course of reviewing insurance companies which were to handle Medicare payments, the Social Security Administration set up a task force to evaluate employment practices in the upper ranks of the insurance companies. The AJC worked continuously with the Federal Office of Contract Compliance to start similar task forces throughout the federal establishment.

Since the social club is an integral part of executive advancement, strenuous efforts have been made to open these clubs to minority groups. These efforts have included persuading corporations to refuse to pay membership fees and other expenses in exclusionary social clubs. As a result, some of the most prestigious clubs, whose membership policies have been biased since their inception, began to open up to minorities.

On the basis of considerable experience, the AJC has developed a number of effective methods to help uncover and overcome executive suite discrimination. These include corporate self-examination, unequivocal public statements on policy with respect to nondiscrimination, clear and effective instructions to personnel departments on the promotion of qualified minority group members, examination of "third party" pressures; careful watch over prejudiced personnel officers; correction of misconceptions about the supposed characteristics of minority groups, frequently through workshops; and the establishment of appropriate hiring criteria and the elimination of irrelevant marginal ones.

The AJC executive suite program made good use of (1) negotiations, (2) scientific research, (3) appeal to company self-interest (also the industry's best interest), and (4) appeal to democratic ideals. The intelligent utilization of all these techniques was probably an important factor in the success of the program.

Statement by Rabbi A. James Rudin on "Full Employment" Before the Equal Opportunities Subcommittee of the House Committee on Education and Labor, March 15, 1976 — Washington, D.C.

My name is Rabbi A. James Rudin of New York City, and I am the Assistant Director of Interreligious Affairs of the American Jewish Committee. The AJC, founded in 1906, is America's oldest human relations organization. During the past 70 years, the American Jewish Committee has inaugurated and promoted many programs that have directly related to improving inter-group relations in this country. I speak, then, as a representative of an organization that has a deep and continuing interest in shaping a just American society; but I believe the views I reflect today are also shared by the general American Jewish community as well.

I heartily welcome the basic principles of the proposed Full Employment and Balanced Growth Act of 1976. My enthusiastic support for the bill's goals comes from two major sources—one source is profoundly rooted in Jewish tradition and teaching and the second source of support stems from recent American history.

The Hebrew word for labor is AVODAH, and from its very beginnings as a religion, Judaism has invested AVODAH or labor with the highest ethical values. For some people of the ancient world, labor was despised and relegated only to the lowly masses. (Indeed Aristotle believed that laborers and even merchants were unsuited for citizenship.) But Judaism has always insisted that AVODAH was a positive and creative good. In time AVODAH, labor, also came to mean service and religious commitment, an inextricable bond between labor and religious redemption, between meaningful work and human liberation. Labor is no necessary evil, no humiliation, no degradation, rather it can lift a man or woman to heights of religious fulfillment and self-respect.

Jewish religious literature is filled with many references to labor and its positive potential. Three brief examples will suffice to make this point:

A person should love work, and no person should hate work. [7]

When a person eats of his own labor, his mind is at ease, but when a person eats of the labor of his father or mother or children, his mind is not at ease. How much more so when he has to eat of the labor of strangers. [8]

Great is labor, for it honors those who perform it. [9]

Thus it is clear that Judaism, as a value system, never saw a workless society as a social ideal. Even a scholar, the most esteemed person in Jewish life, was expected to earn his livelihood by creative labor. Some of Judaism's greatest Rabbis were blacksmiths, carpenters, and farmers. An elite leisure class as well as an unemployed working class were to be avoided in Jewish life. Both are inadequate responses to AVODAH. Labor fulfills two major goals. First, it provides the goods and services vital to sustain life. Second, labor fulfills a person spiritually by creative effort. Through AVODAH, a person gains self-esteem and the respect of others.

In emphasizing the importance of the seventh day, the Sabbath as a day of rest and refreshment, we tend to overlook the Biblical injunction, "Six days you shall labor and do all your work. . . ."

The opposite to all this is obvious. A person who is without work often is lacking in self-respect. A person who is dependent upon the labor of others, even of his own family, eats the bread of bitterness and frustration. A person without meaningful work is often spiritually shortchanged. A person without work is an unfulfilled, though not an unredeemable man or woman. The blessings, both economic and emotional of AVODAH (work), are enormous both for the individual and for the society as well.

Judaism, through its teachings, was not content to extol the concept of labor, nor did it merely describe the blessings of meaningful work. To diagnose a problem is necessary, but insufficient. A program of prevention and/or cure is also required if the person and a society are to be productive and creative.

Classic Judaism taught the importance of learning a trade, a skill, or a profession. It was the religious duty of every parent to guarantee that his child has a meaningful occupation:

A man is obliged to teach his son a trade, and whoever does not teach his son a trade teaches him to become a robber.[10]

I deeply believe that this ancient teaching can be applied to a total society as well. If I may paraphrase and place it in modern terms:

A society is obliged to teach its citizens a trade and to provide opportunities for employment. A society that does not do this, encourages its unskilled and unemployed citizens to become robbers, robbers from others and robbers from themselves.

From the Jewish perspective, to provide aid for the unemployed is to restore that person to wholeness, it is to provide the rightful means for self-respect. The elimination of unemployment is a necessity, it is not an option, an alternative, nor is it simply an act of charity. Charity comes from the Latin word for love, and it has come to mean in our day an act of assistance based on sentiment or good will. Charity plays a vital role in our relationships with our fellow human beings, and it is, in many cases, an enobling concept.

However, charity is *not* an appropriate response to unemployment. There is no word in the Hebrew vocabulary for charity as it is used in the modern sense. Rather, the word that applies here is "Tzedakah," which means "righteousness." Tzedakah is an act of justice, no act of condescension. I think this is a helpful and critical distinction in addressing ourselves to the human problem of unemployment. If the political and religious leadership of our nation view the question in terms of charity alone, and if we do not view it in terms of righteousness and justice, we are doing a grave disservice to ourselves, to our society, and above all to those who are without jobs and who seek employment.

One of Judaism's greatest sages, Moses Maimonides (1135-1204) saw the problem in a profound, yet clear way. Maimonides defined the various kinds of charity and he listed them in his famous "eight steps or degrees of charity." The eighth or highest of which is literally no charity at all!

The eighth and most meritorious degree of charity is to eliminate the need for charity by preventing poverty; that is, to assist the reduced fellow human, by teaching him a trade, or by putting him in the way of business, so that he may earn an honest livelihood and not be forced to the dreadful alternative of holding out his hand for charity....This is the highest step and the summit of charity's golden ladder.[11]

Thus, the values of the Jewish tradition provide some extraordinary insights and guidelines when we confront the modern American problem of unemployment.

My second major source of support for the principles of this bill comes from modern American history. My organization, the American Jewish Committee, a leader in the human rights field for 70 years, declared at its 1975 Annual Meeting: "Full and fair employment for all is an essential ingredient of a democratic society, and that democratic government can have no more urgent goal than to assure to all its citizens the opportunity for gainful and dignified work. We call for immediate, comprehensive, and effective back-to-work measures, including adequate stimulation of the private economy and the creation of substantial numbers of meaningful public service jobs." The lack of gainful and dignified work is not only debilitating to the individual who seeks work, but the mass unemployment that we are currently experiencing is fraught with dangers for our society. Unemployment creates inter-group tensions between races, sexes, religions, and ethnic groups. Mass unemployment has the potential to foment hostility among various population groups. As the struggle for a piece of a shrinking employment pie becomes more intense, polarization sets in among our people, those who have jobs vs. those who are without work—those who hold seniority and those who were last hired and first fired—the young people without work and the older men and women with work—those unemployed workers in depressed industries vs. those employed workers in other less hard hit industries—the list is a long one that indicates how corrosive unemployment is for all of us.

The tragic cost of this unemployment in both financial and human terms is enormous. The staggering losses in the production of goods and services, in wages and salaries, in federal, state and local taxes, and in private business investment can be calculated only in the *trillions* of dollars. In the last two years our nation has lost $400 billion in Gross National Product. The struggle for justice for racial and religious minorities, and for women, has been impeded, poverty has increased, the preservation of our fragile environment has been weakened and health care and educational opportunities have been curtailed because of the continued persistence of mass unemployment.

The American Jewish Committee believes the principles underlying the Full Employment and Balanced Growth Act can help to end the tragic waste of human and fiscal resources. Adequate stimulation of the private economy is needed, joint Congressional and Executive action is called for, and the Federal Government, (itself committed to the goal of full employment by the Employment Act of 1946) should employ the men, women and youth who are unable to locate jobs in the private sector.

The long and bleak litany of unemployment figures are well known to this Committee. The cruel attempt of some to use the unemployed as a damper on the inflation rate is also well publicized. Nor do I need to rehearse before this Committee the novel suggestion of some frustrated economists and political spokesmen that this country accept a 6 per cent jobless rate as the "equivalent" of full employment. The grim unemployment statistics (the official figure is over 7.5% with 7,100,000 unemployed), and the mean spirited rationalization and explanation of unemployment merely contribute to a sense of hopelessness and helplessness.

By my testimony I have sought to indicate that chronic mass unemployment breaks the spirit of an individual citizen, it corrodes the general society, it tears at the very fabric of constructive intergroup relations, it extracts enormous financial cost from everyone, and it simply can not be accepted as the norm in American life.

I have also attempted to portray Judaism's positive view of the concept of labor, the importance of creative work in human self-fulfillment, and the theological and moral foundation of a healthy society.

Too often unemployment is seen in cold percentage figures, in chilly economic indicators. Unemployment must also be seen in human and spiritual terms, and the commitment to end chronic mass unemployment must be rooted in those same human and spiritual terms. I am grateful to the members of this Committee for the opportunity to share my views with them. Thank you.

AJC Statement on Affirmative Action

The American Jewish Committee is committed to helping eliminate discrimination and achieve full civil rights for all Americans, regardless of race, creed, color, sex or national origin. However, experience has demonstrated that the legal requirement of non-discrimination is by itself not sufficient to erase within the foreseeable future the accumulated burdens imposed on the disadvantaged in America who have historically suffered from systematic discrimination. Consequently, Federal, state and local governments have mounted special programs requiring employers and public and private institutions and corporations which receive government funds to undertake Affirmative Action programs that would recruit, train and upgrade those who have been historically disadvantaged or discriminated against.

The American Jewish Committee believes that such efforts are in accord with the American tradition of giving special assistance to categories of people on whom society has imposed hardship and injustice or who have special needs that could not otherwise be met.

The principle of non-discrimination requires no definition. Affirmative action, however, does require spelling out, and the following are some of the basic conditions of such a program:

A) Special efforts to identify and recruit qualified or qualifiable members of previously excluded groups for job openings which become available. This means going beyond the referral sources traditionally used, and especially employing all those community resources that reach out to members of groups previously excluded.

B) Programs to help the potentially qualifiable become qualified, including tutoring, apprenticeship and in-service training programs, and other special efforts. These should be meshed with job-placement programs for successful trainees.

C) Continued review of all tests to make sure they are completely relevant to the job and as free as possible from cultural or other bias, at the same time maintaining and strengthening objective selection standards and criteria.

D) A continuing review of all jobs to make sure that the essential prerequisites for them are still valid. In some jobs this may mean that some kinds of academic pre-job requirements should be dropped. In other jobs, it may mean that demonstrated experience and ability to work with the minority population should be taken into account. However, we reject the concept that belonging to a particular group is an absolute qualification for any position.

E) Within the context of the affirmative action principle, the granting of special consideration to those applicants from among those discriminated against or disadvantaged who are substantially equal in qualifications to others being considered.

F) A program of continuous dissemination and communication within the employer organization of the objectives and procedures of the Affirmative Action program, particularly to those holding positions of responsibility.

In higher education, also, the affirmative action principle requires: (a) scrutiny of admission tests and standards for admission to make sure they contain no cultural or other bias; (b) special recruitment programs to identify and bring into the student bodies members of disadvantaged groups; and (c) special remedial education programs so as to enable those who need such assistance to meet the existing requirements for graduation and for admission into graduate schools.

We believe that the above programs are essential to enable members of disadvantaged groups to compete on an equal basis within the system. They deserve the highest priority in the allocation of resources. The American people must be prepared to make the investment necessary to achieve this end.

*   *   *   *

The search for means of assuring the effectiveness of affirmative action programs has led to demands for the imposition of quota systems. However, the use of quotas to give members of disadvantaged groups special consideration would undermine the concept of individual merit and the principle of equal opportunity itself. We therefore completely reject the concept of quotas. They are wrong in principle, bad in practice, destructive of individual rights and contrary to the best interests of all Americans, including the disadvantaged.

Such quotas have become the actual practice on numerous occasions as a result of improper and unauthorized application of "goals and timetables" as actual quota systems, that is, allocation of given numbers or percentages of positions for one or more particular group. The use of specific numerical goals and timetables must not be permitted to disguise a de facto quota system. On the other hand, the opposition to quotas must not be converted into a blind opposition to goals and timetables. We believe that carefully and sensitively developed goals and timetables can be an effective means of monitoring the effectiveness of an Affirmative Action program.

During the past few years, official pronouncements and regulations of the principal Federal agencies have included assurances that numerical goals not be allowed to be applied in such a fashion as to, in fact, result in the imposition of quotas. Adherence to these official criteria has not always been adequate. We therefore urge that the new Administration take appropriate steps to make official policy one that clearly differentiates between good-faith goals and de facto quotas and that this be made absolutely clear to all those responsible for carrying out Federal affirmative action programs. Such programs will continue to have the closest scrutiny of the American Jewish Committee.

We recognize that the use of numerical data and statistical techniques may be necessary to assure the effectiveness of Affirmative Action programs. To help safeguard that such measurement techniques do not result in the kinds of abuses that have brought protests in the past, we offer the following guidelines:

1) The procedures and standards must be clearly spelled out by the enforcing agency and made public in advance of being put into effect.

2) Quantitative measurements should be used only as management tools to assess the over-all effectiveness of the programs and the progress achieved, taking into account the availability of qualified or qualifiable talent within the area or job market, which will vary with the different occupations and professions. In so doing the use of the principle of proportional representation must not be permitted.

3) Periodic aggregate enumerations of work forces, student bodies, etc., may be used as bases for evaluating and effectuating compliance with Affirmative Action policies, provided, however, that: (a) questions as to race, color, ethnicity, nativity or religion do not appear on application forms; (b) individuals are at no time required to identify themselves by any of the foregoing; and (c) no records are maintained by an employer or educational institution of an individual's race, religion or ethnic origin.

4) Government has the responsibility to vigorously enforce Affirmative Action programs. It has equal responsibility to prevent abuses in them. Accordingly it should build into the programs appropriate safeguards and provisions for periodic review which meet both these responsibilities. In addition, every affirmative action program should also be subject to periodic review to ascertain whether it has attained and maintained its goals with such consistency and reliability that it is clear that continuance of the program as such is no longer required.

5) There should be effective and speedy grievance procedures so as to permit redress to an individual who claims either discrimination or "reverse discrimination" by the administrative abuse of the program. (One such procedure, the appointment of an ombudsman, has been incorporated into the HEW guidelines.) Certainly, no one who is performing satisfactorily should be dismissed to make room for a member of a previously disadvantaged group.

The responsibility for monitoring adherence to the foregoing guidelines rests not only with government but with business and private organizations as well.

The above principles, procedures and guidelines for Affirmative Action are essential for the full achievement of equality of opportunity for all Americans—an objective to which the American Jewish Committee remains deeply committed.

We must, at the same time, urge the creation and furtherance of national policies and programs that would greatly expand employment and educational opportunities for individuals of all groups and thus diminish the intense competition for scarce existing opportunities.

Adopted at the
71st Annual Meeting
Waldorf Astoria Hotel
May 14, 1977

The Tavistock Model of Laboratory Training[12]

The Tavistock model, a group relations technique comparable to the T-group process, is practiced in comfortable and isolated surroundings. The model was initiated at the University of Leicester in England in the early 1960s and is now used widely in the United States through the A. K. Rice Institute with headquarters in Washington and a number of related regional organizations. It was originally a small-group process focusing on authority and leadership of the group. Efforts to examine the group itself as an organization were subsequently added to the process.

A number of workshops sponsored by the A. K. Rice Institute are held throughout the country. The staff of consultants for the technique usually consists of persons who have had experience with similar workshops and whose backgrounds are in the social sciences. Participants tend to be a homogeneous group, depending on the special focus of the conference; they come from middle management in a wide variety of institutions—industrial, educational, and religious.

The Tavistock process involves participants in small-group, large-group, and intergroup exercises. The learning process is applied to problems which participants meet in their daily activities, and the model is aimed at assisting participants to learn about those factors which inhibit organizational task conferences. The Tavistock process focuses on the group rather than the individual. Hence, the individual with psychological problems is not encouraged to attend the conference.

The final exercise of the process deals with application groups. Small groups study the way in which the various exercises and components of the entire program are interrelated. The probability is that these groups will show a trend toward cohesion, friendliness, and interaction.

The relation of the Tavistock methodology to attitude modification is not too clear. However, if there is validity to the assumption that understanding of individual and group processes is related to understanding of the self as a member of the group, and particularly to the dynamics of group action, this technique can be of value.

Laboratory Confrontation or Communications Laboratory[13]

The Laboratory Confrontation or Communications Laboratory technique developed by Dr. Irwin Goldaber in 1968 appears to have some success in conflict situations between community groups, such as police-youth and black-white. The technique aims at achieving a working relationship between adversary groups which have been engaged in controversy and conflict.

The concept of the laboratory is to provide a situation which would result in what is called win/win. Most arbitrations or negotiations result in the feeling that one group has lost and the other side has won, or that both have lost. Through a carefully controlled laboratory process, the objective of the Goldaber technique is to leave each group with the belief that both have won. Even though participants may not leave the process in complete agreement, they do gain better understanding of each other. The process has succeeded if each side can leave with the feeling that they have not suffered some loss.[14]

In developing this program, the following are emphasized: a sense of trust between groups; the improvement of communication skills resulting in better understanding of different points of view; the knowledge that adversary groups share at least some common goals; the realization that each group in a conflict situation has need for the other if society is to function; the emphasis on area of agreement as well as focus on disagreements which groups realize they must learn to live with; and the realization that they must handle diverse conflicts and differences of opinion in a constructive way.

The program consists of two phases:

1. The pre-laboratory phase. In this preliminary action, each adversary group meets separately and is asked to name representatives who will participate in the laboratory program. It is important that the leaders selected have influence with their groups. Complete equality must be accorded each group—each must be given the same rights and responsibilities. An equal number of representatives is selected by each group.

2. The laboratory phase. The representatives chosen by each adversary group develop a written list of concerns and questions affecting relationships with the opposing group. These may be written on large sheets of paper and tacked up in the room for easy reference. The rules are clearly laid down and scrupulously observed. Only one person speaks at a time for as long and as often as he desires. Participants speak when signaled by the facilitator. Any subject which the participant feels is relevant is discussed, and discussion continues until the group feels it has exhausted the subject. During the laboratory phase, the facilitator strictly enforces the rules of procedure.

The facilitator is crucial in this lab process. He must be completely neutral, respect all sides and all positions, and not attempt to influence or become involved in the issues. Trust in the facilitator has been encouraged because in the pre-laboratory phase (a form of shuttle diplomacy), an intense effort has been made to secure the confidence of both sides and to encourage the expectation of a win/win situation.

When the dialogue phase of the laboratory has concluded, the group is split into two heterogeneous groups consisting of those formerly opposed to each other. These groups work on recommendations for implementing solutions to problem areas.

The laboratory takes place in comfortable surroundings and may stay in session for long periods of time. For example, a group may meet for twelve hours, adjourn, and return the next day for another twelve-hour session.

Followup meetings may be required. Although the extent of attitude modification resulting from this laboratory technique has not been fully determined, there is solid evidence that this method does lead to the amelioration of conflicts, and this could hardly occur without attitude modification. There is every likelihood that this technique and variations of it will be tried as community conflicts continue to plague the American scene.

Simulation Games

Some so-called simulation games should not be so designated since they do not embody real-life situations. They may involve a number of steps that depend on the drawing of cards or throwing of dice, and the like. As a rule, such games call for the attainment of certain objectives with obstacles to be overcome en route. The obstacles, however, do not necessarily relate to real-life problems or to the attitudes of participants.

Simulation games offer little opportunity for self-examination, interaction, or developing skills to deal with problem situations. They can be interesting, exciting, and fun, but the impact is short-lived and the process does not offer the participants opportunities for meaningful practical application. Many such games have been commercially marketed, and claims as to their efficacy are difficult to substantiate. The game of Ghetto, for example, is supposed to help players understand what it is like to be a poor person in the ghetto. Another popular game, Starpower, is designed to help players understand the difficulties attendant upon upward social mobility and to realize what it is like to be powerless. The Poverty game is in part an effort to arrive at an understanding of the dynamics of poverty and the feelings of those suffering want.

The effectiveness of these vicarious experiences is doubtful. Games are not likely to provide insights into the problems of powerlessness or poverty. They may be compared to popular games like Monopoly. A player may be a champion at Monopoly, but his playing skill has little bearing on his financial or business ability.

Some simulation games, however, do have meaning and appear to be quite successful. One such game devised by a school teacher in Riceville, Iowa, was made into a motion picture.[15] In this game, over the course of several days, the class was divided into "brown-eyed" and "blue-eyed" children, and first one and then the other group was accorded special treatment as "superior" to the other. When "blue eyes" were designated as superior, they were allowed second helpings at lunch, or when "brown eyes" were so considered, they were granted an extra five minutes recess. In each case, the deprived group felt and behaved in an inferior fashion; even their classroom performance suffered drastically. The children, as they came to understand the nature of deprivation, became deeply involved, especially when roles were reversed. Moves in games such as this one are not dependent on the drawing of cards or a roll of the dice; they are real deprivations, exaggerated to be sure, but they give children an understanding of what it is like to be a member of a rejected minority group.

A somewhat similar game was devised by a teacher who developed a make-believe Nazi-like movement which was supposed to become an elite society through rigid discipline. Members of the group pretended to be part of a national movement, which after great excitement and profound involvement on the children's part turned out to be false. As in the case of the blue-eyed/brown-eyed children experience, the results were discussed and analyzed in the classroom.[16]

These games do generate personal involvement and deal with genuine human emotions and aspirations that young people can understand; from both a cognitive and therapeutic point of view, they are highly effective.

Notes

1. Herbert H. Hyman, Gene N. Levine, and Charles R. Wright, "Studying Expert Informants by Survey Methods: A Cross-National Inquiry," *Public Opinion Quarterly* 31, no. 1 (Spring 1967): 11.

2. Ibid., p. 12.

3. Based on data in the *American Jewish Year Book*, 1966, p. 8. Early in 1966, the AJC surveyed 775 institutions of higher learning; at that time, only 6 were headed by Jews.

4. Most of the material that follows was taken from Edwin Kiester, Jr., "The Case of the Missing Executive—How Religious Bias Wastes Management Talent . . . and What Is Being Done About It," American Jewish Committee, January 1973, rev.

5. Lewis B. Ward, "The Ethnics of Executive Selection," *Harvard Business Review* (April 1965): 6-28, 171-72.

6. Robert P. Quinn, Joyce M. Tabor, and Laura K. Gordon, "The Decision to Discriminate: A Study of Executive Selection," Institute for Social Research, Ann Arbor, Michigan, 1968.

7. Avot De-Rabbi Natan 11:23A.

8. Ibid., 31

9. Nadarim 49b.

10. Tosefta Kiddushin I, 11.

11. Mishneh Torah, Matanot Aniyim X, 7.

12. Kenneth D. Benne, Leland P. Bradford, Jack R. Gibb, and Ronald O. Lippitt, *The Laboratory Method of Changing and Learning* (Palo Alto, Calif.: Science and Behavior Books, 1975), Chapter 14.

13. Ibid.

14. *National Observer* (April 7, 1973).

15. "Eyes of the Storm," broadcast by the American Broadcasting Company, May 11, 1970, distributed by Xerox.

16. Ron Jones, "You Will Do As Directed," *Learning* (May-June 1976): 20-26.

Appendix B

Professional Preparation

What kind of staff should we seek for an intergroup relations (community relations) agency? Obviously, this question can only be answered in terms of the objectives and functions of the agencies themselves, and these, as is readily apparent, are abundant and diverse. The problem of staffing for highly specific areas is the comparatively simpler one. It involves matching the particular skills and training of an individual to the tasks to be performed, e.g., legal training and experience to compliance and enforcement work, and so forth. One element in intergroup work, however, which is rarely if ever covered by the specialized training available, is, broadly speaking, the ability to accept, deal with, and relate to people of all races and creeds. The problem of selection and training becomes enormously more complex when, as is too often the case in the intergroup relations field, the objectives and tasks are neither as distinct nor as simple as in the above example.

Some informants felt that a good intergroup relations worker is "born and not made," primarily one who "relates well to others." On the other hand, some attributed more importance to the type of disciplines required to prepare a person for effective functioning in this complicated and elusive field.

In regards to a query about the qualifications of suitable staff members for the intergroup relations field, the general response elicited was: "It's a little tough for me to answer that." Some of our informants attempted a general appraisal by listing the qualifications. One official in a federal agency stated:

I should think that the people we take on would have to be first, bright and resourceful people. If they have good education in social psychology, it would certainly be helpful. If they have had an education in law, it is of tremendous importance. If they have had some experience in the field of social welfare, that is indeed good for more and more I think that approach is going to count.

As reported by the informant, the required qualifications for staff members in the agencies studied ranged from highly specialized backgrounds to those of generalists from lawyers, educators, social workers, journalists, mass media specialists, to persons equipped with psychological, sociological, economic, and anthropological knowledge and training, as well as a comprehensive understanding of community organization. The latter is considered to be of particular importance in helping people to help themselves.

At the time of our interviews, in an organization such as the National Urban League, persons with social work backgrounds were engaged less frequently than in-

dividuals specifically trained in economics, housing, education, and other special-
ties. The executive of one "extremist" organization observed that he had been trained
as a chemist and that talent and knowledge were the unofficial credentials.

In the Jewish organizations, workers with "Jewish motivation" and Jewish background—Jewish history, culture, and religion—were desired for general social action
purposes or for interfaith activity. Some informants added "Jewish commitment"—
by which they meant an "internalized" form of Jewish identification—on both the
cognitive and effective levels.

In the Community Relations Service of the Department of Justice, the field staff
consisted of individuals with community organization training and/or experience,
plus one or two special skills. For the most part, however, staff members of intergroup relations agencies are not necessarily experts in specific areas. Specialists are
available to assist with the technical aspects of intergroup problems. They (the
specialists) are support people in the fields of education, housing, employment, law,
public relations, religion, and so forth. The Community Relations Service makes use
of resource persons with skills related to individual programs in the manifold federal
and state government departments who can be of assistance to local groups. A
specialist in the formulation of policy in the intergroup relations field is often
necessary.

Specialists in the Community Relations Service are also utilized in the police-community relations sectors; generally in the administration of justice; in connection
with manpower resources and economic development problems; and in media relations and community planning.

Most professionals in the field tend to be generalists with a sociopsychological
background and have skills in dealing with group relations and intergroup discord in
particular. However, since the field has become increasingly concerned with the
wider aspects of human relations, politicoeconomic knowledge and skills are being
given greater weight than formerly.

One administrator characterized a good intergroup relations worker as "a technician with soul," adding that it is easier to teach community relations to the specialist than specialist skills to the community relations worker. The field people working
in local communities are usually generalists; they may include former antipoverty
and/or social workers.

The intergroup relations worker can be regarded primarily as a "change agent"
rather than as an educator or researcher—although these two skills are also involved—
because the problems he encounters involve changes in community and individual
behavior. Moreover, behavior change usually precedes attitude modification in the
various forms of social intervention.

In an organization such as the American Jewish Committee, the tendency is to select individuals with formal training in social work and in sociology and psychology.
Those experienced in government and private agencies are also given consideration.

It seemed that the contract compliance officers who are responsible for enforcing
nondiscrimination clauses in government contracts did not require special qualifications. Of course, the personality of the worker is a factor in selection.

According to the director of an urban affairs department of a Catholic archdiocese,
training in the public agency is generally of a less professional nature than in the private agency. One reason is that, with few exceptions (notably the Community Rela-

tions Service of the Department of Justice), the public agency function is confined to the business of compliance and compliance procedures. More frequently, this function can turn into a mechanical process. One gets a complaint, investigates it, holds a meeting, settles the complaint, and then proceeds to deal with the next complaint.

The problem of routinization that is characteristic of compliance responsibilities in public agencies and in the investigative process that goes along with compliance is not always a simple one. It needs to be looked at in terms of linkages between these functions and the usual intergroup relations activities in which insightful human relations skills are essential. This type of examination could result in the application of processes that would transform compliance and investigative responsibilities into a human relations kind of approach. Otherwise, it may become necessary to separate the usual intergroup relations activity from the specific compliance and investigatory functions (in the consideration of professional training). Experimentation with this "new look" is worth the effort.

Obviously, the specialists employed in private agencies possess skills applicable to the tasks in which the particular organization is engaged. In litigation, legal training for civil rights experience is required. In the field of education, education experience is a qualification.

At present, the additional training required is primarily obtained on the job itself. Sensitivity training, when necessary, is available at human relations workshops. A small percentage of the staffs of various agencies have taken such training. For instance, in one agency where social science plays an important role, candidates who had either social science or social work backgrounds were favored. Where there are no or very few specialists in the organization, the staff is augmented with part-time consultants as needed. Such consultants are frequently utilized because of their familiarity with specific regions as well as their specialization in substantive areas.

At the time of our interviews, the U.S. Commission on Civil Rights[1] was staffed primarily with lawyers, but also with political scientists, psychologists, sociologists, statisticians, and economists; some staff members had training in social work. The Commission found that in order to fulfill its responsibilities the staff (in addition to having the necessary legal qualifications) had to have the ability to appraise civil rights situations in terms of their sociological, psychological, and economic aspects.

An interesting experiment in training top management personnel was undertaken in 1970 by the International City Management Association (ICMA). The executive of this organization described a seminar in Kansas City, where, with a small grant from a service foundation, he brought together twenty city managers. While it was not, strictly speaking, a sensitivity training program, it did involve elements of this approach. The ICMA executive said: "They were shoved into the nose of each other's problem so that they had to understand what the viewpoint of the other was." Although this was only an experiment, some interesting results had already been achieved. The manager of one midwestern city went back and shortly thereafter was confronted with a very serious, violent situation on the university campus. He reported that "he came out of it beautifully" because the skills he had learned and developed had changed his viewpoint immeasurably. He would not have been able to deal with the campus violence, he said, if he had not had the confrontation experience at the Kansas City session.

The ICMA considered three different ways of conducting the seminars for experimental purposes. The first was to bring in managers from different areas of the country. They had already come to the initial conference held in Kansas City—all the way from the West Coast to Mississippi. The second approach involved a metropolitan area—bringing together local government officials from the cities and counties of this one area, including minority group leaders from the same metropolitan region. All of these representatives had worked together, but not in one jurisdiction—not necessarily in one city or in one county, but within the same metropolitan area. The idea was to bring all of them together for a similar kind of training experience. The third approach was to go into one jurisdiction and invite the mayor, some of the councilmen, the manager, the department heads, and selected community minority leaders. Within the various groupings, there would be a determination as to the required modifications in approach. It was thought that each approach might have its own merits and that therefore it might even be advisable to combine all three and utilize them on a national basis.

In the interreligious area, the National Conference of Christians and Jews no longer looks solely for persons with religious backgrounds or primarily those who are of Protestant persuasion. Catholics and Jews as well as nonwhites are now represented on the staff. Knowledge of the specific region in which the vacancy occurs is required.

In some states, the human relations staff places great reliance on investigators who can determine the legitimacy of complaints. These investigators are generally qualified lawyers, as well as paraprofessionals who "come from the streets" and who can relate to community groups and communicate well. The executive of a local Catholic urban organization maintained that the paraprofessionals coming into the field gave them new insights, and as he put it, "I am afraid that they have given us more than we have given them." An executive of a state human relations agency pointed out: "There are some people today who have an innate capacity to relate to people."

The former executive of a large municipal human relations agency spoke of "some people who by dint of special education, training and competence and personal sensitivity, are able to bring people together and have the capacity of building bridges." Here, too, it was felt that the government intergroup relations worker is necessarily far more of a technician than is the private intergroup relations worker; that is, the government worker has to be familiar with the intricacies of government operations and other public programs—federal, state, and city. "If he is any good, he has got to know almost as much about those nuts and bolts as the line bureaucratic civil servant does in order to see what the intergroup relations components really are."

Private intergroup relations workers have a wider spectrum of functions, and they must, accordingly, use a variety of approaches. According to the head of a private agency in the public field, however, they are not necessarily expert on how programs work in the public sector; nor do they know precisely what has to be done to translate equality of opportunity under a particular law or a particular regulatory procedure into action. All intergroup relations workers, he continued, are obliged to know something about how the various institutions actually function. Furthermore, it is impossible "to be intelligent" in the field of intergroup relations without knowing a good deal about urban development—how housing is provided in this society, how education gets or does not get "delivered" to people.

Public compliance workers, he maintained, can do a satisfactory job, even if they have merely adequate understanding of the program for which they have compliance responsibility. Although important, theirs is a more limited job because that is all bureaucracy will let them do. If they work for HUD, they are not going to be doing much with respect to manpower programs and related matters.

At the same time, he felt that it would be advantageous for an intergroup relations worker to know a certain amount of economics, especially economic stratification in our society and how it affects society—what causes it and what perpetuates it. The intergroup relations worker should be concerned especially with how economic hardship or economic opportunity falls unequally on different ethnic, racial, or religious segments of the population. He felt that the business of conquering poverty as such, apart from its minority group aspects, is far too broad a function for the intergroup relations worker. When he reaches that point, he becomes something else, according to this executive.

Almost all respondents observed that the group identity factor in personnel selection is also becoming increasingly important among Jewish and other groups in the population. There was a widespread belief that as a result of the increasing complexities of our society, the intergroup relations field is shifting from a sociopsychological to a politico-economic orientation. Hence, there may be corresponding changes in the required qualifications of the intergroup relations worker.

In a recent symposium,[2] William C. Martin and Karen Hopkins described a similar development in sociology where the emphasis is shifting from the classroom to a concern with social action and social policy-making. This shift became increasingly important at the beginning of the 1960s. Even before then, however, social research had already assumed an important place in the sociological discipline. The conflict among the races and the developing class struggle made this evolution a compelling necessity.

Martin and Hopkins point out that a new generation of sociologists came out of the G.I. Bill "committed to sociology as a profession rather than solely to a scholarly discipline." This group, on the whole, has been unafraid to venture into areas with a potential for conflict. And conflict is indeed a model in intergroup relations.

In general, the matter of professionalism in the intergroup relations field might be put this way: at the present time, although a professional discipline has not yet been worked out, there is a body of knowledge that is basic to the equipment of all intergroup relations workers. This consists of a sound grounding in sociology, psychology, economics, and political science. Knowledge of urban anthropology is also helpful. Acquaintance with the law is desirable, particularly in the area of litigation, which requires knowledge of civil rights laws.

A few of our informants described future workers in the field of intergroup relations in approximately these terms: They ought to be men and women of vision with comprehensive sociological and psychological insights. This is a broad definition indeed. It is obviously intended to apply to the "generalist" among intergroup workers. But perhaps it can also be taken to include the specialists among them. Clearly, the narrowly based specialist whose acts and thinking are confined to his own specialty will be unable to function comfortably or productively in the more amorphous field of intergroup relations. "Vision" and comprehensive sociological and psychological insights are hard to come by. Formal training in sociology and psychology or law can be had, but insight can be acquired only with experience.

Perhaps one solution to the problem lies in the establishment of rotating internships, somewhat on the lines of medical practice. Formally qualified men and women would be given the opportunity of serving in various sections of functioning intergroup relations agencies for specified periods of time. Only after completing such a rotating internship and an evaluation by experienced professionals would they undertake further in-service training in their chosen specialty. In this way, a true professionalization of the intergroup relations field could in time ensue.

As indicated by one informant, the field of private consultation in intergroup relations was expanding slowly but was not restricted to intergroup or human relations per se. Included in this category are all those related activities which have to do with model cities, community action programs, antipoverty programs, and problems that arise in connection with urban renewal. This is true also of projects in which the focus is on some fairly specific urban problems such as housing developments, renewal of urban areas, or working with police on law enforcement.

Generally, the areas in which the private consultant functions comprise the "human resources elements of the planning program." There is also the consultant on "urban social problems" who handles a wider range of projects than human relations as such. Federal agencies such as HUD and HEW, as well as foundations and city executives, use consultants. As one informant put it, "Public housing in this country has gotten very sick"; hence, studies are being made as to why tenants rebel and why they threaten rent strikes. The consultant may be called in to examine the social environment in public housing. However, the intergroup factor as such is not always involved because a high percentage of public housing in big cities is occupied by blacks only, and, to a large extent, by the poor.

Cities generally do not retain consultants in intergroup relations unless federal dollars finance the activity. At the time of our interviews, the federal government was not yet willing to finance consultations in black-white conflict situations. A consultant may be called in during the planning process and considered primarily as a "consultant on urban social problems."

"Manpower" is at present a tremendous field for consultation purposes, partly because the federal government has made large amounts of money available for manpower development. The function of the federal "manpower" program is to develop marketable skills so that trainees can go out into the private enterprise field and function successfully. However, the private consultant whom we interviewed told us: "And I, as an intergroup relations professional going into private consulting, soon found that while there was a demand for my kind of skills, there wasn't any money to pay for them." He also informed us that people engaged in highway programs for many years who formerly did not much care about community relations are now confused and worried because they are running up against community opposition. Hence, they are now looking for help and sometimes bring in persons with community relations experience and know-how. He gave this illustration: In Philadelphia, twenty-five years of indecision as to the route of a proposed highway resulted in a great deal of neighborhood deterioration because in view of the uncertain situation, real estate people were unwilling to make investments there. This consultant was called in to deal not so much with the traffic aspect but with the larger physical and social problems entailed in the project. The hope was that he might help arrive at a broad-scale solution—either to get the highway built or to abandon the idea, or perhaps to evolve alternate proposals, such as building a highway, bridging it over, and erecting structures on top of it, using the air-rights privileges.

He concluded: "If we're talking about intergroup relations in a narrower sense of dealing with black-white conflict, then I can't say that there's very much expansion from the point of view of the private consultant." He added, however, that the field for private consultants who are concerned with rational scientific approaches to solving urban problems is indeed expanding (1970).

Notes

1. The U.S. Commission on Civil Rights is a temporary, independent, bipartisan agency established by the Congress in 1957 "to investigate complaints...study and collect information...appraise Federal Laws and policies...serve as a national clearing house for information...submit reports, findings and recommendations to the President and Congress."

2. William C. Martin and Karen Hopkins, "Sociology, Intergroup Conflict and Social Action: A Political Strategy," *Journal of Intergroup Relations* 2, no. 4 (Summer 1973): 7-20.

Glossary of Abbreviations

AFL-CIO	American Federation of Labor-Council of Industrial Organizations
AJC	American Jewish Committee
ATT	American Telephone and Telegraph
BLS	Bureau of Labor Statistics
CATV	Cable Television
CBS	Columbia Broadcasting System
CETA	Comprehensive Employment and Training Act
C-Group	Clarification-Group
CLEO	Council on Legal Education Opportunity
CORE	Congress of Racial Equality
CRS	Community Relations Service (Justice Department)
CSA	Community Services Administration
CUNY	City University of New York
EEO	Equal Employment Opportunity
EEOC	Equal Employment Opportunity Commission
EO	Executive Order
FCC	Federal Communications Commission
FDIC	Federal Deposit Insurance Corporation
GPO	Government Printing Office
HCDA	Housing and Community Development Act of 1974
HEW	Department of Health, Education and Welfare
HUD	Department of Housing and Urban Development
ICMA	International City Management Association
JOBS	Job Opportunities in the Business Sector
LEAP	Labor Education Advancement Programs
MUND	Model Urban Neighborhood Demonstration Program
NAACP	National Association for the Advancement of Colored People
NCCJ	National Conference of Christians and Jews
NCDH	National Committee Against Discrimination in Housing
NEA	National Education Association
NJCRAC	National Jewish Community Relations Advisory Council
NOIS	National Occupational Information Service
NTL	National Training Laboratory
OEO	Office of Equal Opportunity
OFCC	Office of Federal Contract Compliance
OIC	Opportunities Industrialization Centers

RNS	Religious News Service
RTP	Recruitment Training Program
SEEK	Search for Education, Elevation and Knowledge
T-Group	Training-Group
UAHC	Union of American Hebrew Congregations
UHF	Ultra High Frequency
UN	United Nations
UPACA	Upper Park Avenue Civic Association
USCC	United States Catholic Conference
WCC	World Council of Churches
YWCA	Young Women's Christian Association

Index

About the Author

JOHN SLAWSON is Executive Vice-President Emeritus and Consultant for the American Jewish Committee. A prominent spokesman on social issues for more than five decades, his books include *The Delinquent Boy* and *The Role of Science in Intergroup Relations.*